Elements of Being: Mentalities, Identities and Movements

Edited by

Daniela Hofmann
Jessica Mills
Andrew Cochrane

BAR International Series 1437
2005

Published in 2016 by
BAR Publishing, Oxford

BAR International Series 1437

Elements of Being: Mentalities, Identities and Movements

ISBN 978 1 84171 873 6

BAR Publishing is the trading name of British Archaeological Reports (Oxford) Ltd.
British Archaeological Reports was first incorporated in 1974 to publish the BAR
Series, International and British. In 1992 Hadrian Books Ltd became part of the BAR
group. This volume was originally published by Archaeopress in conjunction with
British Archaeological Reports (Oxford) Ltd / Hadrian Books Ltd, the Series principal
publisher, in 2005. This present volume is published by BAR Publishing, 2016.

Printed in England

BAR
PUBLISHING

BAR titles are available from:

BAR Publishing
122 Banbury Rd, Oxford, OX2 7BP, UK
EMAIL   info@barpublishing.com
PHONE   +44 (0)1865 310431
FAX   +44 (0)1865 316916
www.barpublishing.com

Contents

List of contributors

Andrew Cochrane

School of History & Archaeology,
Cardiff University, PO Box 909,
Cardiff, CF10 3XU
U.K.

Cécilia Courbot-Dewerdt

Direction de l'Archéologie du Douaisis
191 rue Saint Albain
59500 Douai
France

Hugues Courbot-Dewerdt

Eurl Angez, Cabinet d' architectes
12 rue d'en Haut
62130 Roellecourt
France

Oliver Harris

School of History & Archaeology,
Cardiff University, PO Box 909,
Cardiff, CF10 3XU
U.K.

Daniela Hofmann

School of History & Archaeology,
Cardiff University, PO Box 909,
Cardiff, CF10 3XU
U.K.

Gary Jones

School of History & Archaeology,
Cardiff University, PO Box 909,
Cardiff, CF10 3XU
U.K.

Thomas Kador

Department of Archaeology
University College Dublin
Belfield, Dublin 4
Ireland

Marjolijn Kok

Amsterdam Archeologisch Centrum (UvA)
Nieuwe Prinsengracht 130
1018 VZ Amsterdam
The Netherlands

Jessica Mills

School of History & Archaeology,
Cardiff University, PO Box 909,
Cardiff, CF10 3XU
U.K.

Marc Vander Linden

C.P. 175/ Faculty of Philosophy and Arts
Free University of Brussels
Avenue F.D. Roosevelt 50
1050 Brussels
Belgium

Erik van Rossenberg

Faculty of Archaeology
Leiden University
P.O. Box 9515
NL-2300 RA
Leiden
The Netherlands

List of figures and tables

Figures

Tables

Elements of being: mentalities, identities and movements

Daniela Hofmann, Jessica Mills
and Andrew Cochrane

Introduction

Organising a Theoretical Archaeology Group (TAG) conference session is always a bit like a 'lucky dip': you never know what you are going to get. As it happens, we were extremely lucky with *Mentalités and Identities in Motion*, held at TAG in Lampeter in 2003, and we are proud to present all papers held there, and more besides, in this volume. The contributions are widely spread across space and time, ranging from Northern Ireland to Sicily, from France to Bulgaria and covering almost every period from the Mesolithic to the Thirty Years' War. On top of this, they are also very different in methodology, in the ways they have interpreted the session title and approached their evidence. Before rushing headlong into this kaleidoscopic mix, then, it is worth briefly explaining the rationale behind the session title and the selection and arrangement of papers.

In the course of our own PhD research at Cardiff, we became increasingly interested in the role of past ways of thinking, feeling and acting in social transformation. Of course, it is long established that ideological as well as material and economic factors played an important role in past societies. However, most accounts left us dissatisfied and seemed very far removed from the lived experience of the past: either ideology was seen as a restrictive force, a means of social control by an élite (Shanks and Tilley 1987, 75-8), or writing about people boiled down to writing stories, or 'narratives' (Bailey 2000; Spector 1991; Edmonds 1999; Mithen 2003; Tringham 1991). Somewhere in between these positions, we felt, it should be possible to address past worldviews differently. Instead of being relegated to the 'fictional' or anecdotal, we suggest that they are an integral part of every aspect of human life, not just explicit contexts of power struggles and domination, but also approachable from the material evidence.

There are many possible ways to achieve this. One, recently popular in British academic circles, is via the notion of 'being-in-the-world', taken from Ingold (2000; as applied for instance by Whittle 2003). Here, everyday and routine engagements with the world are stressed, as well as the embeddedness of people in the world around them, including its human, spiritual, animal and other components. Little weight is, however, given to the equally important non-routine actions, like ritual, and to questions of change more generally. It became clear that the approach had to be extended and modified to allow for a combination of all the factors we thought of as crucial for understanding past societies as lived: the routine, unreflected actions and movements, but also more special occasions, the conceptions actors had of themselves, their roles and their world and, most crucially, how all of this could be connected.

The project is ambitious, but central if investigation of past societies is to move forward, and hence ideal for a TAG session. However, in order to broaden the appeal of the topic, as well as our horizons, we have not chosen to include 'being-in-the-world' in the title. Instead, we decided to focus on three concepts which we think are crucial for the kind of archaeology we want to write, and invited contributors to reflect on them.

Identities

This is the aspect most intimately concerned with how humans in the past saw themselves. Stated in this broad manner, it can refer to any scale of past identity and link into any number of debates. In archaeology, discussion of identities frequently focuses on gender and age, rank, family or tribal group, household or society, however defined. We wanted to leave contributors as much freedom as possible in choosing which scale or combination of scales was relevant to them. In practice, these scales are not separate entities. People belong to several or all of these groups at once and rupture may occur within certain crises or other situations, instigating feelings of alienation. This can happen at both the individual and the group level through ongoing performances and negotiations during the daily round and at other times, when exposed to unsettling influences (see C. Courbot-Dewerdt chapter 6; Kok chapter 8; Cochrane chapter 2).

Identities are also always interlinked with people's worldviews, their ideas about themselves and their humanness, as well as their place in the world. Recently some archaeological writings have approached this from the perspective of personhood, investigating whether the conception of individuals in the past was similar to our own, (see Hofmann chapter 7; Harris chapter 5). Yet, when focussing on routine aspects, identity can become expressed in differing rhythms and temporalities. These are played out as particular roles, involving interwoven movements, places and encounters. In other circumstances the boundaries between different scales of identity may have to be rigidly defined or negotiated (see H. Courbot-Dewerdt chapter 3, Jones chapter 4).

Mentalités

This concept is originally derived from the French Annales School, where it was conceived as an explicit opposition to the study of individuals, or 'great men' in history. As such, it has generally been assigned to the collective sphere of action and "the attitudes of ordinary people toward everyday life" (Hutton 1999, 381). *Mentalité* as conceived by some Annales scholars, however, has for this very reason a number of important drawbacks. It has been pointed out that *mentalités* are too often seen as homogenous across a society, divorced from other aspects of life such as economy or technology, and function as prison-like obstacles in the way of change (Gismondi 1999, 429-32). The concept has been accused of implicit evolutionism towards "enlightenment" (Burke 1999, 449), being too concerned with rational beliefs at the expense of emotions (Hutton 1999, 386).

We believe that many of these problems can actually be overcome when the concept is applied to archaeology and combined with a study of identities. Shared conceptions and worldviews undoubtedly existed in any society, but as *mentalités* are concerned with the everyday, there is no reason why they should be divorced from material aspects of existence (see van Rossenberg chapter 9, Vander Linden chapter 10). In fact, in an archaeological context, this is often impossible. Coupling these shared concepts with an appreciation of different social actors and interest groups in any one society makes for a far more dynamic concept, in which different timescales and scales of identity can be interwoven and in which causes of change can also be sought.

An application of Annales concepts to archaeology is not a new thing (see very briefly Hodder 1987; more detailed: contributions in Bintliff 1991a; Knapp 1992) and, much like the Annales school itself, is not unified. For example, whilst Bintliff (1991b, 13; *cf.* Barrett 2001) focuses on patterns and outcomes rather than motivations of past actors, Hodder (1987, 2) explicitly calls for an investigation of motivation and meaning. Contributors tread their own path and we have not insisted on a unified terminology, with some authors preferring 'mentality' or '*mentalité*', while others use the terms interchangeably. Some do not even draw upon the Annales movement. Rather than seeing this as a drawback, we believe this fluidity and variability is true to the spirit of the Annales School, whose practitioners distil a variety of sources and inspirations (Bulliet 1992, 133). Following Bulliet (1992, 134), we suggest that archaeology can never import Annales concepts wholesale and dogmatically, rather it should use them to develop alternative stimuli, thereby creating new insights. As contemporary archaeologies are only beginning to thoroughly engage with past worldviews, we regard any artificial limitations to our contributors' creativity as a negative influence.

Movement
Movement is one of the most fundamental aspects of life, whether it is restricted or not. It is therefore surprising that movement remains little theorised within most modern archaeological discourse. Following approaches within other disciplines such as anthropology and geography, we regard movement as one of the fundamental components of identity and *mentalité* (see Mills chapter 11). Previously it has been restricted to purely economic and functional motivations, but this disregards the many social implications behind it (see Kador chapter 12). Differing scales of movement feed into how people view themselves, others and their worlds. Identities and *mentalités* emerge through these differing nodes of thought and modes of movement. In this book movement is the bridge between the concepts of identity and *mentalité*, spanning times and places.

The combination of the three variables presented above is not only new but also very challenging. All these aspects are, in past lived experience, inextricably fused. Therefore, none of the contributors has limited themselves to just one aspect. We have thus decided not to group the papers into artificial sections such as 'Identity', '*Mentalité*' and 'Movement'. Instead, we have loosely arranged them depending on the main source material used, into papers with an architectural, an artefactual and a landscape focus. Between these categories, too, there is considerable overlap, as many authors have used more than one scale of analysis or artefact category. Instead of rigidly pigeonholing our contributors, then, we chose to simply present their work and let it speak for itself; each article has its own position and flavour. The following paragraphs summarise the main aspects of each chapter to guide the reader through the volume in the absence of clear sections.

Andrew Cochrane re-examines the Irish Neolithic monument complex at Loughcrew, Co. Meath. He focuses on the landscape setting of the site and the location and execution of motifs within the tombs. The concepts of the carnivalesque and hyper-real allow us to see these elements as a playful inversion of normality, questioning accepted social status and everyday experience. This leads us to see these sites not as static entities, reflecting a society, but as fluid, ever-changing and lived places of performance.

Hugues Courbot-Dewerdt's case study is set on the northern French border at the time of the Thirty Years' War. The plans of underground shelters dug there for the protection of people and livestock reveal a tension between the necessities of communal defence and the desired privacy of the family group. By outlining the chronological development of shelters and placing them into a wider social context, the author vividly illustrates how people attempted to harmonise conflicting forces in their world. In placing the emphasis on the *mentalité* of the 'common man', Courbot-Dewerdt shows how the study of architectural remains can vastly enrich a field traditionally dominated by written sources.

Gary Jones considers how a desire for privacy is physically and visually expressed on eastern Bulgarian tell mounds in the Eneolithic. He begins by addressing the six kinds of privacy and how these emphasize senses of identity within a society. A comparison of Japanese and English architecture reveals how different societies stress different notions of privacy through scale and arrangement of boundaries within a house. The space syntax methodology of Relative Asymmetry (RA) is used to classify houses according to their internal complexity. On this basis, he suggests that permanent architectural features and the partitioning of internal spaces were increasingly used as mechanisms for the expression of inter- and intra-household privacy.

Oliver Harris utilises an approach based upon *performative practice*, incorporating themes of gender, identity, personhood, emotion and memory, to recreate the multiple nuances of human existence. This is achieved by combining the strengths of Barrett's (2001) agency approach with Bourdieu's (1977) *habitus* and Butler's

(1993) theories of the body. The architecture and structural depositions at Etton causewayed enclosure in eastern Britain provide the backdrop for a consideration of variables such as age, knowledge and rites of passage. These engagements are interwoven to produce a novel account of a particular rite through an individual deposit.

The role and importance of enclosure during the late Iron Age and Roman period in north-western Gaul, forms the context for Cécilia Courbot-Dewerdt's case study. Through examining a number of different enclosed places ranging from farmsteads, *oppida*, sanctuaries and households, new interpretations are put forward regarding the significance of continuity and change in the late Iron Age and early Gallo-Roman way of building places. This leads to a rethinking of the place of enclosure in the creation of spatial identity during this transitional period. Analysing change and continuity in enclosure form reveals that despite the inclusion of Gaul into the Roman Empire, significant strands of Gallic identity and *mentalité* were still being expressed through particular forms of enclosure.

Daniela Hofmann's contribution draws on ethnographic accounts and ideas on the materiality of artefacts to let LBK figurines reveal their makers' conception of personhood. Figurines are characterised as emotionally charged objects, experienced differently by different handlers and created for a particular performance. However, their material characteristics and deposition link them with concepts of the person and of transformations central to other areas of LBK social practice, such as the mortuary domain. By offsetting the individuality of the objects with these wider themes, Hofmann shows how overarching mentalities are always worked through in the unique, specific encounter, where the roots of change ultimately reside.

Marjolijn Kok considers how past identities were expressed and influenced by material culture in the Dutch Broekpolder during the late Iron Age and Roman periods. Kok questions whether the local Iron Age inhabitants shared the same 'reverence' for Roman material culture and social ideas, that is expressed by some modern scholars, or if they incorporated and appropriated Roman artefacts in their own way. The evidence suggests that their worldviews were fluid, with some people selectively engaging with the intrusive Roman material forms. Some forms persist in circulation after the Romans left, and choices were based on an association between the qualities of the objects and the surrounding environments.

Using the Abruzzo region of central Italy as a backdrop, Eric van Rossenberg explores how changing social relationships are sedimented in the landscape. Ranging from the early Bronze Age to the early Iron Age, he analyses the distribution of artefact types on different kinds of site. Over time, new artefacts are first introduced into specific places and existing assemblages, until this previously disparate material is combined in the social microcosm of early Iron Age cemeteries. The new and exotic thus always finds its place in existing *mentalités*, but these end up being creatively transformed as people situate themselves anew in their world.

Marc Vander Linden utilises a polythetic approach to studying the inception of Bell Beakers throughout the central Mediterranean area. Despite strong continuity and similarity throughout central Europe, particular historical trajectories of Bell Beakers are manifest throughout the region. This can be seen to include the take-up of Bell Beakers as a complete 'cultural package' in some areas, with just particular elements being appropriated in others. Notably, the penetration of Bell Beakers throughout this region is assigned to their importance within the domestic sphere, which opposes the traditional view that they were the expressions of social elites, and elite ideology.

Jessica Mills considers a 'movement perspective' for the Neolithic and Bronze Age archaeology of the eastern British river valleys of the Great Ouse, Nene and Welland. Here, patterns and modes of movement are explicitly considered in an attempt to address continuity and change in *mentalités* and identities within, and outside of, each river valley. Through an analysis of sites and monuments, the change from Neolithic mobile lifeways to a more settled existence by the Middle Bronze Age, is explored. It is postulated that movements were actively used to engender particular identities which were expressed at an individual level, and at a much larger corporate, inter-valley sphere.

A Geographical Information System (GIS) approach has been utilised by Thomas Kador to explore the social and economic reasons for later Mesolithic mobility within the Glens of Antrim in north east Ireland. Through analysis of the topography of the region, a series of ideal paths of movement have been created. These are then analysed in relation to later Mesolithic find locations to put forward an interpretation of potential networks of movement. The importance of river valleys as conduits of movement, and the mobility of non-local flint over great distances, suggests the places and scales of social communications and relations being played out at this time.

References

Bailey, D.W. 2000. *Balkan prehistory: exclusion, incorporation and identity.* London: Routledge.

Barrett, J. 2001. Agency, the duality of structure, and the problem of the archaeological record, 141-64. In I. Hodder (ed.), *Archaeological theory today.* Cambridge: Polity Press.

Bintliff, J. (ed.) 1991a. *Annales School and archaeology.* London: Leicester University Press.

Bintliff, J. 1991b. The contribution of an *Annaliste*/structural history approach to archaeology. In J. Bintliff (ed.), *Annales School and archaeology,* 1-33. London: Leicester University Press.

Bulliet, R. 1992. *Annales* and archaeology. In A.B. Knapp (ed.), *Archaeology, Annales and ethnohistory,* 131-34. Cambridge: Cambridge University Press.

Burke, P. 1999. Strengths and weaknesses of the history of mentalities. In S. Clark (ed.), *The Annales School. Critical assessments. Volume 2: the Annales School and historical studies,* 442-56. London: Routledge.

Edmonds, E. 1999. *Ancestral geographies of the Neolithic: landscapes, monuments and memory*. London: Routledge.

Gismondi, M. 1999. 'The gift of theory': a critique of the *histoire des mentalités*. In S. Clark (ed.), *The Annales School. Critical assessments. Volume 2: the Annales School and historical studies*, 418-41. London: Routledge.

Hodder, I. 1987. The historical approach in archaeology. In I. Hodder (ed.), *Archaeology as long-term history*, 1-8. Cambridge: Cambridge University Press.

Hutton, P. 1999. The history of mentalities: the new map of cultural history. In S. Clark (ed.), *The Annales School. Critical assessments. Volume 2: the Annales School and historical studies*, 381-403. London: Routledge.

Ingold, T. 2000. *The perception of the environment: essays in livelihood, dwelling and skill*. London: Routledge.

Knapp, A.B. (ed.) 1992. *Archaeology, Annales and ethnohistory*. Cambridge: Cambridge University Press.

Mithen, S. 2003. *After the ice: a global human history, 20,000-5000 BC*. London: Weidenfeld & Nicolson.

Shanks, M. and Tilley, C. 1987. *Social theory and archaeology*. Oxford: Blackwell.

Spector, J. 1991. What this awl means. In J.M. Gero and M. Conkey, (eds), *Engendering archaeology: women and prehistory*, 388-406. Oxford: Blackwell.

Tringham, R.E. 1991. Households with faces. In J.M. Gero and M. Conkey, (eds), *Engendering archaeology: women and prehistory*, 93-131. Oxford: Blackwell.

Whittle, A. 2003. *The archaeology of people: dimensions of Neolithic life*. London: Routledge.

A taste of the unexpected: subverting *mentalités* through the motifs and settings of Irish passage tombs

Andrew Cochrane

Introduction

Loughcrew, or Sliabh na Callighe, is one of Ireland's most magnificent and abounding archaeological landscapes. It is located at the western end of Co. Meath and incorporates a complex of passage tombs distributed across the four neighbouring hilltops of Carnbane West, Carrickbrac or Newtown, Carnbane East and Patrickstown, in an area measuring 3 km from east to west and 600m from north to south (Fraser 1998, 206; Cooney 2000a, 159). On a clear day the panoramic views from the summits of these hills make it possible to see the Wicklow Mountains, the Mournes, Slieve Gullion and the mountains to the north-east (Shell and Roughley 2004, 22), giving a view of Ireland from sea to sea, about its narrowest part (Conwell 1866, 355). Previous accounts of these passage tombs have addressed individual motifs and how they are related to burials and deposits, the entire complex with the locations and orientations of specific passage tombs, and movements of people through and around the monuments (e.g. Herity 1974; Cooney 1990; Thomas 1992; McMann 1994; Shee Twohig 1996). This paper aims to build upon these previous ideas of landscape context and motif location with physical and visual engagements in order to develop a further argument that includes the possible sequences, differences and repetitions that are being performed by the passage tombs on Carnbane East and West.

Reduplicative visions

I draw upon the Loughcrew passage tombs and settings to explore potential relationships created by the engravers and spectators of the visual images. The passage tomb motifs will be analysed as a flux of images and technological illusions (or the illusion of created technologies, such as an engraved motif or built passage tomb) that may have represented and influenced some Irish Neolithic societies. Although there is indication of some people continually interacting with the summits of Loughcrew from the Mesolithic through to the Neolithic, there is currently no settlement evidence available. The passage tombs and engraved images were therefore probably removed from the context of daily life, possibly thought of as being placed in a liminal zone (van Gennep 1960), involving a strenuous physical exertion in order to reach the summits and the passage tombs (Fraser 1998, 212). Contact with the passage tombs may have been temporal and in some instances physically and emotionally hazardous, potentially acting as some form of social integration or separation (Turner 1982; Foucault 2002).

It is suggested that both the sequential application of images, the topography of the Loughcrew summits and the passage tombs themselves develop visions, gazes and glances that are anchored in the present, with the present being a 'temporally extended field' of retentions of the past in the present, as well as being extensions of the present into the future (Gell 1998, 239-40). Following Gell (1992), I review the Loughcrew evidence and consider how the repeated alteration of the sites in the Neolithic (their 'now'), among a society, was the result of the ways in which people continually renewed their beliefs *in* and *of* the world. By repetitively interacting with the passage tombs, some Irish Neolithic people were devoting effort, play and 'work', which may not be separate operations (see discussions in Ingold 2000, especially chapter 17), to be able to frequently ascertain the currentness of beliefs about events. Although we can never know what these beliefs were, we can detect themes, possible perceptions and repetitive actions; it is through some of these elements that I will construct possible narratives. Furthermore, these perceptions are always 'anchored in the present' (Gell 1992, 173) and in turn informed by a person's horizons, that is the limits of their experiences or outlook (Hirsch 2004, 37) and the residues of their material culture. Appreciating this allows us to further consider the possible worldviews of others.

Recently, Thomas (1990; 1992; 1993; 2001) has explored the view that distances and explorations into other worlds and spheres of knowledge are expressed not only through the internal architectures of the Loughcrew passage tombs, but also via the locations of specific motifs. By moving further into the inner areas of the passage tomb, the spectator is challenged with increasingly managed movement through more complex spatial divisions (Thomas 1990). This is argued to occur in order to facilitate the accumulation and manipulation of communal and 'ancestral' authorities (Thomas 1990, 175). By incorporating textual analogies, Thomas proposed that that the visual motifs acted as symbolic media by which approved knowledges could be 'read' by and aimed at particular members of society, possibly as part of an 'interpretation of reality' (1992, 143, 146, 154). The differing motifs on individual stones are described as being for different people or people at different temporal stages of a particular performance or practice (Thomas 1993, 87). Thomas (1992, 146, 154) does, however, stress that the interpretations and meanings of the motifs may have been fluid, multiple, and capable of change as a result of the ambiguity inherent in abstract images (see also Bradley 1995).

In this discussion the passage tombs, their settings and their motifs will not be regarded as static, but rather 'animate', fluid and transformative. This avoids the paradox created when prehistorians utilise text to understand a Neolithic world in which text did not exist. Better comprehensions of how some Irish Neolithic people perceived their world undoubtedly derives from focusing on what they had seen and what they made of what they had seen (Bloch 1998). Taking my lead from Bloch (1995) and Gell (1998), this paper abandons interpretations founded on unambiguous visual meanings, definable symbolism and decipherable textual codification (see also Dundes 1980; Gell 1999; Gottdiener 1995; Holly 1998). Instead, I seek out alternative metaphors (cf. Thomas 1998) and 'modes of attention' (Baxandall 1997, 135), such as the carnivalesque. We should endeavour to see their 'world-as-a-picture' in flux, rather than their 'world-as-text' in stasis (Mitchell 1994, 16).

To achieve this, detailed accounts are made of episodes and temporalities, multiple meanings and overlapping phenomena. The superimposition and location of motifs is reconsidered within a carnivalesque framework. This perspective is pregnant with conflicts, tensions and paradoxes, all of which allow a more complex understanding of the immediacies and non-uniformities of overlain visual images engraved in passage tombs and their placement within an environment.

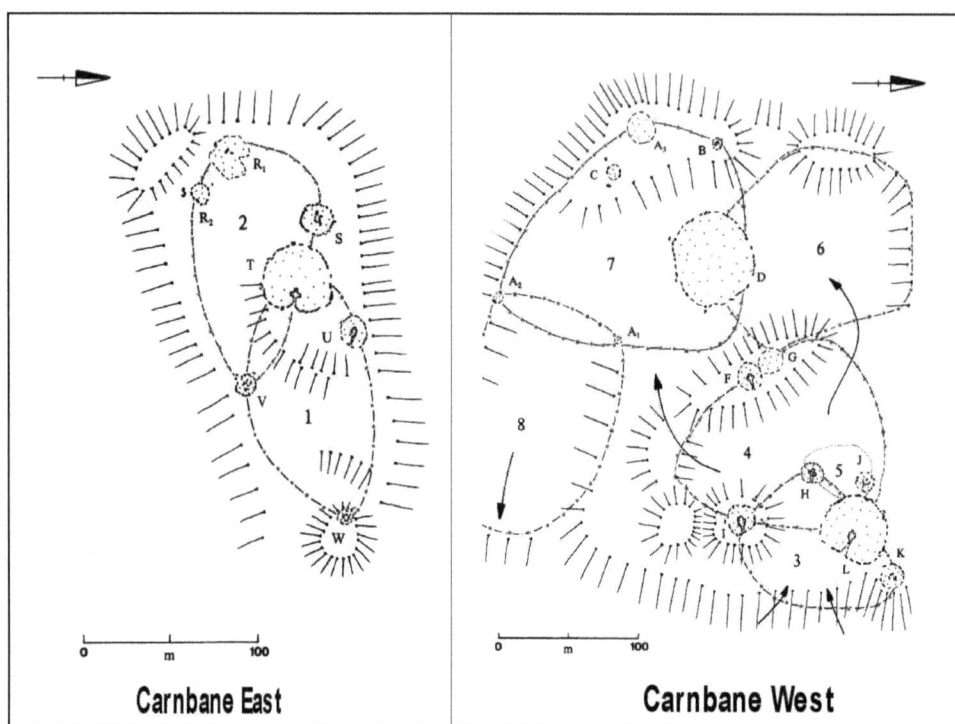

Figure 2.1. The eight possible focal areas (indicated by dash and dot line) as proposed by Fraser (1998) on Carnbane East and West. The black arrows suggest possible movement patterns, while terrain indications are an approximation only (after Fraser 1998, Figs. 8 and 9).

Spectacular spectacular

The Loughcrew cairns are located on an east-to-west axis, with an almost linear structure, with smaller tombs arranged near larger focal ones (see Figure 2.1). In this respect, they can be compared to the Boyne Valley, Co. Meath, sites (Cooney 1990). There are currently over 30 passage tombs in the Loughcrew complex and many of these are engraved with motifs, particularly on the internal structural stones and occasionally on the kerbstones. Patrickstown Hill is thought to have had a further 21 cairns, but that they were totally demolished with no remaining traces before 1864 (Conwell 1864, 48; Coffey 1912, 78; Brennan 1983, 69). Shee Twohig (1981, 94, Figs. 213-41; see also Frazer 1893) recorded over 100 decorated stones (124 decorated surfaces), although the original number was probably higher, and has argued for a distinctive Loughcrew style of imagery. More recently, a Japanese expedition employed a modern rubbing technique to produce a new record of the Loughcrew motifs, but this unfortunately still remains unpublished (O'Sullivan 1993, 30).

The topography at Loughcrew consists of a dominant elongated ridge orientated south-west/north-east on the

interface between the areas of the Boyne/Blackwater and Shannon river systems. This location between rivers is also comparable to the Boyne Valley sites. To the south and west of the hill are the comparatively low, undulating, limestone plains of Co. Meath and Westmeath, and to the north slate rocks occupy the low areas around Lough Ramor (Conwell 1864, 43). The passage tombs are situated along the curving spine of the ridge; with the central component of the complex residing above the 214m contour line (Cooney 1987; 2000b). The passage tombs are centred on moderately flat-topped summits and are again similar to the Boyne Valley passage tombs in that the smaller sites are clustered around larger tombs. The undulating, steep and flattish features of the topography have been argued to directly affect and influence an individual's visual experience through its contrast and transformation (Fraser 1998, 212). The flat features of the summits are only apparent when one reaches the tops of the hills. It is interesting to note that most cairns are located on the margins of the summits, although exceptions do occur (e.g. Cairn D and T). This creates a visual 'island' whereby the internal spaces are framed by the steeper banks on the periphery of the summits and by the cairns, which in turn physically and visually block out the external spaces (see again Figure 2.1). Fraser has suggested that these topographical and artificial features possibly demarcated eight focal areas or as I have proposed 'islands' within the Loughcrew Hills (1998, 212-14; see Figure 2.1). The summits form 'islandscapes' (Cooney 2004, 145), special places where striking features of the land are embellished and special material culture created and used to enhance links with the lived-in-world and 'other' worlds, whilst also delineating boundaries to these liminal places (Bradley 2000, 36). After Whittle (2004), we might therefore describe these aerial locales as 'islands-that-float-to-the-sky'. Indeed, some Neolithic people may have regarded mountains and hills as part of the sky rather than just the land (Watson 2004, 60).

In following Thomas's (1993) desire to create narratives that address more humanised interactions with the environment and associated material cultures, Fraser (1998) discussed the physical stresses involved in ascending the Loughcrew summits and the additional difficulties that would be incurred by leading animals, carrying objects or maybe people in a 'state of crisis' (Foucault 2002, 232), such as adolescents, the elderly, menstruating or pregnant women, the sick, or perhaps the dead. Scaling these slopes might also have impacted upon notions of time and space. The act of climbing might have incorporated different senses of time than were generally used within the daily round. Bloch (1977) has commented that more than one sense of time can often exist in the same society. It is suggested that routine activities may be influenced by the seasons, such as knowing the right times of year to conduct certain events, whereas 'special' activities may involve notions of time that are distinct from or distort the seasons (Bloch 1977). For instance, the summit tops at Loughcrew are generally cooler in temperature than the surrounding lowland areas and can be covered in snow when low-lying areas are not. This climatic feature might deliver the impression that the passing of seasons is respectively progressed or delayed as one rises up the slopes, with the developmental stages and annual cycles of fauna and flora being different to the lowland ones (Watson 2004, 60). Experiencing the Loughcrew Hills with differing climatic conditions and visibility distorted by atmospherics (Watson 2004, 60), may have lead to concrete testaments to the specialness of the summits.

Such features may confirm a worldview, at some level, in which the Loughcrew Hills are regarded as part of a cosmological *axis mundi*, a 'Sacred Mountain', 'Cosmic Mountain' or 'navel of the earth', where heaven and earth meet (Eliade 1964, 268). Hill and mountain tops are often regarded by some Tewa people from the American South-west, as an 'earth navel' an inverted hole into the worlds below that allow spirits access from one realm to another (see discussions in Tilley 1994, 65-66), exposing themselves as 'hierophanies', that is something that reveals itself to be special (Eliade 1964, 32). Foucault (2002, 231-33) describes these sites as 'heterotopias', that is a counter-site which can simultaneously juxtapose in a single place several places. These zones also contest and invert a place while being outside all places, even though one can locate them in a physical reality. These summit tops or island settings may have subverted daily life (see also Bradley 2000, 27). At the Loughcrew summits, at particular times,

some members of society may therefore have inverted their normal networks of relations and disrupted how they thought about themselves, others and the world in general. How these themes interact with the passage tombs and associated visual imagery will be discussed in more detail below.

Appetites for construction and disruption

There is currently a lack of direct datable evidence for the Loughcrew complex and estimated dates generally range from *c.* 4000–2800 BC (McMann 1994, 526). Lithic evidence from the area does, however, demonstrate Mesolithic (some time after 7000 cal BC) and extensive Neolithic activity (Cooney 1987; Dillon 1990, cited in Cooney and Grogan 1994, 13; Kimball 2000, 31). This situation has led Cooney (2000a, 158-163) to propose a speculative three phase sequential model for the Loughcrew complex, based on Sheridan's (1985/6) developmental scheme. Cooney (2000a, 159) believes that such an approach allows one to further appreciate how the complex evolved through the actions of some Neolithic people (see also Thomas 1990; 1992; Fraser 1998). What this scheme highlights is that as with the Boyne Valley passage tombs, the larger Loughcrew passage tombs seem to be built *after* most of the smaller ones (*contra* Herity 1974, 84-7), with the smaller passage being built in the first two phases. The passage tombs were not all built at the same time, rather there were repetitions, episodes and punctuated performances over time. The settings of the tombs in the final stages draw the spectator's attention to the more level areas at Loughcrew, creating 'stage' settings. It is noteworthy that as soon as one creates a stage, there is gaze and distance, performance and otherness, although particular interactions can subvert or abolish these dimensions (Baudrillard 2003, 27).

Of the 31 cairns now visible at Loughcrew today (Cooney 1990, 743), seven have intact ground features, while 21 have remaining interior fragments and 17 have partial or complete kerbs (McMann 1994, 526). Many of the visual motifs are deteriorating (15 cairns still have motifs today) and many more have been lost in the last hundred years as a result of weather conditions, erosion, modern afforestation and even by flourishing nettles (Conwell 1866, 365). The surviving images on do not present the same 'mature' plastic style that was observed at the Boyne Valley passage tombs, and appear more as a collection of random images that are '…crowded onto surfaces in a busy and seemingly unfocused manner…' (O'Sullivan 1993, 30). Following O'Sullivan's (1996, 87) typological sequence, none of the motifs progress beyond the Step 1 standard Irish image designs, with the plastic aspects of the stones rarely explored. Due to restrictions of space here and these preservation issues, I will focus on select cairns and their visual motifs to further understand some of the contradictions, past actions and dramas that may have been played out at these sites. Before engaging in the specifics of the archaeological data, I will briefly introduce the concept of the carnivalesque.

Strange lusts and terrifying actions

In attempting to appreciate the Loughcrew summits, I have recently been drawn to the notion of the carnivalesque and its pervasive and influential visual imagery. The word 'carnival' often evokes an image of an amusement park, Disney theme park, or state fair. Historically, however, carnivals in Europe were quite different affairs. For instance, although they share the same ideas of merriment with their modern counterparts, European medieval carnivals were much more all-encompassing. Contemporary carnivals are diminished examples of the physical lusting, mutating and mutilating activities that were played out during some previous carnival environments whilst consuming excessive psychoactive substances[1]. Mikhail Bakhtin was one of the first authors to coin the term 'carnivalesque' (1968). He describes the carnivalesque as something that is created when the themes of the carnival subvert, distort and invert habitual or established society. In carnival, all that is marginalised and excluded, such as the mad, the scandalous and the uncertain, takes centre stage and liberates in an explosion of otherness (Stam 1989, 86). In this environment, 'negative' bodily expressions such as hunger, thirst, defecation and copulation become a 'positive' corrosive force; life enjoys a symbolic victory over death. Bakhtin (1968) argued that folk-humour based societies in early modern Europe created manifestations of the carnivalesque that laughed at and mimicked those in authority, who believed that social *mentalités*, history, destiny and fate were static and unalterable. The carnival is not 'irrational'; it is the bodily immersion into false façades, monstrous creations, feasts, comic rites and protocols, games and dramas, parodies, processions and visual imagery. It is the 'overlay' of many things and worldviews at once, it is the world turned upside-down, razing and generation coupled with comic, sensuous and abusive performances. It incorporates unbridled juxtapositions, grotesque ruptures and impugnation between binary oppositions and their parodies; it is the mundane routine with fantastical images. Thus it creates an environment where '...everything is pregnant with its opposite, within an alternative logic of permanent contradiction...' (Shohat and Stam 2001, 35). Within carnival, all barriers, norms and prohibitions are temporally suspended (Bakhtin 1968, 15). The carnival incorporates a different kind of communication, based on free and familiar contact (Bakhtin 1968, 17; Stam 1989, 86). The term 'carnivalesque' therefore refers to the carnivalising of normal daily life fluctuating within fleeting permanence. It incorporates a number of themes and these can be summarised as follows:

a) The activation of life and love and the actualisation of myths, with communal and cosmic reunions.
b) Emphasis on sacrifice through the concatenation of life and death.
c) The idea of bisexuality and the practice of transvestitism as a release from socially imposed sex or gender roles. This can also incorporate same-sex orientated practices.
d) A celebration of the grotesque, excessive bodies, orifices and protuberances, with a rejection of social decorum and polite speech.
e) Subversion through the world being turned upside-down, emphasising the permanence of change.
f) Anti-aesthetics that illuminate asymmetry, heterogeneity and the oxymoron, while erasing boundaries between spectators and objects or performers (Stam 1989, 93-94).

Yet the carnivalesque is not only a Western, pre-Renaissance tradition; anthropological examples include the Navajos of Utah who have special social practices for overturning 'good' order and respectable aesthetics. In another instance, the Sioux of North America use ritual clowns or *heyoka* to violate conventional expectations. The *heyoka* are noted to perform seemingly 'foolish' acts; in an example a man is described as riding backwards on his horse with his boots on backwards so that he is coming when he is really going; if it is hot he covers himself in blankets and shivers as if cold and *always* says 'yes' when he means 'no' (Tedlock 1975, 106). These performances are designed to entertain, but more importantly they are designed to open up the spectators through laughter to a desired 'power-filled' and spiritual experience. For the Navajos of Utah, clowns 'open' people up with a mixture of laughter and panic, and when they approach certain spectators '...the smiles of the women and children quickly change to expressions of surprise, tempered with fear...' (Tedlock 1975, 107). The children may have cause for alarm as they are often told that the clowns will carry them off and eat them. Certainly the 'Fool Dancers' of the Kwakiut native Americans occasionally kill spectators by throwing stones or stabbing them with sticks (Tedlock 1975, 107). In these examples not *everyone* has to invert or participate, they can watch if they like (sometimes at some personal risk)[2], while the marginal is briefly brought to the centre. Through these performances the carnivalesque creates more than alternative realities and worldviews, it is life itself, but formed via certain patterns of play (Bakhtin 1968, 7).

Some studies show that often when one finds inequalities of power, wealth and status, one also finds practices that 'turn the world upside-down' (e.g. Tedlock 1975; Gilmore 1998; Bailey 2005). I intend to take the theme of a world inverted, and demonstrate how it is played out by the architecture of the Loughcrew passage tombs and settings themselves. For example, when one enters a passage tomb, there is a sensation of entering the earth itself, or a different 'other' place. This feeling of a 'world inverted' is *magnified* by the processes of engraving images and by overlaying motifs with other motifs. Through 'unfinished'

---

[1] See Gilmore's (1998) description of Andalusian street carnivals in southern Spain for modern European examples.

[2] In a sense there are no 'real' spectators within carnivalesque environments as all near are immersed within it; they live in it with 'normal' life ceasing to exist during its time-span (Bakhtin 1968, 7).

and ongoing processes (see Gell 1998, 80), 'senses' of permanent resistance are literally etched away, as one engraves a permanent and timeless stone. The possible application and erosion of natural pigment[3] (via liquids?) may also have subtly evoked 'energies' against diverse authority that was opposed to change. Whether these authorities were the dead, mythic entities or social elders will remain unknown. We can, however, argue that the idea of the carnivalesque allows people to move beyond the limits of the material, beyond the stone and beyond the motifs themselves. At Loughcrew there are two episodes of the superimposition of one motif with another (Jones 2004, 209, Fig. 21.6). The superimposition of motifs in this context may be a sublime celebration of a world layered upon layer and turned upside down, the celebration and animation of life in a place of the dead. Such a proposition recalls Nietzsche's description of a Dionysian fête, in which the revellers under the influence of narcotic drinks forever exult in the transformation of appearances (Stam 1989, 89).

This paper incorporates Jones's (2004; see also O'Sullivan 1986; Eogan 1996) position, but was initial inspired by C. S. Lewis's (1971) paper 'meditation in a toolshed', in which he stressed the differences between looking *at* and looking *along* a particular idea. I am concerned that past models regarding Irish passage tomb motifs have focused more on the structural forms of motifs than the processes that helped produce them (see also Jones 2004, 202-3). They therefore are more about looking *at* the forms rather than looking *along* the processes. Indeed, Conkey (1982) stated that archaeologists tend to focus more on the 'secretions' of a process (that is the structured motifs), because they do not know how to deal with the process itself (see also Thomas 2004, 145-161). The motifs on the Loughcrew passage tombs offer a unique opportunity to focus on these processes of 'secretion' as they were produced in chronological sequences. By citing specific examples from Carnbane East and West, I will demonstrate how the initial creation of images and the superimposition of particular motifs may be viewed as the embodiments of eternally creative carnivalesque principles. Individual stones are described in detail to emphasis the repetitions and differences that are played out at Loughcrew.

East meets west

Cairn T
This cairn is the focal tomb on Carnbane East and is a cruciform passage tomb 10m long (Figure 2.2). It is also a 'stalled' structure similar to Tumulus J at Dowth, Boyne

[3] Unfortunately, there is no hard evidence at the moment for the stones in Ireland ever being painted. Breuil and Macalister (1921, 4) suggested that some stones were originally painted and that environmental conditions have not permitted survival. Certainly, paint survives on some Iberian megalithic imagery, where motifs in red and/or black were applied to a white background (Shee-Twohig 1981, 32-5). Traces of pigment have recently been found by taking infra-red photographs of decorated surfaces in the main chamber at Maeshowe, Orkney (Bradley *et al.* 2000).

Valley (Herity 1974, 41). Cairn T, *c.* 35m in diameter, is visually noticeable from the lower plains surrounding Loughcrew and from most of the uneven topography below the hills themselves (Herity 1974, 42; Fraser 1998, 214). Interestingly, as one reaches near the summit of Carnbane East, from any direction, Cairn T and the other cairns disappear from view. It is not until one is three-quarters of the way up that the cairns appear again. This feature has been argued to represent the visual capitalisation of the natural aspects of the hill, architecturally creating an additional visual and physical boundary for a particular sense of being or experience (Fraser 1998, 215). The entrance constitutes a V-shaped in-turning in the kerb surrounding the cairn, with the façade emphasised by setting increasingly larger stones towards the entrance (Herity 1974, 42). Both Conwell (1866, 372) and Rotherham (1895, 311) reported loose quartz lumps outside the entrance and base of K29, or the 'Hag's chair' (Conwell 1866, 371). Conwell also described a wall of quartz around the entire base of the cairn (1872, 91). Regrettably, due to undocumented restoration work in the 1940s, there is no surviving evidence for it (Shee Twohig 1981, 214; 1996, 73; McMann 1994, 537). Here, the tomb is thus described in its current state. Two uprights flank the opening to the passage, itself covered by a large lintel block, completing the façade and oriented south-east towards the Boyne (McMann 1994, 535). There is a central octagonal chamber (2 – 2.5m in diameter) with three adjoining recesses and a corbelled roof. All the recesses and main passage have a high sill (c. 0.5m high); above each of these there is a limestone lintel that interlocks with the uprights of the central chamber. In total, there are 19 decorated orthostats, 2 decorated sillstones, 8 decorated roofstones and 1 decorated kerbstone at Cairn T (Shee Twohig 1981, 214; see Figure 2.4). The entrance to the passage is demarcated with a decorated sillstone marked with irregular motifs (including 3 parallel arcs), and the two stones facing the passage (C1 and C15) also have similar designs to each other. Located near the entrance on the left hand side are two heavily decorated stones: L1 has motifs covering the entire front face of the stone, producing a striking arrangement of dots and concentric circles. Similar designs are presented on the nearby jambstones L2, L3, L4 and the opposing R4, while R5 and L5 are similar yet with more concentric circles and cupmarks (Shee Twohig 1981, figs. 232-34; 1996, 73). The stones R5 and L5 mark the last part of the passageway into the main chamber, and it has been suggested that the cupmarks on them were deepened artificially by chalk and stone balls, such as those found in Cairn L (Conwell 1866, 368-9; also see below here), being repeatedly inserted into them (McMann 1993, 28). These repeated interactive performances are thought to possibly be part of processes that dissolve boundaries between humans and stone or even worlds during 'normal' or altered-states of consciousness (McMann 1994, 541). Indeed, the actual cup-hole may have been understood as a circular tunnel extending into the surface of the stone (Bradley 1995, 113). Such acts that incorporate the inversion of surfaces fit well with the discussions of the carnivalesque. All the chamber orthostats include motifs (C1, C5, C10 and C15), predominantly circles arcs and serpentiforms, as do the sills at the entrances (Shee Twohig 1981, 214-5). Speculating on the possible stimuli especially for these

Figure 2.2. Cairn T, Carnbane East with the 'Hag's Chair', K29 at the front (source: Michael Fox).

Figure 2.3. The façade at Cairn T, Carnbane East (source Michael Fox).

'snake' images on some of the stones, we can consider schizophrenia as a pathological condition, which induces not only entoptic phenomena[4], but also auditory hallucinations (Al-Issa 1978). A recent study conducted by Horowitz (1964) investigated the differences and associations between what schizophrenic patients described and drew after hallucinations in an attempt to determine their etiology. For example, initial descriptions of 'vicious snakes' were drawn as wavy lines, whilst 'two

---

[4] The term 'entoptic' refers to visual sensations derived from the structure of the optic system anywhere from the eyeball to the cortex (see Klüver 1926; Knoll *et al.* 1963; Siegal 1977). These images are generally multicoloured geometric or abstract shapes and are perceived when the eyes are closed, although they can occur as external hallucinations (Hodgson 2000). Helvenston and Bahn (2002, 11) have recently requested that archaeologists

dispense with the term 'entopic', but I will continue to use it here, as it has been adopted into the general archaeological literature (e.g. Clottes and Lewis-Williams 1998; Hodgson 2000; Ross 2001), and because this reduces possible misunderstandings.

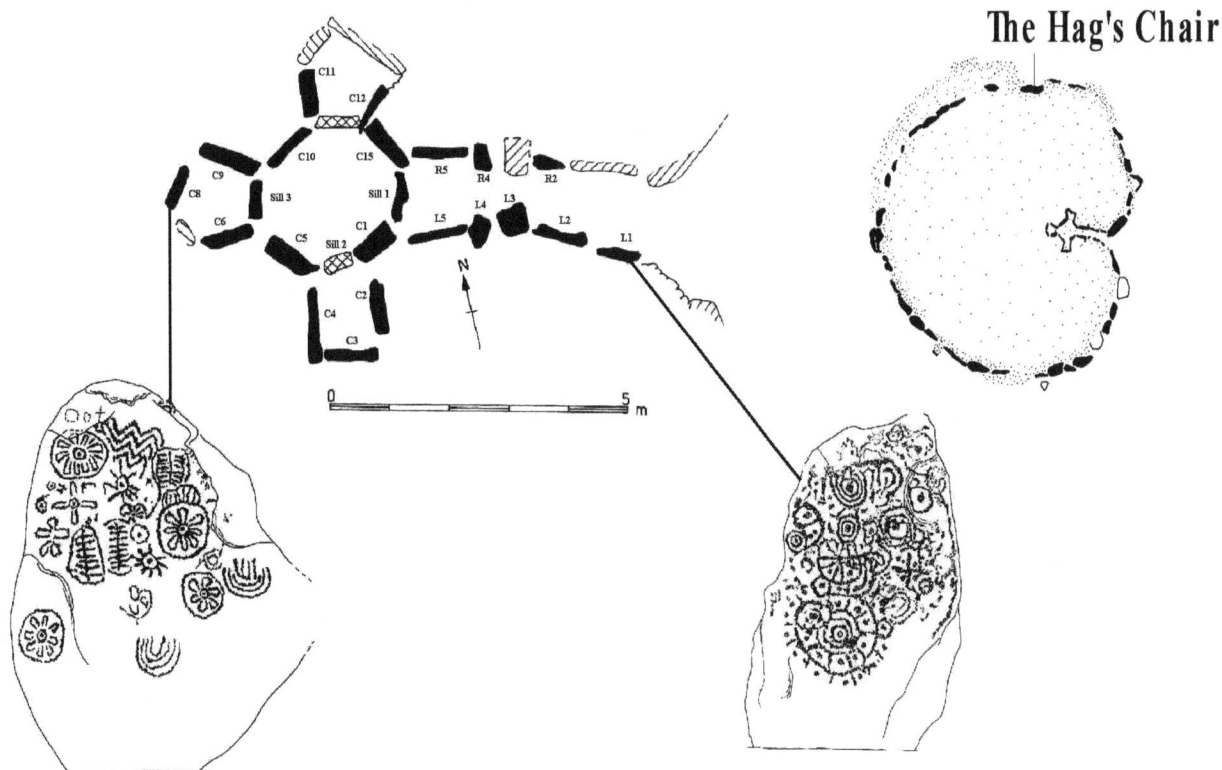

Figure 2.4. Plan of Cairn T with illustrations of C8 and L1, Loughcrew, Co. Meath. Scale represents internal plan only
(after Shee Twohig 1981, Fig. 232, 325; McMann 1993, 26).

armies struggling over my soul' arose from the subjective experience of seeing moving sets of dots (Horowitz 1964, 513). Horowitz's (1964; 1975) studies are interesting, as they suggest that once entoptic or geometric images are experienced, subjective interpretation and social rhetoric automatically consume them and that the designs can readily be converted into descriptive frameworks. It is possible that if some modern people assign these patterns to conversations and thoughts, then the inhabitants of Neolithic Ireland may have as well.

Cells 2 and 3 both show some repeated concerns that can help us appreciate the ways in which the tomb was experienced, the histories of its creation and its relationships with the cosmos. Both cells are heavily decorated, and it has been suggested that some motifs are deliberately placed in relation to sunlight. This is the case for Cell 2's central stone, C8, where particular motifs are illuminated by direct sunlight at the equinoxes (Brennan 1983; O'Brien 1992; see Figure 2.5). It has been suggested that the reflected sunlight then illuminates the roofstone (Brennan 1983, 169). There are, however, inherent dangers in focusing on the particular images that are highlighted by the sun, as a result of the extensive OPW (Office of Public Works) restorations that altered the original shape of the entrance (McMann 1994, 537).

In terms of decoration, Shee Twohig (1996, 74) has noted that fine, coarse and medium point methods were employed in decorating C8. The particular images made with medium point continue under the supporting corbels, and suggest that the other fine and coarse images were made whilst C8 was *in situ*. Similarly, three grades of

picking tool were used to create the panel on the roofstone in Cell 2 (Shee Twohig 1981, 217). This roofstone has imagery all over the underside face. As the motifs continue beyond the supporting corbels, it is likely that the stone was decorated before being placed into the passage tomb and in this respect it is similar to the right-hand recess roofstone in Newgrange Site 1, Co. Meath (see O'Kelly 1982, 181). Furthermore, Shee Twohig (1981, 216) has commented that it would have been very difficult to decorate a stone so intensively whilst lying on ones back. Indeed, today the images are best seen when lying on one's back with one's feet facing towards the passage entrance. This feature has led Thomas (1992, 149) to comment that only those people who had access to the deeper areas of the passage tomb would be able to engage with these images. The motifs on the roofstone are varied and generally 'haphazardly' placed, especially near the centre (Shee Twohig 1981, 217, Fig. 238). As the images are basic abstract geometric, and as they do not conform to the modulations of the stone's surface, we can place this roofstone within step one of O'Sullivan's (1996) sequence.

Similar themes are played out in Cell 3. The underside of the cell lintel has a picked dot with six radiating lines, while the underside of the roof slab has an incised image consisting of parallel zigzags (Shee Twohig 1981, 217; Figure 2.6). These angular incised motifs are thought to have occurred before the later picked motifs in the passage tomb (Jones 2004, 209). They therefore indicate episodes of superimposition. As several of the angles producing the zigzag do not meet, they can be considered as an entoptic 'fortification' illusion or *teichopsia* image (see Richards 1971; Niedermeyer 1990; Dronfield 1994). Its location on

Figure 2.5. Photograph taken at 6:51am showing the shaped beam of equinox sunlight illuminating C8 (source: Michael Fox; see also images in Brennan 1983, 100).

the underside of the roof slab, in an inaccessible position, might suggest that the image was produced before the stone was set in place. The notion that entoptic images were created onto/into stone before most other designs has previously been explored in detail on some of the Boyne Valley passage tombs (e.g. Cochrane 2001). That entoptic

images were used might suggest a desire to incorporate otherworldly/alternative influences or interactions, and possibly performances influenced by psychoactive substances or individuals with pathological conditions.

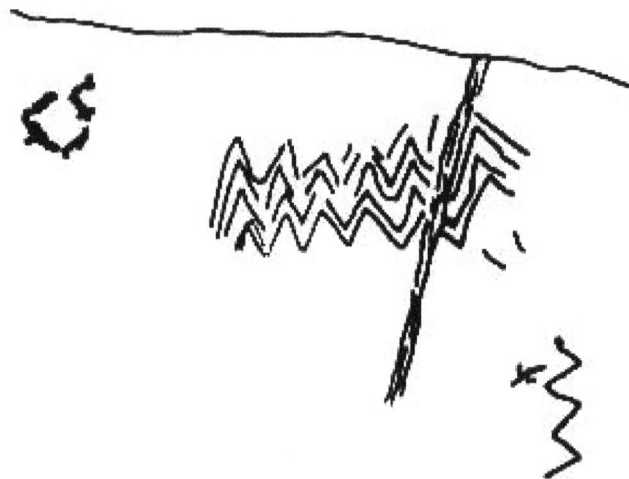

Figure 2.6. Underside of Roofstone Cell 3, Cairn T, Loughcrew, Co. Meath (Shee Twohig 1981, 238).

In the entire Cairn T passage tomb, radial images dominate, being present on 37% of all the carved surfaces. Shee Twohig (1996) has commented that Cairn T demonstrates a desire for coherence, with almost identically styled images appearing in juxtaposition to each other in the passageway, with the 4 main orthostats in the central chamber (C1, C5, C10 and C15) also having similar imagery. Such symmetry fits well with Foucault's (2002, 235) definitions of the roles that heterotopias may play.

The juxtaposition of similar images creates a space of illusions that exposes and enhances the partitioning and ordering of movement within the passage tomb, whilst simultaneously reflecting and inverting the random, messy and jumbled aspects of life.

To the north of Cairn T and on the exterior is located K29 or the 'Hag's Chair' (Figure 2.7). This kerbstone has visual imagery on its front and back face. The top of the central

Figure 2.7. K29 also known as the 'Hag's Chair', Loughcrew, Co. Meath (source: Michael Fox).

part of this kerbstone is believed to be artificially cut to create the chair appearance (Shee Twohig 1981, 217; *contra*. Conwell 1866, 371), and the inlaid cross on the 'seat' surface may have been cut by surveyors engaged in the 'Trigonometrical Irish Survey' (Frazer 1893, 321; but see McMann 1993, 27). Conwell commented that many of the images on K29 were '...much defaced by the action of time and weather...' (1866, 372). The images that we see today, over a hundred years later, are unfortunately even more weathered, so that Shee Twohig (1981, Fig. 238) had to reproduce Du Noyer's water-colour sketch from Frazer's paper (1893, Fig. 45) in her corpus. Six inverted boxed 'U' shapes and several double 'U' shapes and circles, one with central dot, however, still exist on the front face, and there are two roughly executed concentric circles on the back (Shee Twohig 1981, 217). Considering that K29 is the third largest kerbstone, decorated and such a prominent feature, it is surprising that it was not placed diametrically opposed to the entrance, as is seen at some of the Boyne Valley passage tombs (e.g. K52, Newgrange Site 1). That images are presented on the outside of the passage tomb does suggest that they were intended to be seen by spectators in 'public'. Such display may have allowed the passage tomb to operate within networks of opening and closing that both isolated and rendered it penetrable. Performances with these external images may have incorporated differing or mirroring gestures and permissions than the internal motifs.

Cairn L

Cairn L is the focal passage tomb on Carnbane West and is located on the north-eastern edge of the plateau. The passage tomb is orientated east-south-east, in the direction of Cairn M, with the entrance indicated by a curve inwards on the kerb circumference (Conwell 1866, 367; Figure 2.8). On the grounds of their size (*c.* 40.5m in diameter)

and orientations some regard Cairns T and L as the two most important passage tombs in Loughcrew (e.g. Herity 1974, 53; Brennan 1983, 69). As Conwell (1866) first observed, Cairn L is the only passage tomb at Loughcrew with the original corbelled roofing intact, although the central part has been replaced with modern concrete (Shee Twohig 1996, 75). The first 6m of the passage was also restored (Deane 1889-91, 164). The passage proceeds from the entrance into a large asymmetrical central chamber with eight adjoining cells (see Figure 2.9). The central chamber is marked by a large isolated limestone orthostat or monolith (Cooney 1996, 30), and this is suggested to be placed so that it is illuminated by the sun at certain times of the year (Brennan 1983, 110; although see above discussions on reconstructions). This may have enhanced beliefs of permanence, dissolution and disappearance. The pillar may also have been associated with the ones north-west of Cairn D, Carnbane West, and may also have organised movements in and around the hilltop and the passage tomb itself (Shee Twohig 1996; McMann 1994). These movements may have been prescribed for certain festivals at different times of the year. Forty-three of the kerbstones currently survive and none contain visual imagery. The lack of imagery on the kerbstones may be the result of preservation, or it may have been deliberate.

Six of the passage orthostats include imagery (R1, R3, R4, L1, L3 and L4). R4 is covered in deep cupmarks and although Frazer (1895, 64-71, cited in Shee Twohig 1981, 211) stated that they were caused by the burrowing of the sea urchin *echinus lividus*, McMann (1993, 34) has again suggested that these were created for or by the periodical insertion of stone or chalk balls. Other stones that have embellished natural hollows include C1 and C17.

Figure 2.8. Front and side views of Cairn L, Loughcrew, Co. Meath (source: Michael Fox).

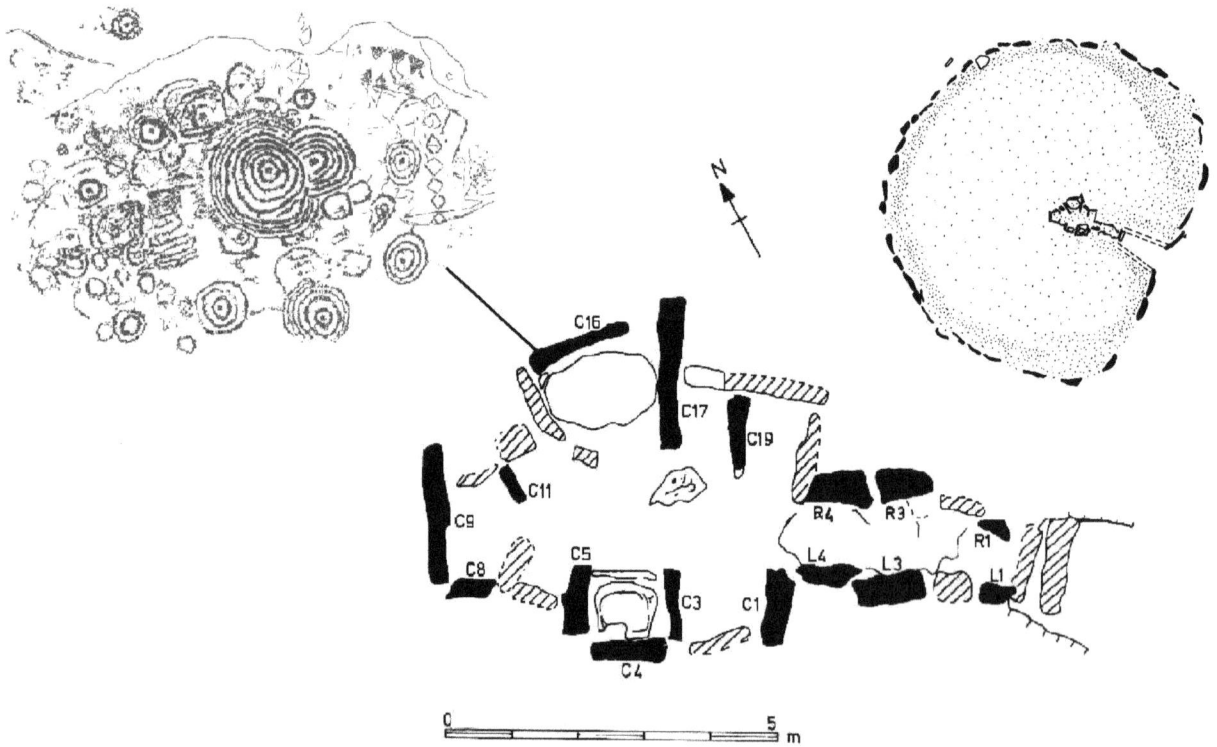

Figure 2.9. Plan of Cairn L with illustration of C16, Carnbane West, Loughcrew, Co. Meath. Scale represents internal plan only (after Shee Twohig 1981, Figs. 222, 226; McMann 1993, 33).

Cells 2 and 6 both contain stone basins under which fragments of more than 900 charred bones, approximately 48 human teeth, 3 stone balls, 8 white balls and a polished oval object were found (Conwell 1866, 368; Herity 1974, 238). The fragmentation and disruption of human remains may have been a deliberate attempt to rupture notions of a given reality, creating new illusions and beliefs that ricochet between secure and destabilised knowledges (Bailey 2005, 183-7). The decorated orthostats surrounding the basin in Cell 2 (C3 west face, C4 and C5 east face) are mainly decorated with circular motifs (see Figure 2.9). This occurrence has led Shee Twohig (1996, 76) to draw comparisons between this left hand cell with a basin, and that of the left hand cell in Newgrange Site 1, Boyne Valley. Cell 6, located on the north and right hand side, is the largest cell in the structure and indeed Loughcrew. Its stone basin is almost 2m long (Conwell 1866, 368) and near the most 'extensively' decorated stone (C16) in Loughcrew (Herity 1974, 54; Shee Twohig 1996, 76; see Figure 2.9). The motifs on this stone are closely grouped together and in some instances actually overlap, which is rare at this site (O'Sullivan 1993, 32), suggesting two chronological episodes. As the images on the lower portion are obscured by the stone basin, it is suggested that they were executed before the basin was set in place (Shee Twohig 1996, 76).

The placement of basins within passage tombs is interesting, as basins are sometimes utilised within carnivalesque environments. For instance, the Hopi of northeast Arizona dress some of their clowns as women and make them wash their 'female' legs in a 'ritual' basin whilst displaying a false vulva. Another clown wearing a false penis then climbs on top of the 'female' and proceeds to '…imitate copulation with her with the utmost grossness right on the sacred shrine…' (Tedlock 1975, 115). This role reversal and perversion of social norms at special zones and with 'ritual' material culture is performed to fragment prescribed realities as a means of enlightenment. This perversion mirrors one of the features of the carnivalesque, with its tendency to laugh at death and violence (Stam 1989, 101). Indeed, this possible subversion of activities and roles within passage tombs may have helped re-establish traditional orders at some level for some people (Gilmore 1998, 4).

Shee Twohig (1996) has reviewed the construction of Cairn L and its visual imagery to contest Thomas's (1992) assertion that the innermost and deepest parts of a passage tomb are the most 'significant' or important and that this is represented via the complexity of the motifs. The evidence suggests that the individual cells, particularly Cell 6 on the northern right hand side and not the deepest (Cell 4), are more visually 'complex'.

Thus, Cairn L repeats many of the themes outlined for Cairn T, such as size and motif repetition, but also adds further dimensions and inversions of use by the incorporation of basins. These similarities and differences will be discussed further below.

Difference and repetition

With the exception of Cairn T, a recurring theme in a majority of the passage tombs at Loughcrew is the prominence of their right sides as you enter deeper into them. In some instances this is emphasised by the right cell being larger than the others (e.g. at Cairns H and U), and in other examples the central cell on the right side is larger (e.g. Cairns I and L) (Herity 1974, 42; Shee Twohig 1996, 78; McMann 1994, 532). Indeed, the right sides of the passage tombs often contain other distinguishing features such as the stone pillar and basin stone in Cairn L, and the basin/slabs in Cairns H and I. The right cells are often more elaborately decorated (Herity 1974, 42, 123), with the sill stones or backstones being the most visually striking, such as is seen in Cairns H, L, I, and U. In multi-celled passage tombs, the cell in juxtaposition to the elaborately decorated right cell is sometimes also stressed, such as in Cairns I and L. What we might be witnessing is the priority of '…dexter over sinister…' (Herity 1974, 123). Shee Twohig (1996) has highlighted these occurrences and suggests that they constitute a choreography of the practices or performances that may have occurred within the passage tombs. She also noted that that the left cells appeared to be dominated by circular images, with the right cells demonstrating greater variety. Whether this is tantamount to more 'complex' panels is open to debate. Thomas (1992, 146-7) creates a 'basic division' and considers spirals, meanders and dots as 'simple', with concentric circles and lozenges as more 'complex' arrangements. He proposes that 'simple' arrangements are rarely found on the same stone as the more 'complex' ones (1992, 149). In attempting to challenge the dichotomy of 'simple: complex', Shee Twohig (1996, 79) has argued that although 'simple' spirals and 'complex' lozenges do not occur on the same stones, spirals and concentric circles do (on 14 stones). She also notes that concentric circles and lozenges only occur on six stones in total, therefore making the distinctions less impressive and removing some of the assertions of Thomas's spatial depth analysis (1992, Fig. 11.3).

Returning to the superimposed motifs within underground settings, and in considering subversive engagements with them, we may think of these processes as the reversibility of perspectives (Merleau-Ponty 1962). By entering the passage tomb itself, we are seeing a reversal of the idea of Plato's cave. It is the people entering the artificial cave (passage tomb) or artificial worlds that are presented with alternatives to a reality, rather than the people who remain outside. We can, therefore, envisage an Irish Neolithic spectator entering a decorated tomb and being absorbed in the pleasures or horrors of an artificially constructed world, the sublime experience of temporary immersion in an inverted world. Irish Neolithic motifs, through their nature or superimposed construct, are therefore not stable, but rather change their relationship to exterior reality at particular moments in time and place (e.g. the illumination of motifs at particular times of the year). As one mode of reality that is represented by an image loses ground, or is superimposed, another takes its place, creating a matrix consisting of realities within realities. Thus the images create difficulties and tensions.

Thomas's (1990; 1992; 1993) proposals create situations in which 'space' as well as 'spectator' are controlled. For Thomas, the Loughcrew passage tombs act as the '...gradual multiplication of bounded spaces... [creating a] greater subdivision of the audience, depending upon how far they were allowed to penetrate into the monument...' (1990, 176). The shapes of the passage tombs enforce a linear pattern of movement within the passageway and physical 'penetration' into the chamber is dictated by the orthostats and by crossing a 'symbolically-laden' forecourt entrance (Thomas 1990, 174; 176; 1993, 85). In some instances a person has to actually hunker-down to enter, such as at Slieve Gullion, Co. Armagh, and even lie down to see particular images (Lynch 1973, 155; and see discussions above). Within this depicted scheme, 'lower ranked individuals' or more 'subservient' persons were only allowed to the outer parts of the passage tombs (Thomas 1990). Thomas's (1990; 1992; 1993) studies are therefore centred around an 'inside: outside' dichotomy, focused more upon the passage tomb interiors. Thomas (1992, 145) does not discuss external or 'public' engagements other than commenting that there may have been approved patterns of movement between the cairns, possibly a linear based one (see Cooney 1990), with the limited intervisibility between some individual passage tomb exteriors indicating possible sequential encounters. For instance, as one could not see the entrance to Cairn H from the entrance of Cairn L, Carnbane West, one would have to physically move closer to it.

As a response to studies that privilege the interiors of passage tombs, Fraser (1998) suggested that greater importance lay in the larger-scale and possibly more frequent social encounters that could have occurred in the spaces *between* and *outside* the passage tombs at Loughcrew. For Fraser (1998, 209), the public spaces did not only add legitimation to specific practices, authorities and beliefs, but also challenged or subverted them, as a direct result of the public nature of the places and events. The spaces in between the cairns (see Figure 2.1) become 'theatres in the round' (Bradley 1998, 116) and as with theatrical performances, may have incorporated elements of apprehension, risk and danger. The notion of risk and danger is amplified if one imagines the Loughcrew summits to be liminal zones where the dead or spirits dwelt or had access to. As with all theatre spaces, they are designed to produce systems of simulation and illusion of place and persons; the aim of theatre is unauthenticity (Pearson and Shanks 2001, 117). Indeed, it is within liminal spaces that all performances operate (Pearson and Shanks 2001, 53). By incorporating notions of performative simulation and the carnivalesque, we can begin to create more emotional narratives. Carnivalesque performances may have been at play within the open spaces, involving larger numbers of people; more people than the passage tombs could hold. As such, we can imagine some people acting with less physical restrictions to movement, deploying festive laughter to momentarily enjoy a symbolic victory over the spirits and death, over all the worldviews that restrict and maybe even oppress within daily life (see Stam 1989, 86). By deploying carnival ideas people may have overcome the confines between passage tomb, cairn, hill topography, bodies that are alive or dead, whole or cremated, and the world in general. Bakhtin

describes these events as 'interchange' and 'interorientation' and proposes that '...eating, drinking, defecation and other elimination (sweating, blowing of the nose, sneezing), as well as copulation, pregnancy, dismemberment, swallowing up by another body – all these acts are performed on the confines of the body and the outer world, or on the confines of the old and new body. In all these events the beginnings and end of life are closely linked and interwoven...' (1968, 317).

Conclusion

We do not have to settle for interpretations that depict either some people operating within passage tombs, or conversely only performing outside cairns. By developing the models presented by Thomas (1990; 1992; 1993; 2001) and Fraser (1998), we can begin to speculate that different people were doing different things and sometimes even the same things, but in alternative settings (i.e. *inside* and *outside* the passage tombs). The Loughcrew settings may represent permanence in flux with punctuated shifts in social orientations. Within the passage tombs the activities may have been more formalised, with spatial distinctions, barriers and the motifs creating fluid and interactive types of communication. These events may have been the 'internal' simulacrum of carnivalesque performances as hyper-real (greater than real) worldview palliatives for the participants (Baudrillard 1994; Cochrane forthcoming). Outside the passage tombs these activities may have been temporally suspended, with the carnival in the 'island' areas erasing the boundaries between spectator and spectacle. We can maybe imagine the laughter of the masses creating an alternative form of free consciousness and unique perspectives on experience, that were no less important than seriousness or even tears (e.g. as seen at some modern Western funeral practices). Carnivals can certainly be transgressive, creating an 'irrational' yet real state of happiness, from miserable situations or locations (Stam 1989, 101, 119). Indeed, the apertures to the passage tombs themselves conform to carnivalesque modes in that they can instantly invert from an entrance threshold into an exit one, with entry leading to exclusion and openings becoming closings (or vice versa).

The conceptual models that were used to create the images on the interior of the passage tombs were made in a 'real' world to '...represent the world as being *capable of being otherwise* than we believe it to be...' (Gell 1992, 217 original emphasis). The images on the Loughcrew passage tombs are simulations of a given reality, a hyper-reality and as Gell suggests, '...the world is as it is, but we think it could be otherwise, and it may be otherwise than we think...' (1992, 217). The Loughcrew passage tombs act as nodes to continuity and rupture, and represent Neolithic simulations and simulacra in that they reference a reality that does or did not exist. Simulation in a Neolithic context is not about referential beings or substances, it is the possible generation of a 'real' without origin or reality: a hyper-real (Baudrillard 1994; Cochrane forthcoming). The motifs, passage tombs, covering cairns and 'island' areas simultaneously represent, contest and invert spaces and place, visually and physically. These features were not static, sanitised and sterile. Neolithic people had no 'physical' access to alternative believed worlds, for if they had physically accessed them, they are no longer alternative believed worlds, but rather the actual world itself. Carnivalesque performances may have therefore facilitated at some level a feeling of being able to temporally rupture one world and access others. Experimentation with simulations of a worldview via motifs on passage tombs, 'real' or 'imagined', possibly allowed some Neolithic people mental access to the other beyond (see Cochrane 2001). The visual motifs are therefore sources for invention and belonging, or processes with dimensions of creativity and 'reason', although they could have also been 'inept' and 'unreasonable', creating gaps and absences within the appearances of the solidity of the world in which they lived in (Shanks 1992, 118, 137). These processes can lead to an escalation of what is thought to be true, of the lived daily experience, through modes of display, engagement and disengagement. This can create feelings of anxiety, and can also create an increase in the material production of images that are of the real. These anxieties can produce subversive and inversive technologies or strategies. The individual motif and the passage tomb within a specific location might therefore be an intensified expression of a chain of images, discourses and material realities that helped support and distort people's perceptions of their worlds in direct and indirect ways.

Acknowledgements

I would especially like to thank Dani Hofmann and Jess Mills for their comments and suggestions on earlier drafts of this paper – I have complete respect for you both! Michael Fox from www.knowth.com was very kind in giving me permission to use his photographs of Loughcrew – it is an impressive website. Discussions with Doug Bailey on the carnivalesque and visual culture were invaluable. Thank you also to Andy Jones for discussing ideas with me and allowing me access to his work. I am grateful to my supervisor Alasdair Whittle; he has supplied unfailing help and guidance throughout my research and this paper. The recommendations made by these people have undoubtedly improved this work, but the errors and mistakes are still mine alone.

References

Al-Issa, I. 1978. Sociocultural factors in hallucinations. *International Journal of Social Psychiatry* 24(3), 167-76.

Bailey, D.W. 2005. Prehistoric figurines: representation and corporeality in the Neolithic. London: Routledge.

Bakhtin, M.M. 1968. *Rabelais and his world*. Trans. by H. Iswolsky. Cambridge: MIT Press.

Baudrillard, J. 1994. *Simulacra and simulation*. Trans. by Sheila Faria Glaser. Ann Arbor: University of Michigan Press.

Baudrillard, J. 2003. *Passwords*. Trans. by Chris Turner. London: Verso.

Baxandall, M. 1997. *Shadows and enlightenment*. New Haven: Yale University Press.

Bloch, M.E.F. 1977. The past and the present in the past. *Man* 12, 278-92.

Bloch, M.E.F. 1995. Questions not to ask of Malagasy carvings. . In I. Hodder, M. Shanks, A. Alexandri, V. Buchli, J. Carmen, J. Last, and G. Lucus (eds), *Interpreting archaeology: finding meaning in the past*, 212-15. London: Routledge.

Bloch, M.E.F. 1998. *How we think they think: anthropological approaches to cognition, memory and literacy*. Oxford: Westview Press.

Bradley, R. 1995. Making sense of prehistoric rock art. *British Archaeology* 9, 8-9.

Bradley, R. 1998. *The significance of monuments: on the shaping of human experience in Neolithic and Bronze Europe*. London: Routledge.

Bradley, R. 2000. *The archaeology of natural places*. London: Routledge.

Bradley, R., Phillips, T., Richards, C. and Webb, M. 2000. Decorating the houses of the dead: incised and pecked motifs in Orkney chambered tombs. *Cambridge Archaeological Journal* 11(1), 45-67.

Brennan, M. 1983. *The stars and the stones: ancient art and astronomy in Ireland*. London: Thames and Hudson.

Breuil, H. and Macalister, R.A.S. 1921. A study of the chronology of Bronze Age sculpture in Ireland. *Proceedings of the Royal Irish Academy*, 36C, 1-9.

Clottes, J. and Lewis-Williams, D. 1998. *The shamans of prehistory: trance and magic in the painted caves*. New York: Harry N. Abrams.

Cochrane, A. 2001. Between heaven and earth: contextualising the alien art of Irish passage tombs. Unpublished MA dissertation. Cardiff University.

Cochrane, A. forthcoming. The simulacra and simulations of Irish Neolithic passage tombs. In I. Russell (ed.), *Image and meaning in archaeology and the heritage industry: towards a counter-modern approach to the past*. New York: Springer-Kluwer.

Coffey, G. 1912. *New grange and other incised tumuli in Ireland: the influence of Crete and the Aegean in the extreme west of Europe in early times*. Dublin: Hodges, Figgis and Co. Ltd.

Conkey, M.W, 1982. Boundedness in art and society. In I. Hodder (ed.), *Symbolic and structural archaeology*, 115-128. Cambridge: Cambridge University Press.

Conwell, E.A. 1864. On ancient remains, hitherto undescribed, in the County of Meath. *Proceedings of the Royal Irish Academy* (1st series) 9, 42-50.

Conwell, E.A. 1866. Examination of the ancient sepulchral cairns on the Loughcrew Hills, County of Meath. *Proceedings of the Royal Irish Academy* (1st series) 9, 355-79.

Conwell, E.A. 1872. On the identification of the ancient cemetery at Loughcrew, Co. Meath; and the discovery of the tomb of Ollamh Fodhla. *Proceedings of the Royal Irish Academy* (2nd series) 1 (Literature), 72-106.

Cooney, G. 1987. *North Leinster in the earlier prehistoric period (7,000 – 1,400 bc): a settlement and environmental perspective on foragers, farmers and early metallurgists*. Unpublished PhD Thesis submitted to University College, Dublin.

Cooney, G. 1990. The place of megalithic tomb cemeteries in Ireland. *Antiquity* 64, 741-753.

Cooney, G. 1996. Standing stones: marking the Neolithic landscape. *Archaeology Ireland* 10(2), 29-30.

Cooney, G. 2000a. *Landscapes of Neolithic Ireland.* New York: Routledge.

Cooney, G. 2000b. Sliabh na Callighe through time: Loughcrew, Co. Meath. *Archaeology Ireland,* Heritage Guide No. 12.

Cooney, G. 2004. Neolithic worlds; islands in the Irish Sea. In V. Cummings and C. Fowler (eds), *The Neolithic of the Irish Sea: materiality and traditions of practice* 145-59. Oxford: Oxbow.

Cooney, G. and Grogan, E. 1994. *Irish prehistory: a social perspective.* Dublin: Wordwell.

Deane, T.N. 1889-91. On some ancient monuments scheduled under Sir John Lubbock's Act, 1882. *Proceedings of the Royal Irish Academy* 1 (Third Series), 161-5.

Dillon, F. 1990. *An analysis of two lithic collections.* Unpublished M.A. thesis, University College, Dublin.

Dronfield, J. 1994. Subjective visual phenomena in Irish passage tomb art: vision, cosmology and shamanism. Unpublished PhD Thesis submitted to Cambridge University.

Dundes, A. 1980. *Interpreting folklore.* Indiana: Indiana University Press.

Eliade, M. 1964. *Shamanism: archaic techniques of ecstasy.* Princetown: Princetown University Press.

Eogan, G. 1996. Pattern and place: a preliminary study of the decorated kerbstones at Site 1, Knowth, Co. Meath and their comparative setting. *Revue Archéologique de l'Ouest,* supplément n° 8, 97-104.

Foucault, M. 2002. Of other spaces. Trans. by J. Miskowiec. In N. Mirzoeff (ed.), *The visual culture reader: second edition,* 229-36. London: Routledge.

Fraser, S.M. 1998. The public forum and the space between: the materiality of social strategy in the Irish Neolithic. *Proceedings of the Prehistoric Society* 64, 203-244.

Frazer, W. 1893. Notes on incised sculpturings on stones in the cairns of Sliabh-Na-Calliaghe, near Loughcrew, County Meath, Ireland. With illustrations from a series of ground-plans and water-colour sketches, by the late G. V. Du Noyer, of the Geological Survey of Ireland. *Proceedings of the Society of Antiquaries of Scotland* 3 (Third Series), 294-340.

Frazer, W. 1895. On cup markings on megalithic monuments due to Echinus Lividus. *Journal of the Royal Society of Antiquaries Ireland* 25, 64-71.

Gell, A. 1992. *The anthropology of time: cultural constructions of temporal maps and images.* Oxford: Berg.

Gell, A. 1998. *Art and agency: an anthropological theory.* Oxford: Oxford University Press.

Gell, A. 1999. Vogel's net: traps as artworks and artworks as traps. In A. Gell (edited by E. Hirsch), *The art of anthropology: essays and diagrams,* 187-214. London: Routledge.

Gilmore, D. 1998. *Carnival and culture: sex, symbol and status.* New Haven: Yale University Press.

Gottdiener, M. 1995. *Postmodern semiotics: material culture and the forms of modern life.* Oxford: Blackwell.

Helvenston, P.A. and Bahn P.G. 2002. *Desperately seeking trance plants: testing the 'three stages of trance' model.* New York: RJ Communication LLC.

Herity, M. 1974. *Irish passage graves: Neolithic tomb-builders in Ireland and Britain, 2500 BC.* Dublin: Irish University Press.

Hirsch, E. 2004. Techniques of vision: photography, disco and renderings of present perceptions in Highland Papua. *The Journal of the Royal Anthropological Institute* 10(1), 19-39.

Hodgson, D. 2000. Shamanism, phosphenes, and early art: an alternative synthesis. *Current Anthropology* 41 (5), 866-873.

Holly, M.A. 1998. Patterns in the Shadows. *Invisible Culture: an electronic journal for Visual Studies,* 1. http://www.rochester.edu/in_visible_culture/Issues-IVC.html.

Horowitz, M.J. 1964. The imagery of visual hallucinations. *Journal of Nervous and Mental Disease* 138(6), 513-23.

Horowitz, M.J. 1975. Hallucinations: an information-processing approach. In R. K. Siegal and L. J. West (eds), *Hallucinations: behaviour, experience, and theory,* 163-95. New York: John Wiley.

Ingold, T. 2000. *The perception of the environment: essays in livelihood, dwelling and skill.* London: Routledge.

Jones, A. 2004. By way of illustration: art, memory and materiality in the Irish Sea and beyond. In V. Cummings and C. Fowler (eds), *The Neolithic of the Irish Sea: materiality and traditions of practice* 202-13. Oxford: Oxbow.

Kimball, M. 2000. Variation and context: ecology and social evolution in Ireland's Later Mesolithic. In A, Desmond, G. Johnson, M. McCarthy, J. Sheehan and E. Shee Twohig (eds), *New agendas in Irish prehistory: papers in commemoration of Liz Anderson,* 31-47. Bray: Wordwell Ltd.

Klüver, H. 1926. Mescal visions and eidetic vision. *American Journal of Psychology* 37(4), 502-515.

Knoll, M., Kugler, J., Höfer, O. and Lawder, S.D. 1963. Effects of chemical stimulation of electrically induced phosphenes on their bandwidth, shape, number, and intensity. *Confinia Neurologica* 23(3), 201-226.

Lewis, C.S. 1971. Meditation in a toolshed. In W. Hooper (ed.), *Undeceptions: essays on theology and ethics,* 171-4. London: Geoffrey Bles.

Lynch, F. 1973. The use of the passage in certain passage graves as a means of communication rather than access. In G. Daniel and P. Kjærum (eds), *Megalithic graves and ritual: papers presented at the III Atlantic colloquium, Moesgård 1969,* 147-61. Copenhagen: Jutland Archaeological Society.

McMann, J. 1993. *Loughcrew the cairns: a guide to an ancient Irish landscape.* Oldcastle: After Hours Books.

McMann, J. 1994. Forms of power: dimensions of an Irish megalithic landscape. *Antiquity* 68, 525-44.

Mitchell, W.J.T. 1994. *Picture Theory.* Chicago: University of Chicago Press.

Merleau-Ponty, M. 1962. *The phenomenology of perception.* London: Routledge.

Niedermeyer, E. 1990. *The epilepsies: diagnosis and management*. Baltimore: Urban and Schwarzenberg.

O'Brien, T. 1992. Light years ago: a study of the cairns of Newgrange and Cairn T Loughcrew, Co. Meath, Ireland. Dublin: Black Cat Press.

O'Kelly, C. 1982. Corpus of Newgrange art. In M. J. O'Kelly, *Newgrange: archaeology, art and legend*, 146-185. London: Thames and Hudson.

O'Sullivan, M. 1986. Approaches to passage tomb art. *Journal of the Royal Society of Antiquaries of Ireland* 116, 68-83.

O'Sullivan, M. 1993. *Megalithic Art in Ireland*. Dublin: Country House.

O'Sullivan, M. 1996. Megalithic art in Ireland and Brittany: divergence or convergence? *Revue Archéologique de l'Ouest*, supplément n° 8, 81-96.

Pearson, M. and Shanks, M. 2001. *Theatre/archaeology*. London: Routledge.

Richards, W. 1971. The fortification illusions of migraines. *Scientific American* 224(5), 88-96.

Ross, M. 2001. Emerging trends in rock-art research: hunter-gatherer culture, land and landscape. *Antiquity* 75, 543-548.

Rotherham, E.C. 1895. On the excavation of a cairn on Slieve-na-Caillighe, Loughcrew. *Journal of the Royal Society of Antiquaries of Ireland* 25(3), 311-6.

Shanks, M. 1992. *Experiencing the past: on the character of archaeology*. London: Routledge.

Shee Twohig, E. 1981. *The megalithic art of western Europe*. Oxford: Clarendon Press.

Shee Twohig, E. 1996. Context and content of Irish passage tomb art. *Revue Archéologique de l'Ouest*, supplément n° 8, 67-80.

Shell, C. and Roughley, C. 2004. Exploring the Loughcrew landscape: a new airborne approach. *Archaeology Ireland* 18(2), 22-5.

Sheridan, J.A. 1985/1986. Megaliths and megalomania: an account, and interpretation, of the development of passage tombs in Ireland. *Journal of Irish Archaeology* 3, 17-30.

Shohat, E. and Stam, R. 2001. Narrativizing visual culture: towards a polycentric aesthetics. In N. Mirzoeff (ed.), *The visual culture reader*, 27-49. London: Routledge.

Siegal, R. K. 1977. Hallucinations. *Scientific American* 237 (4), 132-140.

Stam, R. 1989. *Subversive pleasures: Bakhtin, cultural criticism and film*. London: The John Hopkins University Press.

Tedlock, B. 1975. The clown's way. In D. Tedlock and B. Tedlock (eds), *Teachings from the American earth: Indian religion and philosophy*, 105-18. New York: Liveright.

Tilley, C. 1994. *A phenomenology of landscape: places, paths and monuments*. Oxford: Berg.

Thomas, J. 1990. Monuments from the inside: the case of the Irish megalithic tombs. *World Archaeology* 22, 168-178.

Thomas, J. 1992. Monuments, movement and the context of megalithic art. In N. Sharples and A. Sheridan (eds), *Vessels for the ancestors*, 143-155. Edinburgh: Edinburgh University.

Thomas, J. 1993. The hermeneutics of megalithic space. In C. Tilley (ed.), *Interpretative archaeology*, 73-97. Oxford: Berg.

Thomas, J. 1998. The socio-semiotics of material culture. *Journal of Material Culture* 3, 97-108.

Thomas, J. 2001. Archaeologies of place and landscape. In I. Hodder (ed.), *Archaeological theory today*, 165-186. Cambridge: Polity Press.

Thomas, J. 2004. *Archaeology and modernity*. London: Routledge.

Turner, V. 1982. *From ritual to theatre: the human seriousness of play*. Maryland: PAJ Publications.

van Gennep, A. 1960. *The rites of passage*. Trans. by M. B. Vizedom and G. L. Caffee. London: Routledge and Kegan Paul [first published 1908].

Watson, A. 2004. Fluid horizons. In V. Cummings and C. Fowler (eds), *The Neolithic of the Irish Sea: materiality and traditions of practice* 55-63. Oxford: Oxbow.

Whittle, A. 2004. Stones that float to the sky: portal dolmens and their landscapes of memory and myth. In V. Cummings and C. Fowler (eds), *The Neolithic of the Irish Sea: materiality and traditions of practice* 81-90. Oxford: Oxbow.

"Un pour tous, tous pour un", communal identity and individualism in northern French villages during the Thirty Years' War

Hugues Courbot-Dewerdt

Introduction

This paper will deal with "village *mentalité*" during the sixteenth and seventeenth centuries in northern France. A first study of rural behaviour in this period has already been attempted by many archive studies. Social history, since the 1960's, has focused on the most important human group in a mostly rural world: the villagers' community (Goubert 1998, Gutton 1979). A history of *"mentalité"* was thus built on particular sources, like legal archives, leading us to adopt a historical point of view on villages and the countryside in the modern period. Research has described the social relationships existing between and outside the community. It meant to investigate the modern period with a specific, and thus limited, point of view. Some studies, essentially based on legal archives, made it possible to investigate the villagers' behaviour, characterised by a daily and accepted violence, particularly in some areas of northern France (Muchembled 1989, Paresys 1998). In fact, on the northern frontier of modern France, the higher authority forgave numerous murderers for killing people in tense situations. In this troubled time, Robert Muchembled has described country people as very exclusive communities, acting as a group in and against a hostile world (Muchembled 1989). This historical point of view can be complemented by archaeological artefacts, the underground shelters. In this area of northern France, numerous villages owned their own retreat, dug and occupied from the sixteenth to the eighteenth century. These collective retreats can be considered as an architectural and an archaeological structure, fixing and revealing social relationships in the chalk. Some local historians and experts of the nineteenth century have realized the prime purpose of these structures, but they have not fully appreciated their historical importance. An important recording program was begun in 1988, based on the previous work of François Vasselle after 1945, and of Jean-Pascal Fourdrin (Fourdrin 1979). As a result of our research, we have discovered numerous structures in the three departments of Nord, Pas-de-Calais and Somme, and twenty-eight sites were studied by the GEVSNF[1] (Groupe d'étude des villages souterrains du nord de la France) from an archaeological point of view (Dewerdt 2003). These architectural recordings of underground shelters make it possible to develop a social analysis, and to finally attempt a synthesis between archaeological artefacts and historical sources. The act of digging an underground shelter and, afterwards, the occupation of these structures has contributed to the development of a specific mentality in a hostile environment, in a world in motion. However, the social relationships seem to have maintained a sort of immobility and to have perpetuated the same way of life through generations (Muchembled 1990, 87; Goubert and Roche 1984, 47f). The question is: is it possible to understand more about the villagers' behaviour or their communal identity? And how was the latter reinforced by the necessity of creating a secure place for the group?

To answer these questions, I will first briefly outline the historical context of the Thirty Years' War, which created the necessity to dig underground shelters for the village community. I will then describe the last phase of the Domquer and Bouzincourt shelters, as they clearly illustrate how the architecture of these retreats corresponded to the needs of the village community and reflected their ideas on privacy, the sanctity of ownership and their position and attitude with regard to other villages in the area. This will be backed up with some further historical evidence on village life and on the organisation of defence as a whole. Finally, I will show, using the Arquêves and Domquer shelters as examples, how the evolution of the underground dugouts reflects the attempts of villagers to find the ideal layout for their retreat, one which would alleviate the tension between the needs of the community and those of the family group. The fact that so many shelters have a very similar layout, in spite of the secrecy surrounding their construction, shows how their spatial organisation mirrors social principles and mentalities which were deeply rooted in northern French rural society at this time. This shows clearly how the use of archaeological evidence, in conjunction with written sources, can shed light on aspects of past mentalities and identities which are too often neglected by a purely historical narrative with its focus on legal issues and seigniorial prerogatives.

Modern Europe at war

The villages considered were situated in an area which formed the frontier between France and the Spanish Netherlands (Figure 3.1). From the time of François I, at the beginning of the sixteenth century, to the beginning of the eighteenth century under Louis XIV, there were frequent disputes between these countries. During different conflicts, the armies or, more precisely, different armed bands were defending the frontier. Individuals from all parts of Europe were encamped in this area, because mercenaries constituted an important part of the belligerents (Chagniot 2001, 50, Corvisier 1992, 312) especially during the sixteenth century. As mercenaries, they would fight for whoever paid them.

---

[1] This survey was undertaken by the GEVSNF and the results were established in a special collaboration with Frederic Willmann.

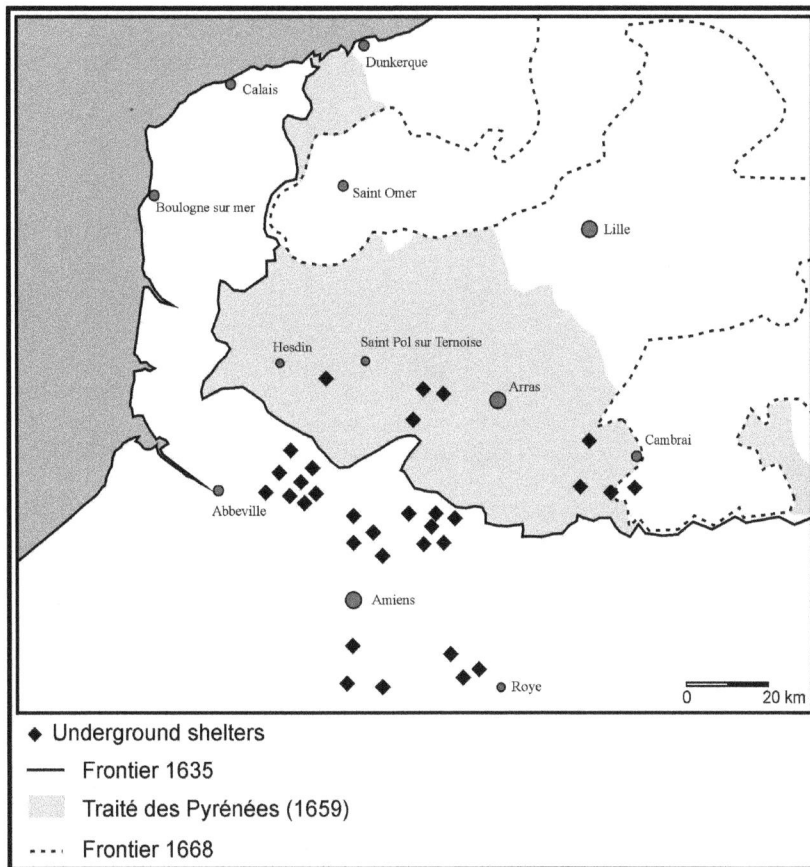

Figure 3.1. Map of frontier development in the XVIIth century, showing location of underground shelters (GEVSNF).

Also, villagers were under a specific military pressure, trapped in an area surrounded by small or more important troops for days, weeks, months, even if the villages and the countryside presented no strategic interest (Bois 2002, 201). They had to suffer two different kinds of persecution: on the one hand, they had to live with the soldiers, and on the other they were seen as secondary but necessary objective, as complement to a war of sieges (Chagniot 2001, 72). The military troops had to live off the land at the expense of the local population, because their board and lodging was not organised. As a consequence, the enemy tried to turn the countryside around the principal fortified towns and places into a desert. In this period, it seems to be important for the armies and for countries at war to have the possibility to take some booty in order to pay mercenaries and to contribute to the global effort of war (Peschot 2002). As a result, the villagers had to endure large-scale and sometimes constant pillaging and robbery (Figure 3.2). Where studies have been undertaken, they show that the consequences appeared to be significant for the population in the countryside (Stévenin 1996, Louis 1996, Bois 2002). The soldiers were seen by the villagers as foes, even if they served the same country. Sometimes, the insecurity and the pressure during the modern period were projected into the image of the "bad mercenary" in frontier areas. Thus, the community took their vengeance with violence against the small troops whenever that was possible (Muchembled 1990, 63). This atmosphere of great tension towards the troops caused some mistakes as well, for example in certain cases the death of some villagers mistaken for mercenaries because of the darkness at night,

or under the effect of alcohol (Muchembled 1989, 115). The villagers' society in northern France can thus be seen as existing in a world in motion, causing reaction and contributing to the development of the specific mentality of this human group.

The armies' movements frequently caused poverty, famine, illness and damages for a long time. In response to this danger, and from the end of the Medieval period onwards, the villagers and, step by step, the community of the inhabitants with more and more independence, organised a defence centred around the cemetery or the church (Contamine 2002, 31). In fact, the villagers often had to leave their villages when the conflicts were too hard to live with. But the fortified cities could not offer shelter to so many people. In addition, country people had to interrupt work on their fields, even if they were not living too far away from their land. Another solution was to leave the village to find a retreat in the wilderness next to the land they farmed, like woodlands, caves or mines (Buridant 1996, 195, Louis 1998). Finally, some villagers in the eastern Picardie fortified their church tower, using it as a lookout and a kind of civilian keep (Corvisier 1996). During the sixteenth and seventeenth centuries, the villagers in the north of Somme and the south of Pas-de-Calais dug underground shelters to protect themselves, their possessions and their cattle when they were under pressure from occupying forces, whether they were friend or foe. The record of these retreats shows a close connection with the frontier fluctuations during this period and especially during the Thirty Years' War. Different

21

Figure 3.2. "Les Misères et les Mal-heurs de la guerre". Engraving by Jacques Callot, XVIIth century (private collection).

artefacts, such as graffiti, finds and a few archives, appear to demonstrate that the digging and occupying of those underground shelters date from the beginning of the sixteenth to the eighteenth century. For example, at Domqueur we can see a graffito of 1697, while at Maison-Roland, some miles away, another one indicates 1550 (Dewerdt, Willmann and Carette 2004). The record of these undergrounds gives us a chance to understand more of the social relations fixed in the spatial organisations.

Mirroring the village: the underground retreats

The morphological characteristics of these underground retreats present some invariant fundamentals. The layout of all these shelters is characterised by a central corridor or several galleries giving access to separate rooms on both sides. For Bernard Bivert, it is thus possible to distinguish mines and underground shelters by their plans (Bivert 1988, 37). Our records show us that the villagers planned the digging of these undergrounds precisely, and after several different attempts they approved the same layout. For instance, when we compare the map of an underground shelter, such as Bouzincourt, and the register of a northern French village, for instance that of Quiévrain, drawn at the end of the sixteenth century, we notice the similarity between the spatial organisation of the two (Figures 3.3 and 3.4). The village is structured by a set of streets giving access to different plots and buildings, just as the underground is designed as a frame of corridors connecting separate cells. The abbot Goddé, in a chronicle dated 1738, described the digging of the Hiermon's retreat in 1647. He called the two corridors 'streets' and explained how the villagers decided to organise and pay for the work, which lasted two years (Fourdrin 1979). The symmetry between the layout of the underground shelters and the village is to be noted. This reinforced the fact that the hide-out was created by and for the community, in the case of Hiermont under the leadership of the most important inhabitants. From the architectural record of these structures, it is difficult to understand what part the public powers played in their construction, but it seems to be the act of the villagers or even the *sanior pars* of them, that is to say the richer ones. Philippe Contamine underlines that in this way, the villagers' community played a vital role in organising its own security at the end of the Medieval

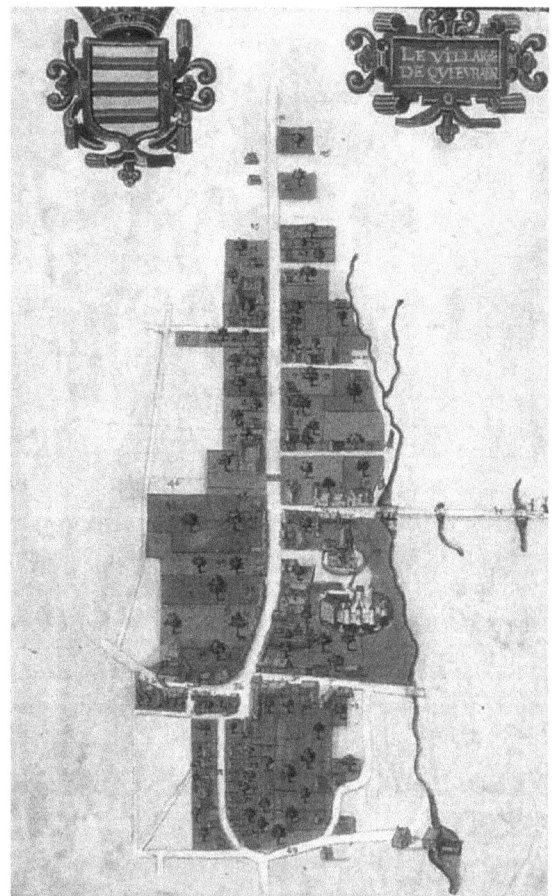

Figure 3.3. Register of Quiévrain at the end of the XVIth century (Duvosquel 1985-1996, t. I, pl. 192).

period (Contamine 2002, 29). The archaeological artefacts, like the structures, cannot be used to understand the different parts the public powers played in the defence and the security of the countryside and countrymen. The most important characteristics of the layout of the underground shelters could explain, nevertheless, how the villagers' mentality was focalised in these specific and communal structures. These archaeological data can thus make us understand some aspects of the rural society that cannot be easily appreciated through the written sources traditionally used. The first point is to notice that, in our study area, the records show us that nearly all villages had dug their own retreats. The underground shelters were created by and exclusively for, the villagers who had contributed to the endeavour.

Since 1970, a history of '*mentalité*' has been constructed from northern French sources. The villagers' communities were quite important groups in northern France during the modern period, the first ones having been formed in the eleventh century. It is possible to see this human group as a collectivity of people who had enough common interests, mainly preserving their own property and their farm rights in a rural society (Fossier 1984). The independence of these communities from the other public powers in the sixteenth and seventeenth centuries was difficult to understand through the study of archives alone. Different situations existed in the same area, depending on the relations and the environment of each village (Gallet 1999, 138, 184). In militarily troubled times, the relationship between villagers and soldiers, based on fear and violence, was managed by the community (Goubert 1998, 223). The villagers' representative dealt with the soldiers, trying to persuade them to leave the land in exchange for some money, or made the security choices on behalf of the people. Robert Muchembled has accurately described the structure of the villagers' relationships in northern France. The community was structured by many interactions and specific solidarities between people of the same area. These social links were embodied in the built environment, as well as learnt. Everyday life unfolded in public spaces: the village square, the church and the inn. Village fairs, religious or not, were frequently organised, as we can see on several Flemish paintings of the sixteenth and seventeenth centuries. Thus, the group identity was very much focused on the village area and was repeatedly reinforced by the defence and the affirmation of many rights around this perimeter (Paresys 1998, 72-77). For example, in Annoeullin in 1537, two groups of youths were fighting to defend a grazing right, encouraged by the adults. The story ended with a murder (Muchembled 1989, 57). However, violent action, while not the only way to create a strong community spirit, also reinforced the ties of villagers to each other, and their opposition to outsiders. Violence and fear characterised a world where life was rather hard. The community spirit thus created led to the rejection of strangers and to fear of others, including neighbouring villages. This sentiment of specific 'xenophobia' was reinforced in troubled times.

Each village cares for its own

The layout of many underground shelters shows us that the conception and the digging mirrored and reinforced the community '*identité*'. In some areas, we have clear records for an underground retreat for each village. It seems that every village was in command of its own defence. The strategy and the safety structures of two neighbouring villages could be different and were not necessarily created at the same time. The record of many underground shelters shows differences between these structures, which reveal that the experience of digging shelters and hiding from soldiers was not shared in a large circle. Probably, a neighbouring villager was never allowed to see the shelter of another community. But it is a fact that many villages in this area have followed the same layout when digging their hideaways. Some transfer of technical aspects and design took place between some close villages. For example, three

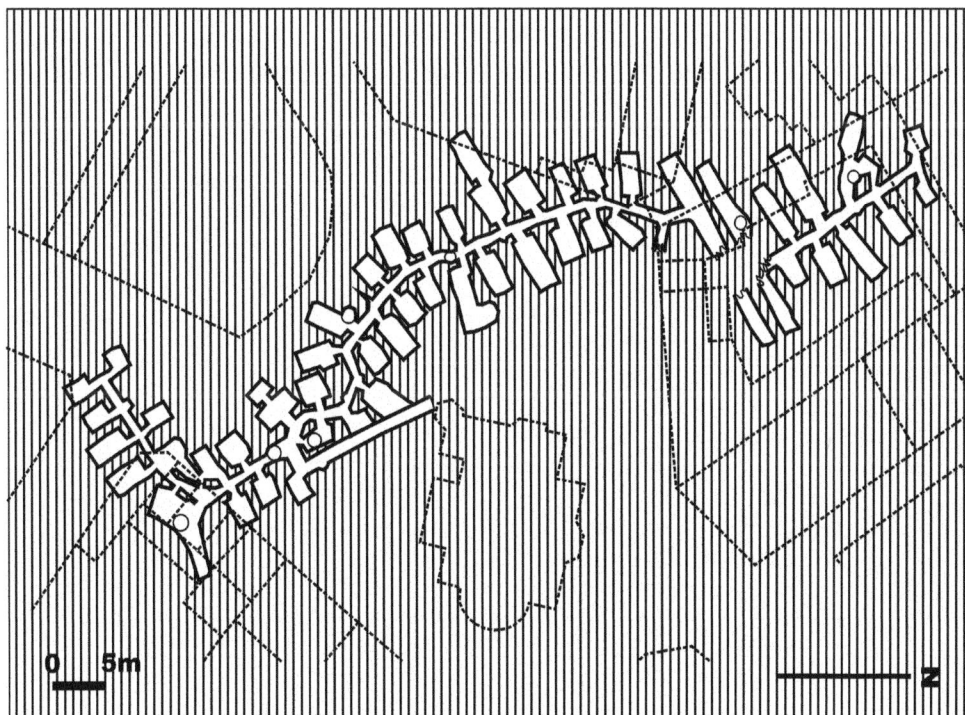

Figure 3.4. Bouzincourt underground shelter (J.-P. Fourdrin 1979).

3.5a

Figure 3.5. Berles-Monchel church tower.
a. First floor. A chimney and some floors were added to create a refuge for the villagers during troubled times.
b. Drawing of the tower. 1-part rebuilt in 1759 (crenellations were present before 1605; Duvosquel t. XVIII, pl. 62); 2-level of the bells; 3-level of shelter; 4-fireplace (H. Courbot-Dewerdt).

villages - Franqueville, Vauchelles les Domart and Lanches - were in possession of shelters which have some strange similarities. These three undergrounds were situated under hills in woods, comprised a small number of cellars, dug like stone quarries, and these structures seem to have been fully equipped for animals and not for people (Dewerdt and Willmann 2003). These specificities allow us to identify a specific group of villages in a little area between which technical transfers were more important than with the other villages. But there is a strong suspicion that no villagers were invited to see the neighbouring retreat. The locations, the layouts and the number of these underground shelters – one retreat for each village - indicate clearly that it was a structure created by and for the single villagers' community.

In any case, these shelters could be seen as only a part of a larger defensive organisation. The feeling of communal property was expressed in the structure and also in the location under the village. For example, in Domqueur (Figure 3.8) the quarrymen made sure they were only digging under the communal space. The central corridor forms a U-shape under the square and respects patterns of land ownership. Taking a larger point of view, we can notice that the access routes to the underground shelters are quite often located in the village churches, like in Grand-Rullecourt or Domqueur. The property management of the church was in the hands of a group of villagers, the parochial council, often consisting of the same people as the villagers' assembly. The ownership of the church and the square of a village were part of the seigniorial belongings, but the management was organised by the villagers with a certain self-sufficiency. Sometimes, conflict of interest developed between these two powers (Goubert 1998, 212). The defence was probably organised by the villagers - sometimes the *sanior pars* of them - under the seigniorial authority. To draw a complete picture of the villagers' system of defence against adversity, it is necessary to point out that the built structures needed a human component, for instance observation from lookout points had to be organised and people's security had to be managed. The entire shelter consisted of the church complemented by an underground. Careful observations offer the possibility to recognise that certain church-towers

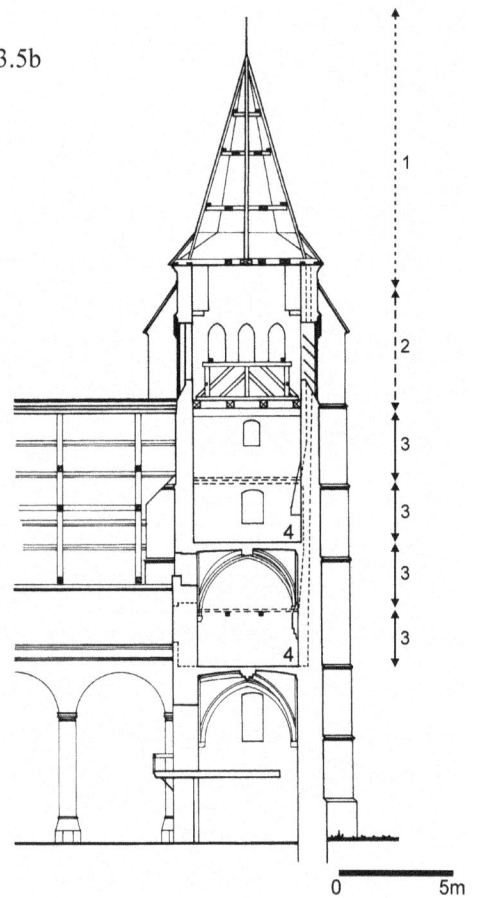

3.5b

also constituted shelters, just like an underground. In Berles-Monchel – in south Pas-de-Calais – the towers are equipped for posting a villager as lookout. Two chimneys were built in the first floor, where we can observe some windows from which to watch the countryside (Figure 3.5a). Probably, this tower was used for defence with an upper wall presenting a crenellated parapet (Duvosquel 1985-1996, vol. XVIII, pl. 62; Figure 3.5b), and for people's safety it was upgraded to create many floors. The fact that some communities decided to dig an underground shelter, like in Linzeux, or instead to build a shelter in the church's vaults, like in Le Fresnoy some miles away, clearly shows the autonomy of each village (Dewerdt and Willmann 1996). With an accurate and critical look at these structures of defence, it is possible to evoke the social relations between villages. Even if some of them show us certain technical transfers, the choice and the organisation seem to be managed by the villagers with autonomy and secrecy, and with little consideration for neighbouring rural communities. Inside the villager's community, the danger reinforced the communal identity through daily attention to safety measures, beginning with posting a lookout and leading all the way to organised evacuations in several steps, depending on the dangers foreseen. The village identity was thus reinforced precisely because of the adversity.

Inside the group: the necessity for privacy

As far as each village community goes, the archives permit to understand more about the individuals who formed the group. A very important social structure in the rural world of the villagers was the "foyer", a fiscal term. This group comprised the members of a family, usually centred upon the conjugal couple (Goubert and Roche 1984, 141). In the social landscape of the village, the private areas of each family were limited by the walls of the house, and the doorstep was understood as a frontier which was never to be crossed, especially at night or by people who came with bad intentions. Even if walls at the time were made only with daub, they had to be seen as a strong limit by the others.

The legal archives show us that most conflicts happened in public areas (the square, the inn and the borders of the village territory), but a sufficient percentage of crimes tells us about the defence of property and morality inside the private space (Muchembled 1990, 132; Paresys 1998, 113). The accepted behaviour considered night assaults against a dwelling to be a serious crime. Even a convicted culprit could be secure under his own roof. For example, a witness cried out to a man named Simon, who had come to attack another man at his home on the twentieth of May 1525 at Laventies: "Simon, be contented, I beg you. Leave this man peacefully in his home. He asks you nothing. He has to feel comfortable in his house" (Muchembled 1989, 63). The walls of houses, although of poor quality at the time, thus create a specific place, often open during the daytime, where the owners could find a safe space during the night. These representational limits were quite well understood by everyone, even strangers or soldiers. In the sixteenth century, a few soldiers entered by force into the Jehan Caillou house. To rape his wife, they needed to take their victim into the garden (Paresys 1998, 85f). The significant and vital space within the house ensured a well-defended private sphere and ties in with the predominant sentiments towards property, even though the villagers were usually poor. Many of them owned only a few objects and not a lot of money, but their property seems at times to be more respected than human life.

The same need for privacy can be seen in the layout of the underground shelters. The communal corridor led to different and private cells. In the later underground shelters, like Domqueur or Hiermont, dug in 1647, these are arranged in staggered rows in order to preserve intimacy even when the doors were opened to ventilate. Each private space comprised a first cell for cattle and a second one beyond for the family. The first cell was fitted out for animals, as we still can see the remnants of hay racks and feeding troughs. This organisation thus creates a greater distance from the public corridor and strengthens the feeling of intimacy. The transition between the cells and the main corridor was achieved by a lobby closed by a door (Dewerdt and Willmann 2003). It had the same purpose as the doorstep on the surface, i.e. it permitted to control access to the inner space.

A focus on the lobby reveals an important part of the villagers' mentality. Many facts demonstrate how a limit was built between communal and private areas. First, the lobby was dug to restrict the entrance to the cell. Even when the room was larger, the door opening itself, made of wood, left only a small passage. For example, in the Lanche shelter, the lobby was very well made and included wooden elements. The entrance had the following dimensions: one meter twenty height per eighty centimetres width. The quarrymen did not build the lobby this way for a defensive purpose, but to show where the limit of the private space was. Some complementary elements permit to demonstrate that the mentality of ownership was very significant in modern society in northern France. In Chirmont or Lawarde, some keys have been found on the ground (Figure 3.6). This shows us that the cells were closed when the owner was not inside, but also that every cell belonged precisely to one family. A graffito, found in Bouzincourt on the exterior of the entrance, told everybody that this cell belonged to "Jean Rouvillain, dit Jano" (Dewerdt, Willmann and Carette 2004). Closing the cells and building lobbies was intimately connected to the social organisation of the village and to the way that villagers planned to defend themselves and their principal possessions. In fact, villagers were not living in these shelters for long periods of time.

Figure 3.6. Key found in an underground shelter (reproduced with permission of the owner).

Even though the layout of the different retreats allows us to see them as underground villages, they are not dug as an alternative place to live like troglodytes. People were hidden only in case of danger, whereas cattle and grain were hidden more frequently. During troubled times, the villagers probably organised the lookout rota and the grain was stocked in the underground cells. Cattle were hidden at night and left the retreat during the day for grazing. Only when the danger was serious and close to the village or the church would the whole population climb down to the shelter. The retreats were thus only planned to permit life for the villagers and their property for quite a short time.

25

Lobbies and doors were created to protect property when the villagers were not in the underground and to give some privacy when they were. Thus, in these two cases, the lobby was not only an entrance to the cell but also a means to maintain the distinction between two realms of the villagers' mentality: communal identity and intimacy.

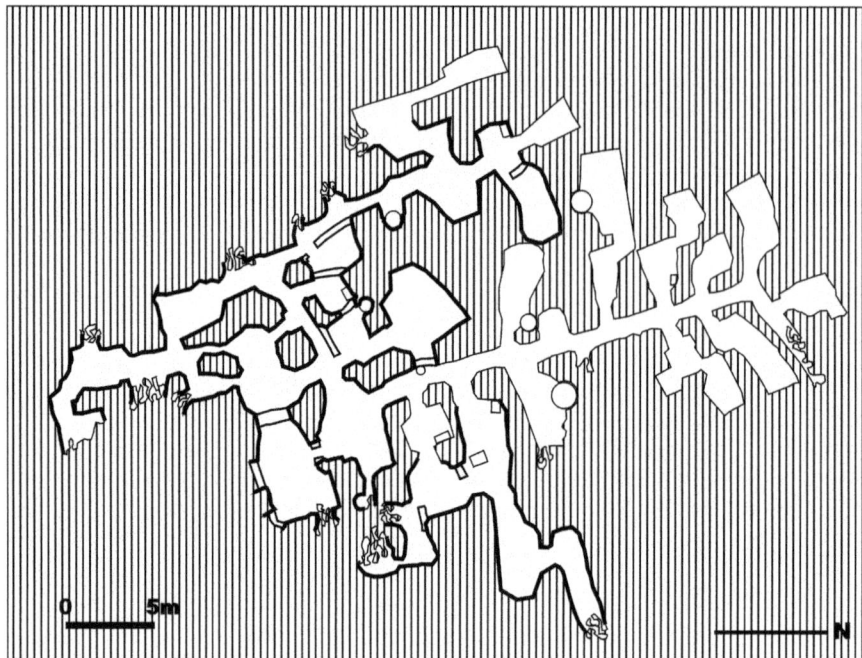

Figure 3.7. Arquêves underground shelter. The thick line indicates the quarry, the thin line the extension and the added walls (GEVSNF).

Private feelings versus communal interest

An important part of this research has been to investigate the origin of the specific layout chosen in the digging of underground shelters in this large area of northern France. After an important survey, we can tell that villagers' first underground retreats were old stone quarries. The record of these man-made quarries shows the evolution of the preferred layout, which culminated in a corridor giving access to separate rooms. At Arquêves (Figure 3.7), the investigation of different remains has allowed us to understand the main principles of the earliest spatial organisation (Dewerdt and Willmann 1998). People and cattle were divided between three different areas. After some time, the villagers built walls inside the quarry to close different cells and added a corridor to communicate with the whole retreat. Finally, they began to dig an enlargement of the existing quarry. After several re-organisations of this quarry, they settled for a corridor connecting different cells. The first entirely collective underground shelter failed to respond to their needs. It demonstrates that, despite troubles and dangers, it was not possible for them to go against their *mentalité*.

Similarly, the history of Domqueur's underground shelters could be described as comprising three important phases (Dewerdt and Willmann 1994; Figure 3.8). In the first phase, the villagers came to the church and then went down into a former quarry. To fit it out, they began to dig some little cubicles into the chalk, allowing them to preserve their privacy to an extent. But it seems that this solution was not really sufficient and we can tell, with the aid of historical sources, that it probably caused a tension between communal and individual identity. Thus, they decided to create a new underground shelter near the quarry, but closer to the church. This second phase shows us an experimental layout. To the right of the entrance gallery, they decided to place some cells for the cattle and, on the other side, they dug different cells for people. The animals were thus regrouped in one specific place. Even if it was a pragmatic solution, we can imagine how hard it was for the villagers to recover their own property at the end of each episode of hiding. The dilemma between communal interest and private feeling was probably so great as to create a need for a new shelter. For this last phase, quarrymen adopted a now classic layout with a central corridor connecting private cells. In fact, the villagers dug this new shelter and abandoned the old one completely, backfilling it with digging waste. With the Domqueur and Arquêves examples in mind, it is possible to consider how strong the engrained scheme of social relationships was, especially when reinforced by the fight for survival.

In conclusion, when I begun this research, quite a long time ago, my objective was to discover a bit more about society in the Modern period. We have seen, for the modern villagers' society, that in troubled times, the existing group's identity as a community, separate from other similar villages, was reinforced. The archaeological data are thus crucial for assessing the tension between, on the one hand, the necessity of acting as a community against a common threat and, on the other, protecting one's own property and preserving some intimacy for the family group. The development of shelters over time clearly shows how these tensions were negotiated. As such, the underground shelters are good witnesses of the villagers' reaction to pressure from soldiers. A complementary survey is now needed to get a better understanding of the whole defensive system. It would necessarily include other archaeological evidence like loopholes, seen in the walls of several churches. Thus, these archaeological structures show us a repeated pattern of spatial relationships, which it is possible to investigate in terms of how it mirrored and helped to build communal identity in the sixteenth and seventeenth centuries. With another sufficiently informed historical context, this kind of research seems possible for other archaeological data sets.

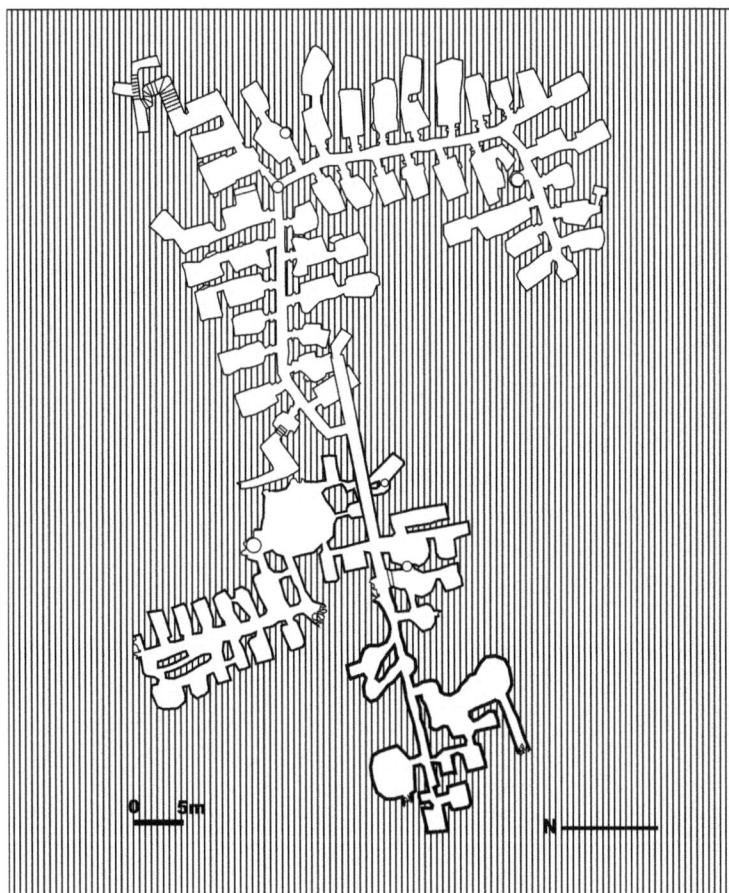

Figure 3.8: Domquer underground shelter, dug in three phases (the thickest line is the earliest, the thinnest line the youngest phase). The two older shelters were abandoned once the youngest one was created (J.-P. Fourdrin, J.-P. Ver Eecke et F. Willmann).

References

Bivert, B. 1988. *Les souterrains du Nord-Pas-de-Calais*. Cuincy: Conseil Général du Département du Nord.

Bois, J.-P. 2002. Les villageois et la guerre en France à l'époque moderne. In C. Desplat (ed.), *Les villageois face à la guerre XIVe – XVIIIe siècle, Actes des XXIIes Journées Internationales d'Histoire de l'Abbaye de Flaran 8, 9, 10 septembre 2000*, 185-208. Toulouse: Presses Universitaires du Mirail.

Buridant, J. 1996. Guerres et paysages forestiers : l'exemple de laonnois au XVIIe siècle. In A. Corvisier and J. Jacquart (eds), *De la guerre ancienne à la guerre réglée, les malheurs de la guerre I*, 193-200. Paris: éditions du Comité des Travaux Historiques et Scientifiques.

Chagniot, J. 2001. *Guerre et société à l'époque moderne, coll. L'histoire et ses problèmes*. Paris: Presses Universitaires de France.

Contamine, P. 2002. L'impact de la guerre de Cent Ans en France sur le « plat pays » et sur la vie au village. In C. Desplat (ed.), *Les villageois face à la guerre XIVe – XVIIIe siècle, Actes des XXIIes Journées Internationales d'Histoire de l'Abbaye de Flaran 8, 9, 10 septembre 2000*, 15-34. Toulouse: Presses Universitaires du Mirail.

Corvisier, A. 1992. *Histoire militaire de la France des origines à 1715, Tome I*. Paris: Presses Universitaires de France.

Corvisier, C. 1996. L'architecture et l'âge des églises fortifiées, l'exemple de l'est de la Picardie. In A. Corvisier and J. Jacquart (eds), *De la guerre ancienne à la guerre réglée, les malheurs de la guerre I*, 77-98. Paris: éditions du Comité des Travaux Historiques et Scientifiques.

Dewerdt, H. and Willmann, F. 1994. Les souterrains-refuges de Domqueur (Somme). *Subterranea 92*, 133-45.

Dewerdt, H. and Willmann, F. 1996. Le souterrain-refuge de Linzeux. *Ternesia, Cercle Historique du Ternois* 11, 56-58.

Dewerdt, H. and Willmann, F. 1998. Les muches d'Arqêves (Somme): une approche de la genèse des linéaires du nord de la France. In Société Belge de Recherche et d'Etude des Souterrains (eds), *Archéologie et Histoire en Milieu Souterrain, Actes du deuxième congrès international de subterranologie (Mons, 2-4 août 1997)*, 239-46. Bruxelles: Société Belge de Recherche et d'Etude des Souterrains.

Dewerdt, H. and Willmann, F. 2003. Conception des muches de Lanches. In H. Dewerdt (ed.) *Concepteurs et conception d'espaces souterrains. Actes du colloque d'Auxi-le-Château 1999, Bulletin Spécial n°2*, 105-23. Auxi-le-Château: Cercle historique d'Auxi-le-Château.

Dewerdt, H., Willmann, F. and Carette, F. 2004. Des villageois face à l'adversité, les souterrains-refuges du nord de la France aux XVI-XVIIème siècles. *L'Archéologue-Archéologie nouvelle* 73, 38-40.

Duvosquel, J.-M. 1985-1996. *Albums de Croÿ, t. I à XXVI*. Lille/Bruxelles: Conseil régional du Nord-Pas-de-Calais, Crédit communal de Belgique.

Fossier, R. 1984. Les communautés villageoises en France du Nord au Moyen Age. In R. Fossier (ed.), *Hommes et villages d'occident au Moyen Age*, 215-44. Paris: Publications de la Sorbonne.

Fourdrin, J.-P. 1979. Cinq souterrains du Ponthieu. *Subterranea* 29, 9-24.

Gallet, J. 1999. *Seigneurs et paysans en France, 1600-1793*, coll. De mémoire d'homme: l'histoire. Rennes: éditions Ouest-France.

Goubert, P. 1998. *Les paysans français au XVIIe siècle*, coll. La vie quotidienne. Paris: Hachette littératures.

Goubert, P. and Roche, D. 1984. *Les français et l'ancien régime, 1 – la société et l'Etat*. Paris: Armand Colin/Masson.

Gutton, J.-P. 1979. *La sociabilité villageoise dans la France de l'Ancien Régime, coll. Pluriel*. Paris: Hachette littératures.

Louis, G. 1996. Les misères de la guerre de Trente Ans en Franche-Comté. In A. Corvisier and J. Jacquart (eds), *De la guerre ancienne à la guerre réglée, les malheurs de la guerre I*, 181-92. Paris: éditions du Comité des Travaux Historiques et Scientifiques.

Louis, G. 1998. *La guerre de Dix Ans, 1634-1644*. Besançon: Annales littéraires de l'Université de Franche-Comté, 651.

Muchembled, R. 1989. *La violence au village*, coll. Violence et société, Brepols.

Muchembled, R. 1990. *Société, cultures et mentalités dans la France moderne, XVIe – XVIIIe siècle*, coll. Cursus. Paris: Armand Colin.

Paresys, I. 1998. *Aux marges du royaume, Violence, justice et société en Picardie sous François Ier*. Paris: Publications de la Sorbonne.

Peschot, B. 2002. Les « lettres de feu » : la petite guerre et les contributions paysannes au XVIIe siècle. In C. Desplat (ed.), *Les villageois face à la guerre XIVe – XVIIIe siècle, Actes des XXIIes Journées Internationales d'Histoire de l'Abbaye de Flaran 8, 9, 10 septembre 2000*, 129-42. Toulouse: Presses Universitaires du Mirail.

Stévenin, M. 1996. Une fatalité : les dévastations des gens de guerre dans l'Est de la France (1620-1660), l'exemple de la Campagne. In A. Corvisier and J. Jacquart (eds), *De la guerre ancienne à la guerre réglée, les malheurs de la guerre I*, 161-80. Paris: éditions du Comité des Travaux Historiques et Scientifiques.

Private lives, public identities: a spatial analysis of privacy within Bulgarian tell architecture

Gary Jones

Introduction

The purpose of this chapter is to consider how past identities may have been physically and visually expressed within prehistoric settlement architecture. The creation and maintenance of Bulgarian settlement mounds (known as tells) suggests they can be seen as successful symbols of continuity and community. Being the accumulations of occupation debris, these mounds produced an era of physical construction and spatial repetition.

I aim to re-evaluate the dynamic relationships between structures and inhabitants, suggesting that the structural form would have been used to mediate the play of social interaction within the confined nature of the sites. These structures are more than purely physical constructs, they are entities that affect and are affected by those who dwell within them, and are visible indicators of presence and identity. This paper considers this social environment in the light of privacy, which has been termed "an important human need" (Pedersen 1997, 147). It will be seen that the desire for privacy is an important aspect of defining one's identity, and that the cultural mechanisms used in the attainment of such desires can be recognised and studied by the archaeologist. An analysis on the structural horizons of three Bulgarian tell sites, using the Space Syntax method of Relative Asymmetry (RA), will be used to consider social questions that have been asked regarding these societies.

Privacy in the past

In order to reflect on privacy, first it must be defined. Privacy can be seen as an important part of understanding the relationship between behaviour, culture, and environment (Altman and Chemers 1984, 75). It has been defined and redefined in disciplines such as psychology, sociology, anthropology, political science, law and architecture (Altman 1975, 17). A common focus in these studies is the aspect of withdrawal, identifying privacy purely as a right to distance oneself from others (see Chapin 1951; Bates 1964; Jourard 1966; Ozaki 2002, 213). However, such an approach to the subject is narrow, only highlighting the 'keep-out' stigma that can be attached to the desire for privacy (Altman 1975, 17). Instead, privacy is a far more diachronic process related to the ideas of control, regulation and choice (Ingham 1978, 38). Control over access to the self is at the heart of this definition. Within this control is the ability to regulate the boundaries of interaction and exchange with other stimuli. This regulation is a dialectic process involving both the restriction of *and* the seeking of interaction (Altman, 1975, 10; Altman and Chemers 1984, 77). Whether to 'open' or 'close' these barriers of interaction is the choice of the one desiring privacy, and is dependant on the desired level of access to the self at a particular time and in a particular set of circumstances (Pedersen 1997, 147). Therefore, privacy can be defined as a responsive boundary-regulation process that reacts to and changes with the circumstances of the moment (Altman and Chemers 1984, 78), (see H. Courbot-Dewerdt this volume).

Our desire for privacy is directly related to situations, such as the crowdedness of the environment, or individual needs such as concentration on a task at hand (Pastalan 1970; Altman 1975, 20; Newell 1998, 367). Maintenance of these situations can be an important part of the healthy internal physiological and cognitive well-being of people and groups (Altman and Chemers 1984, 81; Newell 1998, 359). These situations can be seen as obligations upon the self, obligations that need to be controlled and regulated (Moore 1984, 12). Any success is an indicator of a person's ability to control life events, and to develop a sense of self, identity and a level of personal autonomy (Ingham 1978, 44). Failure to control, or at least regulate, these situations and the social obligations may have adverse affects on the personal identity, self-esteem and self-worth of the individual (Altman and Chemers 1984, 83).

However, would people in the past have had the same desires for privacy that we can recognise today? To answer this, the fundamentally social nature of privacy must again be explored. The situations a person or group may encounter are dependant on the nature of the society they are part of, suggesting that any society holds potential for obligations and encounters. As the nature of a society alters so does the quantity and type of obligations. Because of this, studies have associated this desire for privacy with the socio-economic orientation of the society (see Steadman 2000, 172). The manifestation of public and private spheres is seen to arise with the concept of the group and co-operation (Moore 1984, 14). Factors such as the collection of resources, increased agricultural surplus, the how and by whom this should be distributed, coupled with potential co-operation in the gaining of the resource, whether hunting or agriculture, all hold great potential for obligations. Even in those societies where the level of potential obligation is deemed to be less by those studying them (although supposed social 'complexity' can be no indicator), the acknowledgment of privacy is still present. In his study of privacy in non-literate societies, Moore argues that privacy appears to be much less of a social necessity, as well as less of a social possibility in those societies where technology and social organisation are minimal (1984 73, 276). Regardless, he concludes that even in extreme cases, such as the Siriono Indians in Bolivia, there seems to be at least a basic desire for privacy from some social situations. All physiological activities of the Siriono can and do occur in the presence of other people; however, the mediation occurs through the verbal grumbling about noises and disturbances within the shared living quarters (Moore 1984, 277). Lovers often go away from camp, suggesting that every culture has a set of mechanisms to regulate interaction between members, regardless of whether outsiders can instantly recognise it (Altman and Chemers 1984, 84).

The regulation of privacy is an important process in the maintenance of relationships between individuals and groups. The successes and failures in regulating these social boundaries are an important element of the society as a whole and integral to the development and nature of the society and to the individuals within that society. Successful regulation can mean potential stresses are mediated, whilst failures may partly account for discord and fracture (Wilson 1988, 100). As such, I suggest that within the tell settlements of Eneolithic Bulgaria (c. 4900-3800 BC), the mediation of social obligations through the regulation of privacy boundaries would have played an intrinsic role in the development of the societies. The manipulation of the built environment is one mechanism of mediating this privacy, and the next section shows how the analysis of architecture can give social insights into the nature of societies and the regulation of desires within them.

Privacy types and spatial form

There are various types of privacy that may be sought, each resulting in different means of mediation. These types reflect behaviours that people would undertake dependant on the situation present. Initially, Westin (1970) separated privacy into four types; solitude, intimacy, anonymity and reserve. These were soon revised through other studies (see Marshall 1972; 1974; Pedersen 1979) where two types of intimacy were identified instead of one, and the desire for isolation was added (Pedersen 1997, 148). Following Pedersen (1997, 149), the full six factors are given below, along with their definitions:

- *Intimacy with family* – the desire to be alone with the members of your family to the exclusion of others;
- *Intimacy with friends* – the desire to be alone with your friends to the exclusion of others;
- *Solitude* – placing yourself in a situation where other people cannot see or hear what you are doing;
- *Isolation* – using physical distance to separate yourself from others;
- *Anonymity* – going unnoticed in a crowd;
- *Reserve* – controlling your personal feelings in front of others.

(Pedersen 1997, 149)

Each represents a desire dependant on the causing factors, and better represents the general concept of privacy as a whole. Obviously, the potential range of triggering situations combined with multiple types of privacy means that the mechanisms by which these may be attained and regulated vary greatly. These mechanisms can be personal, verbal or physical in nature; whether simply asking somebody to leave the room, leaving yourself, or averting your gaze. As such, many mechanisms would not appear within the archaeological record. However, the organisation and manipulation of the built environment can act as one such mechanism, and is recognisable within the archaeological record (Moore 1984, 72; Wilson 1988, 98; Sanders 1990, 50). Research into the interactions between society, architecture, and the use of space has been

considerable (see Steadman 2000, 169). A key aspect to these studies has been that architecture and spatial organisation is influenced by social structures within societies (see Bourdieu 1973; Rapoport 1982; Hillier and Hanson 1984; Rapoport 1990; 1994 as examples). Architecture is the product of a purposeful mind, implying reason within any construction. The seeming lack of such order is taken as our own failure to recognise the pattern rather then the absence of such a pattern. This physical definition provides cues to the social world behind the organisation of the space (Hall 1966). Therefore, the regulation of privacy, as social mechanism, can be facilitated in the construction of structures. As such, any debate in the recognition of privacy mechanisms within structural plans must initially centre on the physical attributes of these dwellings (Lawrence and Low 1990, 462). The ability to define areas within structures is considered vital in this relationship (Altman and Chemers 1984, 168). The creation and control of these spaces assists the regulation of boundaries, as a physically demarcated space means a potential increase in the control over that space. Therefore, the physical layout of these spaces may be influenced by, and indicative of, certain types of privacy, and thus the regulation of specific identities.

In an analysis of the spatial organisation of modern English and Japanese housing, Ozaki (2002, 223) noted a distinct relationship between cultural identities such as 'self' and 'family', and house form. He noted that the individualism of the English culture saw an increase in rooms that can be related to the desire for *solitude*, such as bedrooms and bathrooms, where privacy within the family was prioritised. The group-orientated nature of the Japanese culture was more related to *intimacy* within the family. In these cases, emphasis is placed on control over the boundary between the house and the outside, with strongly defined garden boundaries that contrasted with weak boundaries within the houses themselves (Ozaki 2002, 223). The recognition of these privacy types within structures can therefore potentially indicate an expression of identity by those that built them; in these cases, solitude for the individual, or privacy for the family group. As such, the study of architectural boundaries may offer indications into the regulation of privacy within past societies, and thus suggestions as to the nature of these societies, such as whether they are group-centric or individual-centric, a debate which has been raised in relation to Eneolithic tell settlements.

The Archaeology of Prehistoric Bulgaria

The settlement tells of the Bulgarian Eneolithic (4900/4850 BC – 4100/3800 BC) offer a rich material record of the spatial and temporal durability of the societies that created them. These monumental settlements represent a transformation of space to place, as people constructed new environments in which they lived and dwelt. The traditional chronology of Bulgarian prehistory has been established through a primarily cultural-historical approach. The relative chronologies of identified cultures were synchronised to form a broader chronology and have been complimented through the use of radiocarbon dating, particularly from samples taken from the multi-layered settlement tells (Boyadzhiev 1995, 149). A summary of established dates are given in table 4.1 below.

Period	Phase	Date Ranges (cal. BC)
Neolithic	Early Pottery	6300/6200 - 6000/5900
	Early	6000/5900 - 5500/5450
	Middle	5500/5450 - 5200/5100
	Late	5200/5100 - 4900/4850
Eneolithic	Early	4900/4850 - 4600/4550
	Middle	4600/4550 - 4500/4400
	Late	4500/4400 - 4100/3800
Transitional		3850/3750 - 3200/3150
Bronze Age	Early	3200/3150 - 2550/2500

Table 4.1. The chronology of prehistoric Bulgaria.

Settlement activity during the seventh millennium B.C. in north-eastern Bulgaria (Neolithic) saw two forms of structures being created. A semi-subterranean form labelled as pit-dwellings (found at Ocharovo-platoto I, Ochcharovo-zemnika and Podgoritsa), and surface structures (located at Ovcharovo-gorata II-IV and Polyanitsa-platoto) (Todorova *et al.* 1983; Bailey 2000, 59). Construction techniques were simple, involving the use of mud, clay, and straw and showing an absence of long-term rebuilding. The nature of the evidence suggests that these settlements were not occupied for long periods of time and were not the focus of re-occupation. From this it has been proposed that they were impermanent or semi-permanent with temporary occupation (Bailey 1995, 7; 2000, 61).

The Eneolithic period saw an adoption of tells, influenced by developments in the south (Todorova 1978, 33). Examples from north-eastern Bulgaria include the three which form the focus of this chapter: Polyanitsa, Radingrad and Tărgovište (Figure 4.1). Tells are formed by the continuous re-occupation of a settlement. The landscape is gradually changed as material and debris accumulate following phases of settlement construction, destruction and re-construction. In today's landscapes, they are usually below 10m high, and can range greatly in diameter. The increase in the number of tells was dramatic. In north-eastern Bulgaria alone it is estimated that there were over two hundred new examples during the fifth millennium BC (Todorova 1986, 272-79).

Maintaining these tell communities can be seen as a substantial investment in time and labour towards a specific place in the landscape, something not previously seen in north-eastern Bulgaria (Bailey 1995, 16). Settlement continuity was important, offering fixed points in a previously fluid landscape. The re-occupation of these sites by semi-mobile peoples would have become a central aspect of society, as the physical and social presence of the tell increased with each cycle (Chapman 2000, 214). Re-affirmation of ownership and legitimacy, on the tell and within the society, would have increased; this can be seen by the presence of tectomorphs (figurines of dwellings), domestic representations (for instance, figurines of chairs or tables), and shrines within structures, as well as a repetition in floor plans (see Bailey 1990). The increasing evidence for social differentiation and economic growth and diversity suggests that the need to regulate social interaction and obligation would have played an important role in the successful maintenance and stability of these societies.

The developing nature of the architectural structures on these sites would have provided a means for such mediation. Although I wish to make no assumptions about the creation of the 'house' or the 'household' (Whittle 1985, 63; Hodder 1990), a social focus can begin to be seen in association with these structures. The basic plan of each layer is of a varying number of structures, often organised around paths orientated towards the entrances of the settlements. These substantial structures were constructed of wooden posts sunk into foundation trenches and either joined with wooden planks or interwoven with a matrix of branches, mud and clay (wattle and daub) (Bailey 2000, 157). The renewal and maintenance of these structures suggests a strong relationship between structure and owner. The clay layers inside the buildings have been found to be continually repainted, often with different colours with each renewal. Whilst this has been related to seasonal restoration by Todorova (1978, 52) it is just as likely that some of these layers could represent redecoration by new owners as a sign of ownership, or expressions of individuality and re-legitimisation by existing inhabitants.

Inside the structures, these ideas continue through the association of expressive material culture. The hearth or oven was a focal point, often being the best preserved feature of a structure, and in some cases constructed on a stone base for better durability. It was physically reminiscent of the larger structures in both construction method (often built directly into the building) and form, and was also represented in clay miniatures. Furthermore, hearths and ovens were often associated with items of social significance. On Ovcharovo, a structure was excavated with a model of the house next to the oven, and on the floor one metre away was a collection of 27 miniature cult items - such as figurines, altars, tables, cylinders, dishes and pots (Whittle 1985, 153). Whilst this example may be an extreme, the general association of structures with miniatures of arguably 'domestic' character, coupled with the level of attention in their maintenance and renewal, suggests strong cultural ties between these buildings and their occupiers.

Figure 4.1. Location map showing the tell sites of Polyanitsa, Radingrad and
Tărgovište discussed in the text.

The spatial organisation of Eneolithic structures

The ability of these structures to organise and regulate space has been considered as an important aspect of tell life. These rectangular structures offer the potential to accommodate a greater number of individuals and more tasks taking place simultaneously, an important distinction from previous smaller pit-hut structures. The processes of multiple activities being performed can be seen as providing the contexts for the forging and maintenance of small-group relationships, and would have created the social obligation and opportunity for encounter that would have likely required some process of social regulation. It is through the spatial segregation and the physical partitioning of these structures that those within are seen to have had the means of attaining some measure of privacy. Bailey in particular has stressed the importance of these structural forms in allowing increased choice over what information is included or excluded from specific areas (or groups) (see Bailey 2000, chapter 5). As Ozaki (2002) has demonstrated, desires for solitude and intimacy can be directly related to social models focussing on the individual or the group, models that may have been important to tell-based societies.

Chapman believes the organisation of tell structures is evidence of household lineages (Chapman 1990, 55). His research uses dimensional order (Fletcher 1977; 1984) to explore continuity between settlement levels by analysing the ratio of built to un-built space, house dimensions, and the inter-house spacing. Chapman sees an increase in house dimensions on some tells to be indicative of household competition. For Chapman, the acts of re-occupation, renewal and spatial growth seen in structural plans are evidence of increasing success and status for lineages within the settlements (1990, 55). Successful households gain status within the tells, which lead to greater roles, increased activities, and further structural complexity. Significantly, this increase in activities is related to the temporal economic development of the successful lineages within the societies (Wilk and Rathje 1982; Kent 1990; Rapoport 1990). The physicality of structures is a tangible boundary reflecting the cohesion and membership of a group, and is a powerful expression as to the extent of these memberships (Bailey 2000, 268). The regulation of the entrance to these structures can therefore be a way of gaining *intimacy* within the group, allowing control over the relationship between member and non-member, by purposeful exclusion or inclusion.

Whittle (1996) argues less for strong household lineages and more for an individual-focused *mentalité* within tell societies. The variations in house dimensions so important to Chapman are dismissed as variations within the renewal process. The emergence of the individual within this continuity is believed to be evident from the increase of expressive material culture, such as figurines, burial goods, structural decoration and vessel incision. The control of boundaries within structures, represented by the increase in rooms and more controlled access to the 'deeper' rooms can represent rise in individuality by creating more opportunities for *solitude* (Bailey 2000, 282).

The social development of tell sites has thus been put down both to the growth of family hierarchies and to the emerging status of individuals, although neither has looked at it from the point of view of what kind of privacy should be afforded. By analysing the type of privacy that can be suggested from structural layouts instead of merely its presence or absence, I suggest that new insights can be offered to compliment and advance these earlier ideas.

The Analysis of Privacy

This analysis will be applied to the architectural horizons of Polyanitsa, Radingrad and Tărgovište. These three sites offer a good example of tell settlements across north-east Bulgaria during the Eneolithic period, and have adequately published architectural plans that will allow an analysis of spatial form. My analysis considers the control over the interactions between inhabitant-visitor, and inhabitant-inhabitant. The inhabitant-visitor relationship is focused on the nature of the internal-external boundary of the structure, characterised by the control of entrances into the structure. The inhabitant-inhabitant relationship is focused on the internal boundaries within the structure in relation to each other.

The data set

The data used in this analysis are the architectural floor plans of the three Bulgarian tell settlements of Polyanitsa, Radingrad and Tărgovište, derived from Bailey (1991).

Polyanitsa – lies 6km west of the town of Tărgovište. 80-100m in diameter prior to excavation, Polyanitsa produced eight habitation horizons (levels). The site dates from circa 4750-4350 BC (Todorova 1982). Horizons I-III date to the early period of the Eneolithic, horizon IV to the middle, and V-VIII to the late Eneolithic (Chapman 1990, 59). Evidence suggests Polyanitsa developed successfully over this period without any major hiatus of occupation.

Radingrad – situated 6km east of the town of Razgrad, this site was 45-50m in diameter prior to excavation (Ivanov 1983, 166). Radingrad is dated to circa 4750-4350 BC (Ivanov 1982) and spreads over five horizon levels. Horizon I is dated to the early Eneolithic, II-III to the middle, and IV-V to the late Eneolithic. No breaks in occupation are recorded throughout its life (Chapman 1990, 59).

Tărgovište – Situated just 2km south of and named after the town of Tărgovište, this site stood 1.5 m high and 60m in diameter (Bailey 1991, 163). It dates to circa 4550-4350 BC (Todorova 1982) and excavation produced four habitation horizons. Through ceramic typologies, horizons I-III are dated to the middle Eneolithic, and horizon IV to the late Eneolithic (Chapman 1990, 59). Again, no breaks in occupation are recorded.

In this study, structures are identified as an architecturally defined space. The purposeful construction of such spaces is important to the analysis, so an entrance to the structure must be archaeologically defined for the structure to be included. Although most structures follow the identification made by the original excavators, some structures were deemed too architecturally vague in order to be included within this study (for more detail see Jones 2002). Furthermore, identified external areas such as courtyards were excluded. Although important in their own right in the mediation of privacy, they were archaeologically undefined in comparison to the main structures. A full summary of the number of structures analysed within each habitation horizon is presented in table 4.2 opposite.

Horizon	Structures	Eneolithic Period
Polyanitsa I	14	Early
Polyanitsa II	16	
Polyanitsa III	15	
Polyanitsa IV	30	Middle
Polyanitsa V	18	Late
Polyanitsa VI	19	
Polyanitsa VII	21	
Polyanitsa VIII	22	
Radingrad I	16	Early
Radingrad II	9	Middle
Radingrad III	12	
Radingrad IV	10	Late
Radingrad V	11	
Tărgovište I	12	Middle
Tărgovište II	14	
Tărgovište III	15	
Tărgovište IV	5	Late
Total Structures	**259**	

Table 4.2. Number of structures analysed per habitation horizon.

R.A. analysis (Relative Asymmetry)

The organisation of these spaces in relation to access and boundaries will be analysed using a variation of 'gamma-analysis' defined by Hillier and Hanson (1984, 147). The depth of each space is measured as the number of 'steps' (from space to space) it would take to reach it from the entrance. A space next to the entrance would be one step deep, another space beyond would be two steps deep, meaning that the previous space must be travelled through in order to reach it. These steps are figurative, so each space counts as one step. A distinction is drawn between 'shallow' structures (those with one or two access levels), and 'deep' structures (those with three or more access levels). It is suggested that the 'deeper' a space is within a structure, the greater the degree of boundary control present. In this context, deeper structures have been taken to mean greater control over household space and the level of privacy within (see Chapman 1990, 62).

In this analysis, a space is taken as an area within the structure that can allow an activity to take place within it. A single room can contain multiple spaces, often defined through cues and props such as furniture or temporary partitioning (Rapoport 1990). The spaces within this analysis were defined by the following rules:

- They must be architecturally visible;
- Partitions (where present) must significantly alter the internal layout, or seem designed to guide the use of space;
- Good practicality within each space is considered (due to limitations of the excavation techniques some small partitioned areas are likely to be erroneous);

- Defined areas such as grain silos are designated as a space due to their specific activity and usually substantial size;
- The spaces must be considered in context, and seem to reflect the nature of the structure as a whole.

It was felt that the standard rules concerning the definition of spaces (that rooms/spaces tend to be convex and thus definable through shape, see Hiller and Hanson 1984) can only be applied to the clearly defined nature of more modern structures. The structures in this analysis were deemed more personal in their construction, lacking the sharp definitions of more recent architecture, and thus a more contextual approach was taken.

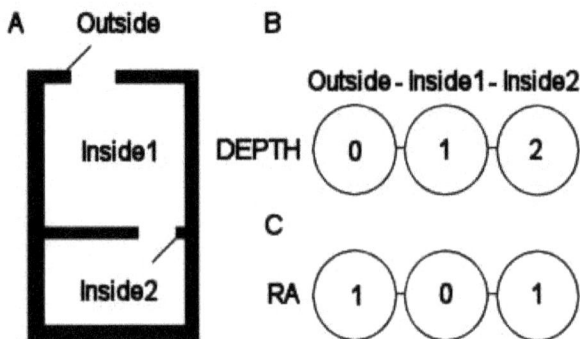

Figure 4.2. Example of Analysis.
A) Structure separated into three spaces. B) Spatial depths using the outside space as the point of origin C) RA values (the closer to 1 the more segregated).

In order to assess the potential control over barriers offered by each space (permeability), their level of integration within the spatial system must be considered. A highly integrated space within a system can be seen to have less potential boundary control (e.g. a corridor). Its purpose is often purely to allow access to other spaces, often with multiple spaces leading to and from the space. In modern architecture, it is this fact alone that often defines the space as a corridor or hallway etc. Size and shape are irrelevant. A space with little integration can be seen to offer greater control over what information passes through that boundary and into the space. En-suite bathrooms typify this in modern homes. They are constructed to be private to all except those in the space that has sole access (the bedroom). Passage to this private space is usually controlled by those in charge of the previous space. Taken as a whole, each space in a structure is connected to others in a system. This system also includes the outside as a single space (regardless of how many entrances/exits) (Figure 4.2). Within such a system, the depth measure of *Relative Asymmetry* can be applied to each space. This measure provides the generalised depth of each space in relation to other spaces within the system, comparing how deep the system is from a particular space with how deep or shallow it could theoretically be (Hillier and Hanson 1984, 108). With this measure, the depth of each space in the system can be worked out when that space is the carrier (point of origin). There are two steps to the process: 1) The Mean Depth of the carrier space must be calculated; 2) The

Relative Asymmetry of the system from the carrier can then be analysed.

The calculation for these measures is as follows:

$$\text{The Mean Depth of a space} = \frac{TD}{k-1}$$

where

TD = the total depth of the other spaces

k = the number of spaces in the system

Then

$$\text{The Relative Asymmetry of a space} = \frac{2\,(MD-1)}{k-2}$$

where

MD = the mean depth of the space

k = the number of spaces in the system

This gives a value between 0 and 1, with low values indicating an integrated space, and high values indicating segregation. In this analysis, two RA values were considered, each chosen to reflect a specific type of privacy.

1. The mean RA for the system reflecting the general level of integration within the structure, related to the privacy of individual spaces within the group.
2. The external space RA, suggesting the level of integration a structure has with the outside. This reflects the level of control over the internal-external boundary and is related to the control of access between the group and others.

Results of the Analyses

Polyanitsa
The RA analysis shows the variation of structural organisation within each horizon, with structural values ranging from 0 to 0.750 across the tell. Within this variation, the mean structural values suggest a temporal increase in spatial segregation (Figure 4.3). However, this overall trend is constantly near the 0.500 level, neither specifically integrated nor segregated. The external analysis shows a more definite trend towards segregation of the external space, with horizons I-III having significantly lower values than the later horizons. Horizon IV can be noted with considerable segregation and a mean value of 0.735, and no structure with a lower value than 0.333 (Figure 4.4).

Radingrad
Although generally shallow structures, the RA trend is of distinct segregation (Figure 4.3). On three of the horizons all structures have an RA of 0.667, showing consistency across the tell. The external values show extremely high levels of segregation and control over the external space, never falling below 0.741 (Figure 4.4).

Tărgovište
The RA values show more spatial integration within the structures. Only horizon IV has a mean structural RA above 0.500 (Figure 4.3). The external RA values suggest levels of segregation, if not as extreme as those of Radingrad. They too follow a slight temporal pattern, increasing in segregation over the duration of the tell (Figure 4.4).

Groups or individuals?

Polyanitsa
Throughout the eight horizons, its inhabitants constructed and reconstructed buildings which are amongst the largest and most complex known from a tell settlement. Most have high degrees of internal partitioning and some have considerable depth, perhaps indicating the potential social pressures that may have been present on such a site. The close proximity of structures and people would have meant that the physical and social organisation of activities and obligations would have been an important element of life on the tell. The regulation of these obligations would likely have merited some clear models of privacy.

In the creation of these large multi-spaced structures, the desire to create deeper spaces was not always very strong (Figure 4.5). Whilst often numerous in spaces, control over boundaries within the structures seems to be less of a

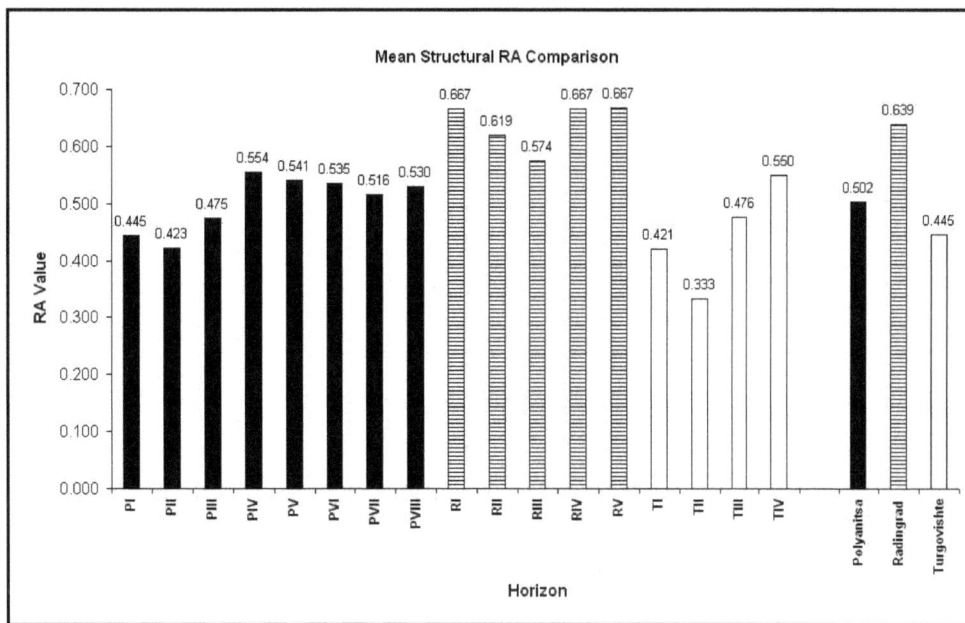

Figure 4.3. Comparison of mean structural RA per horizon, across all tells. Includes tell means.

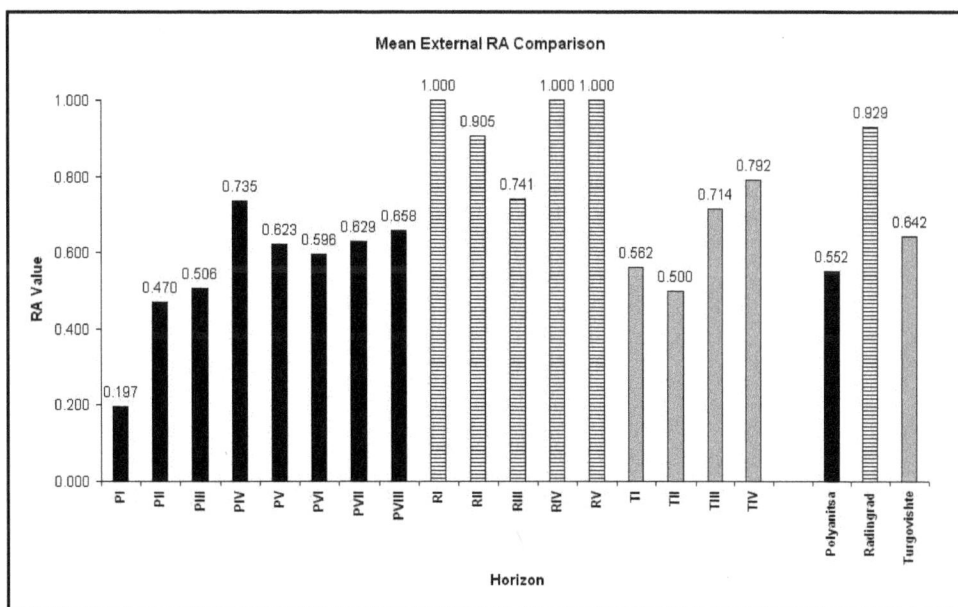

Figure 4.4. Comparison of mean external RA per horizon, across all tells. Includes tell means.

priority, with the site offering a mix of integrated and segregated structures. I suggest that the relationships on Polyanitsa may have been more focused on the control of these large structures and possible associated structures at a group level. The segregation of the external space is noticeable, especially on the later horizons. This increasing desire for control over access may be reflected by the presence of neighbours. As the tell increases in structures

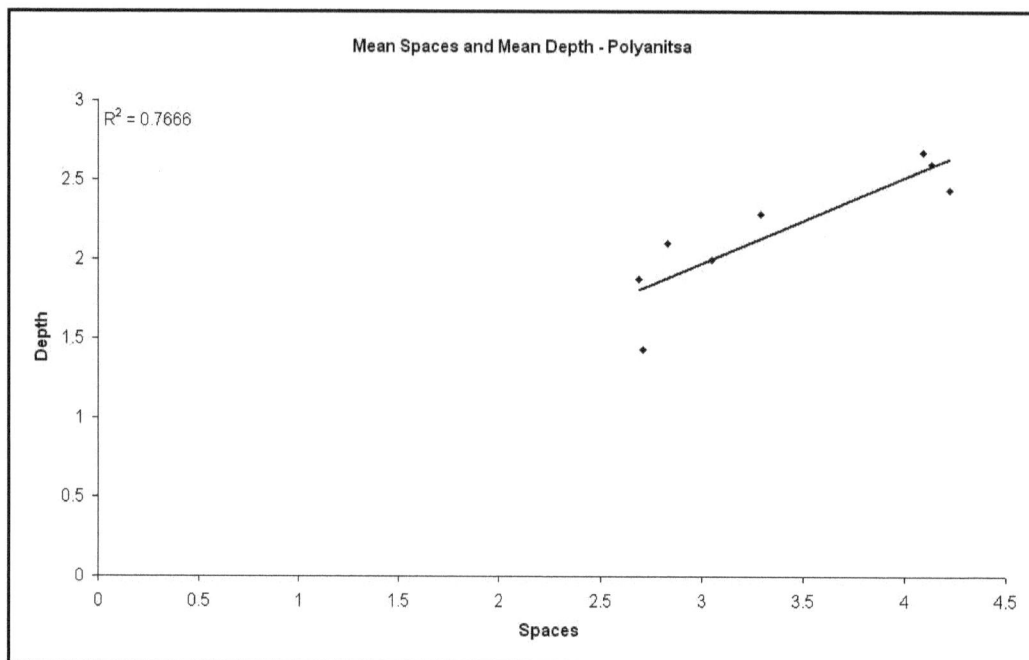

Figure 4.5. Mean spaces compared to mean depth – Polyanitsa.

and built area, this control would have become more important. It may be no coincidence that horizon IV, which has an abnormally large number of structures (30 in this analysis), also has the largest amount of segregation of this boundary. Chapman's suggestion of household lineages (1990, 83) comes to mind, as each strives to maintain the boundary between what/who is inside and what/who is outside. The closeness of neighbours in these cramped conditions may have led to a segregation defined by a limited number of access ways into the structures. The desire and regulation of intimacy seems a possible occurrence within this archaeological framework. Further evidence may be suggested by the structural changes between horizons IV and V. In horizon V the number of structures reduces to 18, yet the number of spaces within these structures dramatically increases, usually to two or three times the previous amounts. As the maintenance of the external boundary is still high (0.623), this may indicate the amalgamation of neighbouring structures/groups or the success of some groups over others.

However, even as intimacy may have influenced spatial form, other factors must be considered. For instance, the need to house more activities as outside space diminished, and the subsequent restrictions on where it was possible to build. This I feel is reflected in the range of structures and values across the tell, perhaps indicating specific tasks within some structures, such as stables, or store rooms. The continued presence of single-celled structures throughout the duration of the tell suggests that some activities were deemed to belong outside the structural system. Within the

structure, it is easy to see activities and privacy merged together in a more controlled environment.

Radingrad
Architecture on Radingrad follows a significantly different trend to that on Polyanitsa. The built area is far less dense, and the space between structures and the outside space actually increase over the life of the tell. A strong trend in shallow structures is noticeable across all horizons, with no increase in spaces across any stage of the tell's life. This may have been because there was always external space to use, in contrast to the externally deprived layout of Polyanitsa. The nature of the spatial partitioning within the structures may well have been temporary, reflecting either a more limited range of activities, or smaller durations in which they were formed. The generally smaller nature of the tell and the structures might reflect this.

What architectural spaces there were, however, would have provided optimum spatial control. This is reflected in the high structural RA values, showing a dominance of structural segregation on all horizons. Although these structures are not of the scale of those on Polyanitsa, the desire for group privacy within them seems even more likely. The shallow, yet controlled structures across Radingrad offer the ability for extreme control over the internal/external boundary and the seclusion of deeper spaces. Notable is the presence of simple two-celled structures, with an integrated 'front' room and a closed 'back' room (as in Figure 4.2). Whether this structural form was built for increased control over this back space is undecided. The RA results suggest this, demonstrating

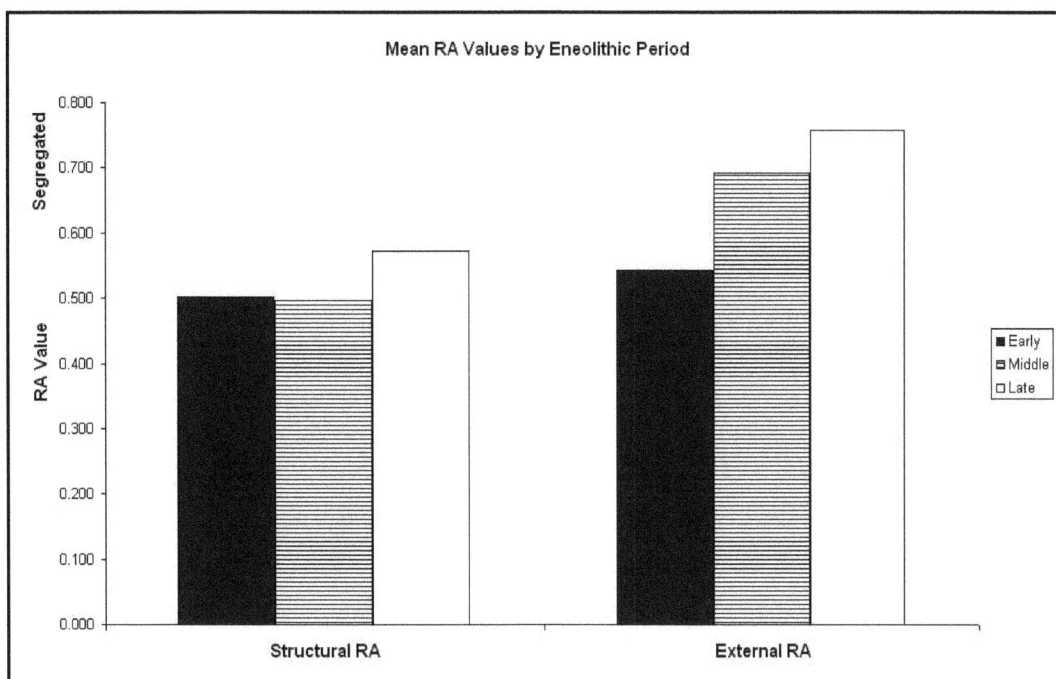

Figure 4.6. RA values per Eneolithic phase.

extremely high external values. Regardless, it is equally likely that this is one of the easiest structural types to construct, the next step from a single-celled structure. However, it is noticeable that this pattern must have been successful, as it was repeated over most horizons. The lack of need to partition within structures to accommodate activities, especially as the tell developed, may have meant that social factors governed structural design more than physical factors. Although there was increasing space between the buildings, control over their access remained a priority (Chapman 1990, 70).

Tărgovište
Initially, the organisation of structures on Tărgovište seems more comparable to Radingrad then Polyanitsa, with a trend for a decreasing built area and shallow, spatially limited structures. However, unlike Radingrad, the organisation of these spaces suggests a changing social model. Although Tărgovište offers the fewest habitation horizons, it is the only site to suggest a clear temporal change in the architectural patterns.

The control over access seen on Radingrad is not present on the initial horizons of the site. The spatial integration of the structures is relatively high, shown in the integrated structural RA values. The low external RA values of the first two horizons suggest that the control over the access to these structures was less defined during these phases. The internal/external boundary was more blurred, seemingly without the desire to physically exclude others from the group. I suggest this desire becomes recognised after the second horizon (an important moment of first deciding how to rebuild, what is to be done differently etc.), a point that corresponds to a sharp increase in the external RA. Overall, Tărgovište can be seen to potentially reflect the desire for intimacy and control over the internal/external boundaries that is present on the other

tells. In this case however, Tărgovište follows a gradual adoption of this social model, with increasing external control that culminates in horizon IV. This horizon is significant, as it shows a re-orientation of all the structures at the site, and offers the most segregated and deepest structures.

Privacy and identity in the Bulgarian Eneolithic

The control over the passage of information through the entrance of structures was a common theme in all three tells. This control has been related to the desire for group privacy (intimacy) that can be physically and socially defined by the structures. Due to the strong contrast in the use of space between Polyanitsa and the other two tells, it is perhaps surprising to find that a similar social model may be influencing some aspects of structural design (i.e. privacy for the group, not the individual). However, whilst the mechanisms for obtaining such privacy are similar, the social obligations triggering such desire may have been different. With consistently decreasing external space within Polyanitsa, more activities would have been present within the structures. This may have led to the inter-house rivalry suggested by Chapman (1990), as the internal/external boundary became an important aspect of controlling the amount of access others outside the group had to those activities, especially considering the close proximity of most structures. Neither Radingrad nor Tărgovište saw this intensification of building activities, yet both produced a similar, if not more noticeable, desire for control. On Radingrad there was immediate and constant control over this external boundary, in Tărgovište this desire was realised more gradually. The triggering factor for control over group privacy within these two tells may have been the increase in the possible activities that could have taken place outside the structures. By

37

controlling this boundary, the ability to regulate the interaction between the outside and the inside was present.

In many ways, these results confirm the importance of architecture within these societies. The importance of exclusion and control seems valid, as these structures can be seen as potential mechanisms through which intimacy is regulated. The importance of the group/household within tells is a factor that may have played an important role in the continued success of the tell. Throughout the 5th millennium BC, the repetition of structural concepts and the renewal of household groups may have become integral to the success of a tell. By breaking down the RA values from all three tells into their respective Eneolithic phases, the increasing desire for control over this external boundary is well defined as the societies grew (Figure 4.6); such aspects would be important in the maintenance of group membership.

The seeming absence of the ability to regulate solitude is less defined within this analysis. Whilst the creation of private spaces within structures seems more than likely at Polyanitsa, in order to assess this fully, better recording of the furniture and artefacts within structures is needed. This would also allow us to define activities. The artefactual evidence suggests that individuality became an important aspect of these groups, with expressive material culture in both the settlement and the burial contexts. Anthropomorphic and zoomorphic figurines have been found in numerous quantities, and changes in burial evidence suggests previously unseen differentiations between age and gender, coupled with exotic grave goods of clay, gold, copper, and *spondylus* (a spectacular aquatic shell). In many ways, this seeming embrace of distinction and individualism contrast with the limited evidence of seclusion within the group in this analysis. As such, I suggest that the regulation of intimacy through the spatial form of Eneolithic structures is only one of the mechanisms that would have been used to regulate social obligations.

Conclusions

In this chapter, I have tried to consider questions of identity within Bulgarian Eneolithic tell settlements using privacy as the main consideration. By demonstrating the relationships between regulating privacy and structural organisation, I have argued that it is possible to consider the nature of societies within tell settlements through the analysis of spatial form. I believe that the conclusions drawn show that the desire for intimacy within a group may have had an increasing influence in the construction of structures on these tells throughout the Eneolithic period. Control over whom or what may pass through these physical boundaries would have been an important part of social mediation within these communities. Ideas of continual 'households', or at least family groups, seem likely, especially on those sites that contain no noticeable hiatus between occupation levels.

Yet, the concept of the individual cannot be easily dismissed just because of a lack of evidence supporting the manifestation of solitude. No archaeological analysis can truly allow for the presence or absence of temporary barriers and divides within such structures. Likewise, there is some evidence of secondary stories that will forever be lost in any modern consideration. Regardless, I suggest that the rise of individuals within these groups was inherent in the mobile nature of the people within the site. People where not anchored to the tells, or to any site. The ability for group members to pack up and leave, to take their animals to new lands, to mediate social pressures through movement, can all be related to privacy types such as isolation, and should form vital considerations in our understanding of the roles tells played in the wider social landscape. Ethnographic studies can show how some social relations are fluid, meaning relations between individuals and groups are changed as and when the situation demands (Moore 1984). The presence of off-tell structures (see Bailey *et al.* 1998) and movement due to activities such as transhumance (Evans 2003) should be considered as important in the ways these people would have lived their lives, and mediated their social needs. Even the desire just to 'get away from it all' and wander out of the settlement for no other purpose then because you can may not be so unreasonable.

Acknowledgments

Academic support for this research came from Dr Douglass Bailey (Cardiff University) and Dr Mark Lake (University College London). Financial support came from the Arts and Humanities Research Council (AHRC) postgraduate awards division. Thanks to all.

References

Altman, I. 1975. *The environment and social behaviour.* Belmont, California: Wadsworth Publishing Company.

Altman, I. and Chemers, M. 1984. *Culture and environment.* Cambridge: Cambridge University Press.

Bailey, D. W. 1990. The living house: signifying continuity. In R. Samson (ed.), *The social archaeology of houses,* 19-48. Edinburgh: Edinburgh University Press.

Bailey, D. W. 1991. *The social reality of figurines from the Chalcolithic of Northeastern Bulgaria: the example of Ovcharavo.* Unpublished PhD dissertation. Cambridge University.

Bailey, D. W. 1995 The analysis of tells in northeastern Bulgaria: settlement behaviour in the contexts of time, space and place. Paper submitted on invitation for publication in *Reports of Prehistoric Research Projects.* Unpublished.

Bailey, D. W. 2000. *Balkan prehistory: exclusion, incorporation and identity.* London: Routledge.

Bailey, D. W., Bass, J., Hamilton, M., Neumann, H., Raduncheva, A., Stevanovíc, M. and Tringham, R. 1998. Expanding the dimensions of early agricultural Tells: the Podgoritsa archaeological project, Bulgaria. *Journal of Field Archaeology* 24 (4), 373-96.

Bates, A. 1964. Privacy - A useful concept? *Social Forces* 42, 432.

Bourdieu, P. 1973. The Berber house. In M. Douglas (ed.), *Rules and meanings,* 98-110. Harmondsworth: Penguin Books.

Boyadzhiev, Y. 1995. Chronology of prehistoric cultures in Bulgaria. In D. W. Bailey and I. Panayotov (eds), *Prehistoric Bulgaria,* 149-92. Wisconsin: Madison Press.

Chapin, F. 1951. Some housing factors related to mental hygiene. *Journal of Social Issues* 7, 164-71.

Chapman, J. 1990. Social inequality on Bulgarian tells and the Varna problem. In R. Samson (ed.), *The social archaeology of houses,* 49-92. Edinburgh: Edinburgh University Press.

Chapman, J. 2000. *Fragmentation in archaeology.* London: Routledge.

Evans, J. G. 2003. *Environmental archaeology and the social order.* London: Routledge.

Fletcher, R. 1977. Settlement studies (micro and semi-micro). In D. L. Clarke (ed.), *Spatial archaeology,* 47-162. London: Academic Press.

Fletcher, R. 1984. Identifying spatial disorder: a case study of a Mongol fort. In H. Hietala (ed.), *Intra-site spatial analysis in archaeology,* 196-223. Cambridge: Cambridge University Press.

Hall, E. T. 1966. *The hidden dimension.* New York: Doubleday.

Hillier, B. and Hanson, J. 1984. *The social logic of space.* Cambridge: Cambridge University Press.

Hodder, I. 1990. *The domestication of Europe.* Oxford: Blackwell.

Ingham, R. 1978. Privacy and psychology. In J. Young (ed.), *Privacy,* 35-58. Chichester: John Wiley and Sons.

Ivanov, I. 1983. Le chalcolithique en Bulgarie et dans la necrople de Varna. In A. Poulter (ed.), *Ancient Bulgaria,* 154-63. Nottingham: University of Nottingham.

Ivanov, T. 1982. *Radingrad. Tell et necropole des Ve et IVe millenaires avant J-C.* Radingrad.

Jones, G. 2001. *The private life of tells: The social implications concerning the manifestation of privacy within the architecture of Ovcharovo, a fifth millennium BC settlement mound.* Unpublished B.Sc. Dissertation. Cardiff University.

Jones, G. 2002. *Mechanisms of control: The manifestation of privacy within Eneolithic architecture.* Unpublished M.Sc. Dissertation. University College London.

Jourard, S. M. 1966. Some psychological aspects of privacy. *Law and Contemporary Problems* 31, 301-18.

Kent, S. 1990. A cross-cultural study of segmentation, architecture, and the use of space. In S. Kent (ed.), *domestic architecture and the use of space,* 127-52. Cambridge: Cambridge University Press.

Lawrence, D. and Low, S. 1990. The built environment and spatial form. *Annual Review of Anthropology* 19, 453-505.

Marshall, N. 1972. Privacy and environment. *Human Ecology* 1, 93-110.

Marshall, N. 1974. Dimensions of privacy preferences. *Multivariate Behavioural Research* 9, 255-71.

Moore, B. 1984. *Privacy: studies in social and cultural history.* London: M. E. Sharpe Inc.

Newell, P. 1998. A cross-cultural comparison of privacy definitions and functions: a systems approach. *Journal of Environmental Psychology* 18, 357-71.

Ozaki, R. 2002. Housing as a reflection of culture: privatised living and privacy in England and Japan. *Housing Studies* 17 (2), 209-27.

Pastalan, L. A. 1970. Privacy as an expression of human territoriality. In L. A. Pastalan and D. H. Carson (eds), *Spatial behaviour of older people,* 88-101. Ann Arbor: University of Michigan Press.

Pedersen, D. 1979. Dimensions of privacy. *Perceptual and Motor Skills* 48, 1291-97.

Pedersen, D. 1997. Psychological functions of privacy. *Journal of Environmental Psychology* 17, 147-56.

Rapoport, A. 1982. *The meaning of the built environment: A non-verbal communication approach.* Beverly Hills: Sage.

Rapoport, A. 1990. Systems of activities and systems of settings. In S. Kent (ed.), *Domestic architecture and the use of space,* 9-20. Cambridge: Cambridge University Press.

Rapoport, A. 1994. Spatial organisation and the built environment. In T. Ingold (ed.), *Companion encyclopedia of anthropology,* 460-502. London: Routledge.

Sanders, D. 1990. Behavioural conventions and archaeology: methods for the analysis of ancient architecture. In S. Kent (ed.), *Domestic architecture and the use of space,* 43-72. Cambridge: Cambridge University Press.

Steadman, S. R. 2000. Spatial patterning and social complexity on prehistoric Anatolian *tell* sites: models for mounds. *Journal of Anthropological Archaeology* 19, 164-99.

Todorova, H. 1978. *The Eneolithic of Bulgaria.* Oxford: BAR.

Todorova, H. 1982. *Kupferzeitliche Siedungen in Nordostbulgarien.* Munich: C. H. Beck.

Todorova, H. 1986. *Kamenno-mednata Epokha v Bulgariya. Peto Khilyadoletie predi Novata Era.* Sofia: Nauka I Izkustvo.

Todorova, H., Vasilev, V., Janusevic, Z., Kovacheva, M. and Valev, P. (eds), 1983. *Ovcharovo (Razkopki I Prouchvaniya 9).* Sofia: Bulgarskata Akademiya na Naukite.

Westin, A. 1970. *Privacy and freedom.* New York: Atheneum.

Whittle, A. 1985. *Neolithic Europe: a survey.* Cambridge: Cambridge University Press.

Whittle, A. 1996. Houses in context: buildings as process. In T. Darvill and J. Thomas (eds), *Neolithic houses in Northwest Europe and beyond,* 13-26. Oxford: Oxbow Books.

Wilk, R. and Rathje, W. 1982. Household archaeology. *American Behavioral Scientist* 25, 617-39.

Wilson, P. 1988. *The domestication of the human species.* London: Yale University Press.

Agents of identity: performative practice at the Etton causewayed enclosure

Oliver Harris

Introduction

Archaeology is often lauded for its ability to study monumental changes over large sweeps of time, be it the evolution and spread of *Homo Sapiens* or the Neolithic 'revolution'. Yet such broad brush strokes miss much of the real lives that people led, and too often do not engage with the real reasons for change and development. Processual archaeology in particular with its emphasis on systems theory and functionalism failed to adequately deal with the people of the past. In contrast, much of recent post-processual writing has concentrated directly on this through an emphasis on agency (e.g. Barrett 1994; Gardner 2004). Yet, this writing on agency has largely ignored the variety of human experience, the multiplicity of forms of identity, gender, personhood, emotion and memory which people experience as central parts of their socialities (Hall 2000; Butler 1993; Strathern 1988; Lutz 1986; Connerton 1989). It has thus been widely criticised for being essentialist and reductive. In this paper I wish to argue that a combination of relevant aspects of agency theory, notably the practice-based understandings of John Barrett (1994; 2001), with a more complex understanding of identity can help preserve the powerful insights of such approaches, whilst dealing with accusations of essentialism. In such a brief paper it would be impossible to deal with the complete spectrum of complex emotions and memories available to people in the past (though these are ideas I am exploring elsewhere in my PhD research). Instead, I shall therefore concentrate on how the notion of identity might be approached.

The opening section of this paper is thus explicitly theoretical, and is intended to develop a notion of *performative practice*, that is a combination of the understandings of Barrett (2001) alongside more nuanced understandings of identity put forward by authors such as Judith Butler (1990; 1993). The second half of the paper will take these ideas and apply them to the Neolithic causewayed enclosure at Etton (Pryor 1998). In particular, I wish to look at how the detailed analysis of particular acts of deposition can begin to allow us to access the moments at which identity was created, maintained and undermined.

Practice and identity

The material archaeologists recover has traditionally been seen as a record either of past cultures or past processes. Instead, John Barrett (2001) has argued that we need to think of the material as the physical conditions of social life. He argues that if we take the material to be a direct record of social conditions, then the material is immediately separated from the processes of agency that brought that material into existence (Barrett 2000a, 25). The task is not so much to recover human agency archaeologically as to recognise that human agency is inherent in the material. As Barrett proposes:

Those who claim the study of agency through archaeology to be impossible because they are unable to see agency in the material can be disarmed simply because the study of agency does not adhere for its validation to such a theory of representation (2000b, 63).

In this argument the objects of study are the principles which structure agency (Barrett 1994, 165). Within these principles we need to ask questions as to what possibilities of being there were. In other words, what ways of living were possible within those material conditions? Barrett's work (e.g. 2001) is explicitly based on the structuration theory of Anthony Giddens (1984). From this perspective, when agents act they are simultaneously constrained and empowered by the material and social structures in which they live, and by acting within those structures they contribute to their reaffirmation. In social practice, the performance of agency requires actions that have ramifications beyond the individual, beyond even their lifespan, as they work and act within institutions that extend beyond themselves (Giddens 1984).

Barrett (1994; 2001) also draws extensively on the concept of *habitus*. The term was first coined by Marcel Mauss, but has become best known through the work of the French anthropologist Pierre Bourdieu (1977; 1990). The *habitus* is based on practical rather than discursive knowledge, that is knowledge of how to act and proceed based on experience, rather than discussion and debate. It is the *habitus* that informs people of when to speak and when to remain silent, when to act and when not to; it tells us what is conventional, acceptable and proper (Barrett 2001, 153). *Habitus* is a concept bound into people's everyday life, as it is created and sustained through their actions on a day-to-day basis. It is also a product of history. As Bourdieu points out, it "produces individual and collective practices - more history - in accordance with the schemes generated by history" (1990, 54). It is thus perpetuated through its own expression. Barrett (1994) uses the concepts of *habitus* and structuration theory to explore the material conditions that archaeologists discover. They allow him to consider the encounters agents had with their world, the experience of living in it and the possibilities they had for action.

Although Barrett's (1994; 2001) argument offers a powerful agency-centred basis for archaeological understanding, there are a number of difficulties with his work. The most crucial difficulty is that the people in Barrett's accounts remain largely undifferentiated, both from each other and from the people of the present. For example there is no sense of variation in age and gender. Distinctions such as childhood, old age, male and female blend together to produce the 'knowledgeable agent'. This not only denies the possibility of multiple genders and complex identities in the past, it also genders power implicitly as male (Brück 2001, 653; Gero 2000, 35).

This a-historical and universal 'knowledgeable agent' also presents a very particular Western view of personhood, that of the bounded, whole individual (Fowler 2000; 2004; Whittle 2003). Ethnographic accounts from India (e.g. Busby 1997) and Melanesia (Strathern 1988) show how we cannot assume that any particular view of what a person is or what can be a person is universal across space and time. Other considerations are absent from Barrett's (1994) account, notably how socially contingent understandings of emotion and memory affected the possibilities for agency in the past. The broader community lacks a real sense of shared values and of aesthetics (Overing and Passes 2000; Whittle forthcoming). Agency is also located uniquely within the human self. Concepts of animal agency or the agency of enclosures themselves, which Joshua Pollard has recently written about, are underplayed (2004; cf. Ray and Thomas 2003; Whittle 2003, chapter 4). Drawing on Tim Ingold (2000), Pollard (2004, 64) shows how agency is not the infliction of cultural forces onto the natural world, but instead is the way in which humans amongst other agencies draw on the affordances of their environment.

In acknowledging these weaknesses, however, we certainly do not need to reject the insights of an archaeology of practice. Instead we can embed it within other perspectives. An archaeology of practice does not inherently require us to reject socially contingent notions of gender or identity, or of emotion or memory for that matter. We can retain its powerful sense of agency and improvisation within these broader understandings of how human beings dwell in the landscape, and draw on values and identities that are socially and historically contextual. Unfortunately in such a brief paper there is insufficient space to discuss all these vital aspects of past socialities. Instead I will focus on one particular aspect and examine how a more complex understanding of identity in the past, set within an archaeology of practice, can benefit our interpretation.

Identity
Identity in archaeology is often treated either as irrelevant (where the true purpose of archaeology is regarded as the recovery and understanding of long-term processes) or unrecoverable, as the top level of Hawkes' *ladder of inference* (1954). Both these attitudes are misplaced. Firstly, they thrust modern conceptions of identity back into the past, and thereby legitimate modern inequalities, such as those between men and women for example. Secondly, both are based on a view that sees the archaeological material as a record. Identity is certainly not irrelevant, it is central to any understanding of the past, and it is certainly not unrecoverable. Just as Barrett (2000b) has argued with reference to agency, I would argue that the archaeological material is already infused with identity because it was produced in, and helped produce, a world in which identities were central. Those that argue that identity is unrecoverable, if I may twist the earlier Barrett quote (2000b, 63), are disarmed simply because the study of *identity* does not adhere for its validation to such a theory of representation. The material conditions in which people lived, that which archaeologists recover, are the material conditions through which concepts of identity were created, performed, sustained and undermined. These conceptions were central to past people's lives and thus must be central to our investigations of the past.

Today, identity is conceived as being the combination of multiple factors such as age, gender, sexuality, status and personhood. Each of these is made up of categories, which can be taken up by the subject in day-to-day life. Being male or female, for example, is a position that we take up that helps to define who we are. Often these notions are perceived and presented as unchanging, eternal, and universal. This assumes an essentialist position with regard to human nature; we are all the same across space and time. It is the same supra-historical position that Barrett (1994) offers on agency. One author who challenged this was the French philosopher Michel Foucault (1977; 1978). Foucault argued that the conception of agency prevalent in the social sciences "places its own point at the origin of all historicity – which in short leads to a transcendental consciousness" (1970, xiv). Instead what was required, he argued, was "not a theory of the knowing subject but rather a theory of discursive practice" (1970, xiv). It is here that identity becomes important, in the attempt by Foucault, as Stuart Hall has argued, to "rearticulate the relationship between subject and discursive practices" (2000, 16). In other words, identity emerges in an examination of how discursive practices can create differing notions of the subject and subjectivity. This begins to form the basis for an argument that rejects an essentialist view of human identity. Foucault views the subject as constituted entirely within the discursive practices of disciplinary regimes and the repeated performances of 'technologies of the self' (Redman 2000, 10). This point is essential. If subjects, and therefore identities, are created through discourse, then they must be produced through historically constituted acts of performance; through conditions, and at moments, that are unique (Hall 2000, 17). This makes identity a historically constituted creation and different across both time and space. Further examinations based on Foucault's work have also turned directly to the materiality of the body, and these have offered insights that develop his work and also build notions of performativity that blend well with the insights gleaned through an archaeology of practice. Judith Butler (1990; 1993) has carried out the most notable of these works, and her thinking is beginning to influence the ways in which some archaeologists in Britain and America understand gender and identity (e.g. Fowler 2000; Perry and Joyce 2001).

Judith Butler: regulatory ideals and performativity
Judith Butler draws on an eclectic range of sources including Foucault (1978), Derrida (1981), Lacan (1977), and Iragary (1985) to problematise all our modern notions around identity. Building on Foucault (1978 *inter alia*), Butler (1993, 1) describes modern notions of identity as being made up of regulatory ideals. These regulatory ideals provide idealised and reified norms which people are expected to live up to. Thus, categories such as male and female, heterosexual or homosexual, young or old are not biological facts, but ideals which we create and recite through performance. As Chris Fowler has pointed out "*the ways that subjects attempt to recite, subvert or reiterate fictions of identity mark them as a specific type of person*"

(2001, 148 emphasis in original). This is not to say that these ideals do not have genuine authority within particular socialities or that people have a free conscious choice to move between them (though in some societies they might). Acknowledging this, however, does not make them 'real' or 'true' or somehow eternal, fixed and unchanging through space and time.

These types of regulatory ideals are thus created, sustained or undermined through performance, or to be more exact performativity. Performativity as defined by Butler is not a singular act, "for it is always the reiteration of a norm or a set of norms, and to the extent that it acquires an act-like status in the present, it conceals or dissimulates the conventions of which it is a repetition" (1993, 12). This reiteration is crucial in understanding performativity. It is through repeated action that these norms are created and lived up to. In relation to discourse, Butler (1993) argues that performative acts are statements which also produce that which they say. Her classic example is that of the midwife's cry of "it's a girl" which is not merely a reflection of a biological given but a performative act, binding a gender onto the body (Butler 1993). In other words, it produces that which it names (Butler 1993, 7). Thus performative acts are the one domain in which "discourse acts as power" (Butler 1993, 225). Through such an understanding, it becomes clear that concepts of male and female, of gender, are historically and culturally unique. These regulatory ideals are indeed *fictions* (Fowler 2000; Haraway 1991). The baby girl is not a girl until the midwife declares her so, and thus curtails the possibility of other genders being created and explored. This does not mean that the midwife makes a conscious choice of gender on behalf of the infant, but that gender is not a statement the body itself makes. In other places, at other times, different genders might be acknowledged and other regulatory ideals stressed. We cannot assume that the same categories existed in the past that exist today. As Butler herself points out: "these regulatory schemas are not timeless structures, but historically revisable criteria of intelligibility which produce and vanquish bodies that matter" (1993, 14). Categories of sex and gender are constructed against an outside, against non-viable choices, that secure the boundaries of sex (Butler 1993, 8). The construction of these categories is through exclusion, through abjection, through making some bodies unthinkable (Butler 1993, 188). In the heterosexual hegemony of modern Western society, these abjected bodies may be homosexual, but in other societies, different bodies may lie outside the regimes of power and discourse constructed through performativity. Indeed there is much evidence anthropologically that shows that other genders are possible, further weakening any position which sees the categories of 'man' and 'woman' as universals (e.g. Busby 1997; Gilchrist 1999). Societies may have 'multiple and fluid gender categories' which refuse to be categorised along the simplistic male/female bifurcation of the modern West (Rautman and Talalay 2000, 2; *cf.* Strathern 1988).

Bourdieu and Butler, practice and performativity
The similarities between Bourdieu (1977; 1990) and Butler (1993) have been noted by several authors (e.g. Gilchrist 1999, 56; Gosden 1999; McNay 2000, 40). Both place emphasis on bodily materiality and the way one carries oneself, on corporeality in other words. Lois McNay has argued that the combination of the two allows each to deal with the other's principal weakness (2000). In Butler's work (e.g. 1990; 1993), this is the way agency is underplayed through her reliance on a negative paradigm of subjection, and in Bourdieu's work his failure to deal adequately with the unstable nature of gender and the ways in which agency can emerge from the margins (McNay 2000, 46-56). Bourdieu's account of agency is generative rather than prescriptive. The concept of *habitus* offers a way of thinking about agency that, whilst creative and temporal, is also historically and socially specific (McNay 2000). Due to her reliance on Foucault (1978 *inter alia*), Butler (e.g. 1993) remains trapped between competing relations of dominance and resistance, whilst Bourdieu offers a more "nuanced view of political agency" (McNay 2000, 56). Butler's proposed view of identity, however, resists the naturalised view of the modern West and allows, in contrast to Bourdieu, the ambiguities and dissonance of performative identity to emerge (McNay 2000, 54). Thus the singular universal agents that have emerged through Bourdieu's accounts are made more complex through combination with the performative understandings of Butler. What is needed is thus an understanding of both practice and performativity, of *performative practice* in fact. This understanding allows us to maintain a sense of improvisation and creative agency within an approach that recognises the performative nature of identity and the ways in which regulatory ideals are created, cited and undermined.

This indicates, I would argue, that both agency and performativity are central to our understandings of human action in the past. Too often in archaeology, simplistic polemics are offered declaring the superiority of *this* philosopher or *that* social theorist (e.g. Barrett 1994; Thomas 1996). Instead, we require more complex, less mono-causal explanations for why archaeology has failed to deal adequately with the complexity of sociality in the past. This may make for less elegant narratives, but that I believe is a small price to pay. Alongside this more complex view of identity which I have concentrated on here, other aspects of being-in-the-world require consideration. Accusations of essentialism do not only apply to the way in which identity has been addressed. We also need to think about the complex ways in which different memories and emotions might have been played out, and the broader concerns that surround this, such as notions of conviviality and shared values (*cf.* Lutz 1986; Rosaldo 1993; Overing and Passes 2000; Whittle 2003; O. Harris 2004). Both memories and emotions are socially contextual and emerge through dwelling and agency, although we do not have the space to deal with these issues in detail here. They remain important, however, and begin to hint at other arenas in which identity might have been important, and other ways in which identity might have been created. Let us turn now to the Neolithic causewayed enclosure at Etton to see how these theoretical insights can deepen our narratives and broaden our understandings of people in the past.

Identity at Etton

Etton causewayed enclosure near Maxey, in Cambridgeshire lies on the floodplain of the River Welland (Pryor 1988, 107). Excavated in the 1980s it had extraordinary preservation, due to the waterlogged conditions and dates to the mid 4th millennium BC. Shaped like a squashed oval, Etton is small in comparison to other causewayed enclosures (Pryor 1998, xix). A stream cuts past the northwest of the enclosure, which would still have been active while the site was in use (Pryor 1998, 4). There was only a single ditch circuit consisting of 14 segments, with what appear to be entrances to the west, east and north (Figure 5.1). It is possible, however, that further segments and a fourth entrance may well have existed at the southern end, now hidden by the Maxey Cut. The north entrance, at causeway F, appears to be particularly important, as a three-metre wide wooden gateway was constructed there (Pryor 1998, 99). Like other causewayed enclosures, such as Windmill Hill (Whittle *et al.* 1999), a huge range of material, both organic and inorganic, was deposited in the ditch segments, including pottery, axe fragments, human and animal bone, along with wood and bark (Pryor 1998).

The enclosure at Etton appears to have been defined as two halves from the outset, on either side of the north entrance (Pryor 1998, 356). The difference between them can be shown in a number of areas.

Figure 5.1. The Etton enclosure (after Pryor 1998, 100, fig.103).

There is a real physical difference with the western half being far wetter, indeed the ditches on this side would have been waterlogged when first dug (Pryor 1998, 364). Pryor (1998) argues that this was a deliberate choice made in prehistory, and I think that is a reasonable conclusion. There are areas nearby, such as Maxey Island where the enclosure could have been situated on dry ground. Instead, Etton was placed in a location that would have been flooded for part of the year and half of the ditches would have been permanently waterlogged (Pryor 1998, 364). Other differences between the two halves of the enclosure are also clear. For example, in terms of deposition, pottery was excluded from much of the western half and wood and bark from much of the east. It is important to note that this latter example is not merely a preservational issue, as some wood was found later in the sequence in the eastern half. Later, this division was formalised with the erection of a fence and the digging of a ditch between the two halves of the enclosure.

There is a strongly discernible sequence of deposits at Etton, partly due to the fact that the entire enclosure was excavated, and partly due to the nature of deposits and alterations that took place in antiquity. In his excavation report, Pryor divides the first phase, the main period of the enclosure's use, into three subphases, 1a, 1b and 1c. The later Neolithic use of the site, which includes pit digging and the construction of a cursus, is known as phase 2 (Pryor 1998, 16-17). The ditches were originally cut in phase 1a and then, in the eastern half at least, recut, with new, increasingly more complex deposits being laid through phases 1b and 1c. This phasing is important as it allows us to examine how different concerns developed over time, through increasingly complex acts of deposition.

One of the strengths of archaeology, as I mentioned above, has traditionally been seen as the huge tracts of time over which changes can be studied, and this is certainly true. Yet as archaeologists we also have access to particular moments, particular sequences of deposition. Within an understanding of performative practice that we developed above we can see that it is here, in these moments, that identities were cited and performed and it was also here that they may have been transformed. As we turn now to examine the detail of two particular moments of deposition at Etton, I want to analyse how these actions may have helped create, sustain or undermine identities through this notion of performative practice. In particular I wish to think about how age, knowledge and rites of passage may have vital roles to play.

Age, knowledge and rites of passage

Age in our society can be divided up into a number of categories following birth, and arriving eventually at death. Beginning with infancy we move through childhood, puberty, adolescence, adulthood, middle age and old age. Each of these categories, although associated with certain biological realities, are, as I argued earlier, regulatory ideals laid down for us to live up to as we move through life. People of different ages are supposed to behave in different, appropriate ways. In current Western society it could easily be argued that these categories are becoming increasingly fluid, the ways in which people act at different ages are much more open to question than they were forty years ago. Often, moving from one age category to the next involves a rite of passage. Within Christian belief, there are rites of passage of christening, confirmation and marriage that take place to mark people's movement through life and are intimately connected with age. In other places, other rites of passage, for instance, are associated with menstruation and circumcision (e.g. Strathern 1988). In the Neolithic, age might have been an important consideration; it might have reflected experience and knowledge just as it would today. These similarities, however, should not prevent us from considering how different ways of thinking about age might be involved (Amoss and Harrell 1981). Different regulatory ideals might exist for different ages, associated with different rites of passage. We also need to consider how knowledge might be tied up in this, knowledge of the location of the enclosure, of what was appropriate to deposit and where. These knowledges may have developed with age, as people became more immersed in the *habitus*, in the knowledge of how to go on. How old people were may have affected how often they had been to the enclosure and the rituals and ceremonies they had seen and experienced before. These in turn would both draw on and create memory. How can we begin to think about age and the development of these understandings in the Neolithic? One way in begins with the concept of rites of passage.

Age and rites of passage
The concept of rites of passage is widespread in the archaeological literature and so requires only a brief discussion here. First developed by the anthropologist Arnold van Gennep (1960), and later by Victor Turner (1969), the concept is based on a tripartite system of separation, liminality and incorporation. Thus when a rite of passage takes place a particular person is first separated from the group, they then go through a liminal phase, betwixt and between normal life, and are then reincorporated again (van Gennep 1960). I believe that

close examination of the deposits at causewayed enclosures can reveal narratives that allow us to talk about how age might have been conceived in the Neolithic, through rites of passage. Ethnographically recorded societies such as the Himba do not count age by the number of years, but by the stage a person has reached (Crandall 1998, 108). Each of these stages may be associated with a rite of passage. It is my argument that many of the deposits at Etton are intimately connected with such rites. This is hardly new in itself, but I hope that I can indicate how certain narratives, certain ways of living within the material conditions of life, might be more likely than others.

Ditch segment 7 lies in the eastern half of the enclosure at Etton, which saw the more complex structured deposits. The phase 1a deposits in this ditch are of particular interest. Beginning at the butt-end at causeway H, and moving away, a sequence of deposits was laid down. The first deposit was a severed inverted fox skull, followed by an upturned Mildenhall bowl, a decorated antler comb and a second vessel, this time a plain bowl placed on its base, with two animal bones nearby (Pryor 1998, 33). Although different sequences might be suggested, with the deposits being laid down in a different order, the relationship with the butt-end suggests that this indeed was the direction they followed (Figure 5.2).

Around these deposits, a narrative related to age, regulatory ideals and rites of passage can be constructed. I would like to make it clear that the following interpretation is an imaginative engagement with the evidence. Of course, other 'readings' or 'performances' are equally possible, but I wish to highlight the potential of a rite of passage approach. The deposits were laid out along two metres of the ditch bottom; this would have allowed many people to watch as they were laid out. The initial deposit was the fox skull. This can be interpreted in two ways: it can be seen as a symbol of the woods, the outside, external to the community, but it could also be seen as symbolic of another group of people perhaps. Maybe these explanations can be combined. In this case, the initial deposit as it was laid down would have represented both an external group, and perhaps that group was seen as dangerous and external. That the fox skull was severed also suggests ritual performance; the cutting off of the head before an audience and then depositing it inverted the ground could create powerful metaphors.

The next deposit was the upturned pot. In the excavation report Pryor points out the similarity between the upturned pot and a skull (1998, 370). The similarity is quite striking, and skulls are found on the base of ditches at other causewayed enclosures such as Hambledon Hill (Mercer and Healy forthcoming). We can also connect pots and skulls in other ways; they both act as containers for example. Skulls contain the brain, eyes and, if one includes the jaw, also the tongue (Edmonds 1999). Pots obviously act as containers, holding water, grain, milk or perhaps blood. Yet, the comparison between the upturned pot and the skull is a peculiarly archaeological one, made in the context of what people find during excavation. The pot could equally represent a human head, as opposed to a skull. The comparison as a container continues to hold, but our emphasis is moved slightly away from the skull, and thus slightly away from death. If the upturned pot represented a human head, perhaps this represented the person who was going through the rite of passage.

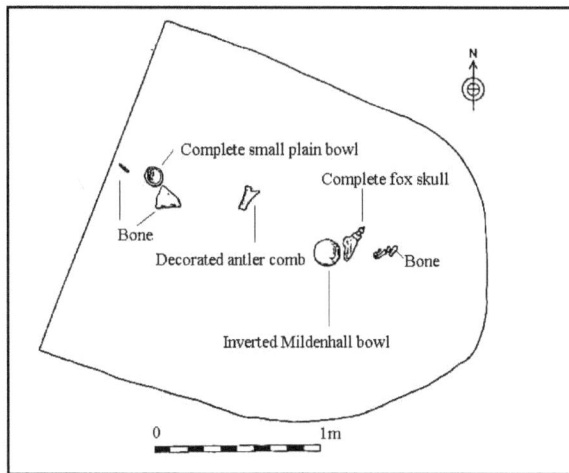

Figure 5.2. The section 7 deposits
(after Pryor 1998, 33, fig. 30).

Next in line was the antler comb, which lay some 40cm from the upturned pot (Pryor 1998, 33). This I argue represents a liminal deposit. The antler comes from a deer, a wild animal, which has then been worked on to transform it into a domestic tool, a comb. Deer in any case may well have been liminal animals in themselves (Sharples 2000). Thus the antler comb lies betwixt and between the wild and domestic (see discussion below), neither one nor the other. Its separation from the fox skull and upturned pot is important from this point of view. It is separated both physically as well as ritually from the previous deposits. The final deposit was the small flat-based plain bowl, this time the right way up, again separated by 40cm from the previous deposit (Pryor 1998, 33). This I believe is more directly representational, as it was placed on its base, but still has qualities that transcend its functional characteristics. The pot perhaps represented domesticity, the group itself, possibly made somewhere away from the wet lowlands in which Etton lay (Pryor 1998). It perhaps spoke of those different lands, where other, less mobile members of the community may have resided. As with the first deposits it was separated both metaphorically and physically from the antler comb.

So we have a possible sequence of deposits moving from the wild, possibly violently removed and inverted fox skull, via an upturned pot, through the liminal antler comb to the domestic pot. This follows the tripartite system we discussed earlier, from separation, through liminality to re-incorporation. So what narrative could we attach to this rite of passage? To me it speaks of the incorporation of an outsider into a particular community, the change in someone's identity from an outsider to an insider. The fox skull represents the wild from which the person came; it might also have been the symbol of their old group; the possible violent removal of the head providing a metaphor for the removal of the person from their old society. Then the upturned pot, close to the fox skull, represented the person involved. We might also think of the inversion of the pot, the emptying of whatever contents it held, as

another act of performance, representative of the separation of the person from their community. Following this after some 40cm came the antler comb. This literal physical separation represents the separate liminal nature of this comb. Other events may have taken place whilst this was being laid in the ground perhaps directly engaging the person involved. After the comb came a second 40cm gap, then the second pot representing the incorporation of the person into their new community. That both the fox skull and the first pot were placed in the ground upside down is surely significant, stressing inversion, the breakdown of normality, perhaps even the *carnivalesque* (*cf.* Bailey 2005; Cochrane this volume).

It might be argued that this narrative draws on the old nature:culture dichotomy which has been prevalent in Western thought for so long (Thomas 2004). To assume such a relationship between nature and culture existed in the Neolithic is deeply problematic, as Pollard has demonstrated (2004, 62). The contexts of wild and tame, outside and inside, are highly contextual here, however. The beheaded, carnivorous fox emerges as external because of the place of its deposition, its rarity in other Neolithic deposits, and the contrast between it and other nearby objects. I am not suggesting that foxes were *always* perceived as natural, wild and dangerous whereas pots were *always* seen as cultural, domestic and safe. Indeed of the two pots that appear in the sequence, one is wild and external, the other domestic and internal. Their status as inside or outside the community is deliberately contextual, depending on the circumstances of their deposition. Even conceptions of community, of anything being wild or domestic, were impermanent. What I am suggesting is that such understandings, which were always temporal and always contingent, emerged during this particular sequence of deposits.

Here we have an individual being incorporated into the community, through action that was not only performative but also *transformative* (Seremetakis 1991, 2). Throughout this, different regulatory ideals were being cited through performance. The audience, perhaps filled with people of different ages watched, remained silent or spoke at the appropriate times. This would act as education to the younger members as they were inculcated in the ways of acting, the *habitus*, which was already unthinking for the older members of the group. We should recognise that both children and adults dwell within their world, and both would have important and different understandings of their world. Human cognition, as Christina Toren (1993, 461) has pointed out, is not an a-historical process. People are not born as somehow natural and then affected by the social to become socialised. Instead we need to recognise that both children and adults "are at once the subjects and objects of history" (Toren 1993, 474). Toren (1993, 463) argues that children often have an inverted understanding of their world in comparison to adults. It is through rituals at sites like Etton that children and young adults would re-imagine their elders' world, and come to understand it anew. Children who knew the importance of Etton as a special, and spectacular place, might come to understand the importance of different artefacts through their deposition in such a place. This could be seen as, in the words of Alfred Gell, the "enchantment of technology"

(1999, 163). In contrast, adults who understood the myriad of associations being cited by the materiality might see Etton as important because these kinds of artefacts were deposited there. This, in Gell's terms again, could be seen as the "technology of enchantment" (1999, 163).

Perhaps people from the person's old group might also have been there, watching as their friend and relative joined another group. Different emotions may thus have been involved on each side. Indeed different understandings might have been reached by different people on each side, about the nature of the rite, and indeed its efficacy. What one community might have perceived as a safe item might be seen by another as dangerous (A. Strathern and Stewart 1999). The person themselves, by moving between communities behaved as they might have been expected, but equally perhaps their move was an act of rebellion, a way of undermining particular regulatory ideals. More likely though the regular movement of people between groups was just one form of exchange that took place. These exchanges may have happened when people were of an appropriate age. Thus I believe this rite of passage shows the incorporation of a person at a key moment in their lifecourse, when their identity changed (*cf.* Sofaer Derevenski 1997; 2000).

Other deposits like this can be seen during phase 1a in ditch section 6 (Pryor 1998, 357). This sequence ran from causeway G into the ditch and included deposits of pyre material, a human cranium 'facing' the causeway, and an antler 'baton', along with other bones (Pryor 1998, 30). Further on, a large calcrete stone was placed on top of two pottery sherds (Pryor 1998, 30). One could easily create a narrative to run through these deposits also.

Elsewhere such explicitly structured deposits are rare in phase 1a. In phase 1c, however, they become more common in the eastern half of the enclosure, although they are much more complex and quite different to the two examples we have just encountered. Rather than discrete items placed in a clear sequence, the phase 1c deposits consist of "integrated linear deposits" (Pryor 1998, 358). We will encounter the detail of these deposits below.

Age and knowledge
Another way in which age can be accessed is through a consideration of knowledge and the particular roles older people play. If we return to the rite of passage detailed above, we can see how knowledge and co-ordination played a crucial role throughout the rite. Only certain people would have had the knowledge of what deposits were appropriate in what particular order to bring about the incorporation of a person within the group. In doing so, this act of performativity cited earlier performances when other people had been incorporated, thus reinforcing the regulatory ideals surrounding the old and the wise.

Other areas of Etton can show clearly how knowledge and memory were important. Multiple small filled pits were dug at Etton throughout the Early Neolithic. Some of these may have been marked, such as pit F711, which had a quern sticking out from it (Pryor 1998, 103). Upturned turves may have marked the locations of others (Pryor 1998). Nonetheless, the majority of them would have faded away, their locations remembered only by those who were 'in-the-know'. Yet these pits never inter-cut, demonstrating the existence of long-term social memory. Remembering their locations might not have been the job of a single individual, and that knowledge would have been absorbed by the next generation. Nonetheless, access to such knowledge would have privileged certain people within the architecture of Etton, giving them special roles within the ceremonies, which they could reiterate and thus reinforce through performance. Even the later phase 2 pits still respect the location of all the small filled pits at Etton, indicating the continuing importance of memory and knowledge. These roles might have reflected the understanding people had of the older members of the community, built up through the *habitus* and quotidian life. It can also be argued that there is an increasing emphasis upon knowledge and memory through time at Etton, as the deposits become increasingly complex. Yet they still respect previous deposits, both physically and thematically. An example of such increased complexity can be drawn from the phase 1c deposits in ditch segment 8 (Pryor 1998, 34). This consists of a complex linear spread of material characteristic of phase 1c deposits across the site. The spread includes a shard of polished stone axe, animal bone, a large number of flints, a piece of human skull, pottery sherds, a piece of decorated limestone, and a pitted cranoid (Pryor 1998, 34). This lay next to a flat piece of limestone and would have originally lain on top of it (Pryor 1998, 34). The pecked hole thus would have pointed vertically down and would have represented the *foramen magnum* of the human skull (Pryor 1998, 34). These deposits, covering less than a metre, were only part of a spread of phase 1c material that ran down the centre of the segment.

The complexity of this deposit, compared say with the phase 1a deposit from segment 7 examined earlier, is clear. I do not believe that a simple rites of passage narrative is sufficient here. Instead we can think of more composite connections in such a deposit. Certainly I would argue that the spread of material drew on both complex metaphors and also on complex memories. The items deposited were undoubtedly metonymic and mnemonic in quality. The polished axe, although its origin is not clear, may have hinted at memories of other places and other people, perhaps of exchange connections and the links that brought people together. Other axes at the site came from as far away as North Wales, so this deposit tied in long distance connections with the intimacy of the deposit. The animal bones may have connected the people watching with their daily lives which were tied in with the animals; the flints too hint at the rhythms and concerns of daily life. Much of this may have highlighted the shared values of the community, indeed may have helped create and sustain these values. The broken pottery may have been redolent of the meals, perhaps feasts, in which it was used. The human skull fragment connects the community itself to the deposit, whilst the pitted cranoid perhaps offered other metaphors around people, stone and deposition. All of this I would argue was connected with memories and emotions. There must have been emotional connections not only to the dead person represented, but also perhaps with the dead animals. Whole people, whole pots, whole axes, whole animals are absent though, perhaps lessening the

46

immediate emotional connections, but aesthetic concerns were still central (*cf.* Overing and Passes 2000; O. Harris 2004). This may well also have been connected to a sense of personhood that was partible (Fowler 2004). People gave up parts of themselves, parts of their animals, parts of their friends for the deposit, thus the community in all its manifestations was represented in this complex deposit along with senses of value, emotion and memory. Alongside such explicit concerns these deposits may also have been about renewing relations with the monument. They may have acted to enhance and enchant the monument itself, and so in turn be enhanced and enchanted by the enclosure (*cf.* Bloch 1998; Gell 1999).

I think it is important to recognise that the complexity of such deposits would have been apparent in the past. Thus the knowledge required not only to interpret but also to dictate what deposits were appropriate must have been greater than in phase 1a. The deposits themselves were acts of creative remembering (Bartlett 1932). What had been deposited before, when and by whom? All of these might have been referenced through the practices caught up in later more complex acts of deposition. If memory, as authors as diverse as Frederick Bartlett (1932) and Tim Ingold (2000) have suggested, emerges creatively through dwelling, practice and action, then memory itself was being formed and expressed in these complex deposits. This, in turn, shows the increasing emphasis upon knowledge through time at Etton, perhaps resulting in the increasing importance of certain older members of the community. Equally, however, this offers us an opportunity to think about how different members of the community may have had very different understandings of what was going on. The same applies to members of different communities watching depositions like this (*cf.* A. Strathern and Stewart 1999). These moments of citation, when metaphors and aesthetic ideals were explicit helped construct the broader understandings of what actions were appropriate when, where and by whom. It was also here where these ideas might be challenged, subverted and overcome. The items deposited in certain orders may have been open to multiple, contradictory understandings in the past, just as they are in the present, and this might have allowed the authority of certain persons to be challenged.

These acts of deposition were still caught up with identity, with who deposited what, where and why. People's identities, their genders and roles were not forgone conclusions, rather they had to be cited and lived up to through performance and citation. Deposition offered a crucial moment at which this might happen. Within the ritualising architecture (Bell 1992) of Etton these acts would take on greater significance and greater meaning. In these moments, which archaeologists have extraordinary, if partial, access to, Neolithic people's identities were being cited, maintained and subverted through performative practice. This does not only apply to the particular person whose rite of passage was posited as central to the segment 7 deposits earlier, nor just to the older members of the community whose knowledge of former deposits and multiple metaphors might allow them to control the deposits in segment 8. Those who watched, those who spoke, those who remained silent; their identities too were being cited. Who was excluded from the enclosure and

who was included, who saw the deposits enter the ground and who did not? These aspects of identity were central to the acts of deposition that took place at Etton.

Conclusion

In this paper I have taken the theoretical insights of an archaeology of practice (e.g. Barrett 2001), with its emphasis upon agency and *habitus* and attempted to meld them with the performative nature of identity advocated by Judith Butler (1993). This notion of performative practice has allowed me to examine the architecture and deposits at Etton from a perspective that emphasises the creation of identity through performance. Thus, I have looked at how at certain ages the performance of particular rites of passage might be appropriate and how these might lead to a change in identity through incorporation into a new group. Equally I have looked at how differential access to knowledge allowed different acts of performativity, particularly how older people might dominate in these discourses. Through particular acts of deposition we can begin to access how these identities were cited, maintained or undermined through performative practice. Yet if we are to move away from essentialist accounts of past agency, it is not only identity that needs to be considered. We also need to turn to a consideration of emotions and conviviality (O. Harris 2004; Whittle forthcoming), of creative rememberings, and of differing notions of personhood (Fowler 2004). Ideas around the rhythms of life, around mood, seasonality and temporality play through all of these concerns (M. Harris 1998; 2000). Principally it is through the combination of all these understandings, rooted in notions of dwelling and performative practice that the people of the past will be able to emerge as differentiated from each other, and historically distinct.

Acknowledgements

I would like to thank Andy Cochrane, Jess Mills and Dani Hofmann for their invitation to contribute to the volume, and for their comments on this paper. I would also like to thank Helen Bradley and Chris Fowler for their views and comments which I know I have only begun to address. Finally special thanks are due to Alasdair Whittle for his criticisms, comments and on-going support. Any mistakes of fact or interpretation remain, of course, my own.

References

Amoss, P.T. & Harrell, S. (eds) 1981. *Other ways of growing old: anthropological perspectives*. Stanford: Stanford University Press.

Bailey, D. 2005. *Prehistoric figurines: representation and corporeality in the Neolithic*. London: Routledge.

Barrett, J.C. 1994. *Fragments from antiquity: an archaeology of social life in Britain, 2900-1200 BC*. Oxford: Blackwell.

Barrett, J.C. 2000a. A thesis on agency. In M.-A. Dobres & J.E. Robb (eds), *Agency in archaeology*, 61-68. London: Routledge.

Barrett, J.C. 2000b. Fields of discourse: reconstituting a social archaeology. In J. Thomas (ed.), *Interpretative archaeology: a reader,* 23-32. London: Leicester University Press.

Barrett, J.C. 2001. Agency, the duality of structure, and the problem of the archaeological record. In I. Hodder (ed.), *Archaeological theory today,* 141-64. Cambridge: Polity.

Bartlett, F.C. 1932. *Remembering: a study in experimental and social psychology.* Cambridge: Cambridge University Press.

Bell, C. 1992. *Ritual theory, ritual practice.* Oxford: Oxford University Press.

Bloch, M. 1998. *How we think they think: anthropological approaches to cognition, memory and literacy.* Boulder: Westview.

Bourdieu, P. 1977. *Outline of a theory of practice.* Cambridge: Cambridge University Press.

Bourdieu, P. 1990. *The logic of practice.* Cambridge: Polity Press.

Brück, J. 2001. Monuments, power and personhood in the British Neolithic. *Journal of the Royal Anthropological Institute* 7, 649-67.

Busby, C. 1997. Permeable and partible persons: a comparative analysis of gender and body in South India and Melanesia. *Journal of the Royal Anthropological Institute* 3, 261-78.

Butler, J. 1990. *Gender trouble: feminism and the subversion of identity.* London: Routledge.

Butler, J. 1993. *Bodies that matter: on the discursive limits of 'sex'.* New York: Routledge.

Connerton, P. 1989. *How societies remember.* Cambridge: Cambridge University Press.

Crandall, D.P. 1998. The role of time in Himba valuations of cattle. *Journal of the Royal Anthropological Institute* 4, 101-14.

Derrida, J. 1981. *Positions.* Chicago: Chicago University Press.

Edmonds, M. 1999. *Ancestral geographies of the Neolithic: landscapes, monuments and memory.* London: Routledge.

Foucault M. 1970. *The order of things.* London: Navistock.

Foucault, M. 1977. *Discipline and punish.* Harmondsworth: Penguin.

Foucault M. 1978. *The history of sexuality volume 1: the will to knowledge.* Harmondsworth: Penguin.

Fowler, C. 2000. The individual, the subject, and archaeological interpretation. Reading Lucy Irigaray and Judith Butler. In C. Holtorf & H. Karlsson (eds), *Philosophy and archaeological practice: perspectives for the 21st century,* 107-33. Göteborg: Bricoleur Press.

Fowler, C. 2004. The archaeology of personhood: an anthropological approach. London: Routledge

Gardner, A. (ed.) 2004. *Agency uncovered: archaeological perspectives on social agency, power, and being human.* London: UCL Press.

Gell, A. 1999. The technology of enchantment and the enchantment of technology. In A. Gell (edited by Eric Hirsch), *The art of anthropology: essays and diagrams,* 159-86. London: Athlone Press.

Gero, J.M. 2000. Troubled travels in agency and feminism. In M.-A. Dobres & J.E. Robb (eds), *Agency in archaeology,* 34-9. London: Routledge.

Giddens, A. 1984. *The constitution of society: outline of the theory of structuration.* Cambridge: Polity.

Gilchrist, R.L. 1999. *Gender and archaeology: contesting the past.* London: Routledge.

Gosden, C. 1999. *Archaeology and anthropology.* London: Routledge.

Hall, S. 2000. Who needs 'identity'? In P. du Gay, J. Evans & P. Redman (eds), *Identity: a reader,* 15-30. London: Sage.

Haraway, D. 1991. Situated knowledges: the science question in feminism and the privilege of partial perspective. In D. Haraway (ed.), *Simian, cyborgs and women: the reinvention of nature,* 183-202. New York: Routledge.

Harris, M. 1998. The rhythm of life on the Amazon floodplain: seasonality and sociality in a riverine village. *Journal of the Royal Anthropological institute* 4, 65-82.

Harris, M. 2000. *Life on the Amazon: the anthropology of a Brazilian peasant village.* Oxford: Oxford University Press.

Harris, O. 2004. *Emotional agents? Conviviality, identity, performance and practice at Windmill Hill.* Paper given to the Theoretical Archaeology Group conference. Glasgow University.

Hawkes, C.F.C. 1954. Archaeological theory and method: some suggestions from the old world. *American anthropologist* 56, 155-68.

Ingold, T. 2000. *The perception of the environment: essays in livelihood, dwelling and skill.* London: Routledge

Iragary, L. 1985. *The sex which is not one.* Ithica: Cornell University Press.

Lacan, J. 1977. *The four fundamental concepts of psychoanalysis.* London: Hogarth Press.

Lutz, C. 1986. The domain of emotion words on Ifaluk. In R. Harré (ed.), *The social construction of emotions,* 267-88. Oxford: Basil Blackwell.

Mercer, R. & Healy, F. forthcoming. *Hambledon Hill, Dorset, England: excavation and survey of a Neolithic monument complex and its surrounding landscape.* English Heritage.

McNay, L. 2000. *Gender and agency: reconfiguring the subject in feminist and social theory.* Cambridge: Polity.

Overing, J. & Passes, A. (eds) 2000. *The anthropology of love and anger: the aesthetics of conviviality in native Amazonia.* London: Routledge.

Perry, E.M. & Joyce, R.A. 2001. Providing a past for 'Bodies that matter': Judith Butler's impact on the archaeology of gender. *International Journal of Sexuality and Gender* 6, 63-76.

Pollard, J. 2004. A 'movement of becoming': realms of existence in the early Neolithic of southern Britain. In A.M. Chadwick (ed.), *Stories from the landscape: archaeologies of inhabitation,* 55-69. Oxford: BAR.

Pryor, F. 1988. Etton, near Maxey, Cambridgeshire: a causewayed enclosure on the fen-edge. In C. Burgess, P. Topping, C. Mordant and M. Maddison (eds), *Enclosures and defences in the Neolithic of Western Europe,* 107-26. Oxford: BAR.

Pryor, F. 1998. *Etton: excavations at a Neolithic causewayed enclosure near Maxey Cambridgeshire, 1982-7.* London: English Heritage.

Rautman, A.E. & Talalay, L.E. 2000. Introduction: diverse approaches to the study of gender in archaeology. In

A.E. Rautman (ed.), *Reading the body*, 1-12. Philadelphia: University of Pennsylvania Press.

Ray, K. & Thomas, J. 2003. In the kinship of cows: the social centrality of cattle in the earlier Neolithic of southern Britain. In M. Parker Pearson (ed.), *Food, culture and identity in the Neolithic and Early Bronze Age*, 37-44. Oxford: BAR.

Redman, P. 2000. Introduction. In P. du Gay, J. Evans, P. Redman (eds), *Identity: a reader,* 9-14. London: Sage.

Rosaldo, R. 1993. *Culture and truth: the remaking of social analysis.* London: Routledge.

Seremetakis, C.N. 1991. *The last word: women, death and divination in inner Mani.* Chicago: Chicago University Press.

Sharples, N. 2000. Antlers and Orcadian rituals: an ambiguous role for red deer in the Neolithic. In A. Ritchie (ed.), *Neolithic Orkney in its European context*, 107-15. Cambridge: McDonald Institute for Archaeological Research.

Sofaer Derevens—ki, J. 1997. Age and gender at the site of Tiszapolgár-Basatanya, Hungary. *Antiquity* 71, 875-89

Sofaer Derevenski, J. 2000. Rings of life: the role of metalwork in mediating the gendered life course. *World Archaeology* 31, 389-406.

Strathern A. & Stewart P. 1999. Dangerous woods and perilous pearl shells: the fabricated politics of a longhouse in Pangia, Papua New Guinea. *Journal of Material Culture* 5, 69-89.

Strathern, M. 1988. *The gender of the gift.* Cambridge: Cambridge University Press.

Thomas, J. 1996. *Time, culture and identity: an interpretive archaeology.* London: Routledge.

Thomas, J. 2004. *Archaeology and modernity.* London: Routledge.

Toren, C. 1993. Making history: the significance of childhood cognition for a comparative anthropology of mind. *Man* 28, 461-78.

Turner, V.W. 1969. *The ritual process.* London: Routledge.

van Gennep, A. 1960. *The rites of passage.* London: Routledge.

Whittle, A. 2003. *The archaeology of people: dimensions of Neolithic life.* London: Routledge.

Whittle, A. forthcoming. Lived experience in the Early Neolithic of the Great Hungarian Plain. In D. Bailey, V. Cummings & A. Whittle (eds), *(Un)settling the Neolithic.* Oxford: Oxbow.

Whittle, A., Pollard, J. & Grigson, C. 1999. *The harmony of symbols: the Windmill Hill causewayed enclosure.* Oxford: Oxbow Books.

'Mending Gauls' fences with the Romans': spatial identities from farmsteads to sacred places in northern Gaul

Cécilia Courbot-Dewerdt

Introduction

This paper is about the part played by enclosures in appropriating space and creating a sense of belonging in north-western Gaul, from the Late Iron Age to the Roman period. Enclosures are ubiquitous features of any Late La Tène archaeological site, from the imposing earthworks of the *oppida* and the walls of the sanctuaries to the banks of isolated farmsteads (Figure 6.1). They helped structure the different sites. Other contemporary buildings were constructed in wattle and daub, and appear to be quite unimpressive in contrast. The word 'enclosure' itself is regularly used as a synonym by archaeologists for Late Iron Age farmsteads, as it is the structure that appears most clearly in aerial photographs and excavations. But from the middle of the first century AD onwards, new kinds of settlements appeared with prominent buildings like Gallo-Roman *villae*. These sites were walled rather than enclosed and what is more, the architecture of the dwelling, inspired by a certain Roman way of life, was the focal point of the settlement. Such changes could not have occurred without significant evolution in the inhabitants' conception of place. The starting point of this thought has been PhD research into the evolution from Late La Tène farmsteads to Roman *villae* in western Gaul (Courbot-Dewerdt 2004). As the primary data derives from rescue excavations, the amount of available information was significant, encompassing a great deal of unpublished material. The possibility thus offered to examine a whole series of farmsteads dated from the second century BC to second century AD, had far-reaching consequences for interpretations of the late Iron Age and early Gallo-Roman way of building places. This has led to a rethinking of the place of enclosures in the creation of spatial identity.

In France, enclosures have mostly been seen as ditches, the actual physical remains found delimiting settlements. However, recent work has begun to show that creating ditches was perhaps the last thing in the Gauls' mind when they dug them, so archaeologists probably need to consider the whole phenomenon, from the ground up and in different kinds of contexts. The first step in that direction has been a seminar entitled 'Enclosures: what for?' presenting several case studies from different areas and contexts (Brunaux 2000a). Using their conclusions as a starting point, this paper will try to illustrate that enclosures played a part in developing the Gauls' conscious identity and thus formed a significant role in the construction of a *mentalité* that survived somewhat after Gaul's inclusion into the Roman Empire.

Iron Age farm enclosures: creating place – creating identity and a feeling of belonging

The study of the archaeological data at hand makes it possible to consider enclosures as a specific form of architecture. The ditches are only the last remnants of the actual limit of the dwelling. In the context of Late Iron Age farmsteads, they are mostly composed of an open trench associated with a bank. The careful stratigraphic analysis of several enclosure ditches has revealed quite the same story (Langohr 2000, 62-64). Immediately after the digging, a primary infill deposit occurred naturally until the sides of the ditch stabilised. This initial silting was followed by a second, generally multi-layered sediment corresponding to various deliberate deposits which differed from place to place within the ditch. Finally, an abandonment layer can be observed after the desertion of the settlement. There is usually no hint of the regular clearing out of farmstead enclosure ditches, although the contemporary field boundaries were sometimes cleaned out, as in the case of Champs d'Aviation (Pluméliau, Morbihan), (Courbot 1998, 130-32). This phasing, with more or less complexity, has been repeatedly observed, thus leading to the understanding that ditches were only quarry-like features for the erection of a bank. The building of the enclosure was therefore a foundation act for the human group as they delimited a new space they could call theirs. Even if they are exceptional in Gaul, special deposits can occasionally be found in the bottom of an enclosure ditch, usually situated immediately next to the entrance, substantiating the notion of the enclosure's symbolic importance (Hill 1995, 50-51).

Even if archaeobotanical surveys are far from systematic for this kind of site, they all indicate the presence of a planted hedgerow composed of different trees, shrubs and other plants (see for example Menez 1996, 158; Rougier 2000, 424-26). The French reconstructions generally show

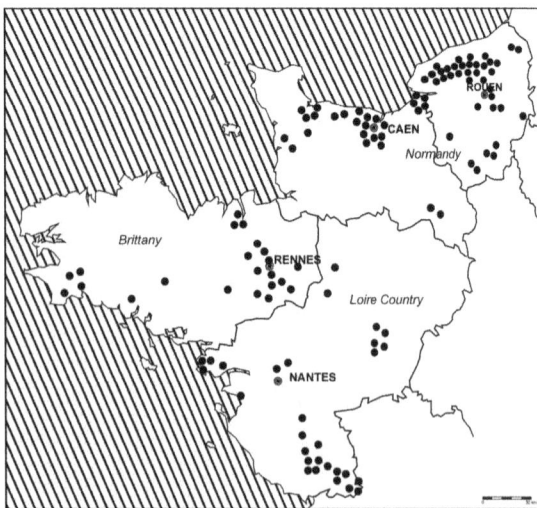

Figure 6.1. Location map of Iron Age enclosures in the study area.

low hedges, but some of the species found grow quite high, like maple, sorb, oak or birch trees. In fact, these species can easily reach more than ten metres in height. This combination of bank and quickset hedge thus creates a fence several metres high, which is of some significance in the landscape. Caesar even mistook these quickset hedges for little patches of woodland, writing in his account of the Gallic wars that 'Gauls' homes are generally surrounded by woods, to avoid great heat by settling down near rivers and woods[1]'. This depiction vividly evokes the wood-like view of modern farmsteads surrounded by similar high hedges in Normandy, called 'clos-masure' (Figure 6.2).

Figure 6.2. Picture of a traditional 'clos-masure' situated in the middle of fields (Photo C.Courbot-Dewerdt).

The comparison between Late La Tène enclosures and 'clos-masures' provides a good starting point for a better understanding of the physical and symbolic significance of these boundaries. The characteristics of the two kinds of site are very similar: ditches, which are quickly backfilled, the importance of the bank, and the vegetation species grown. The Iron Age farmstead enclosures were probably very like the modern 'clos-masures' and had the same prominence in the landscape. For its Late La Tène inhabitants, the visual impact of the enclosure strongly defined this specific piece of space as 'their place', as opposed to the rest of the world, thus creating a feeling of identity and belonging.

Some sociologists have shown how appropriation is achieved by partitioning space and how the strongest way to do so is by creating visual barriers inside which the individual feels at home. For instance, A. Moles wrote that 'the notion of partition is integral to the idea of space appropriation. Human beings only conquer space by dividing it, organizing it and reducing it to his own scale, by making real its subdivisions[2]' (Moles & Rohmer 1998, 62-63). It was probably the case in north-western Gaul that enclosures surrounding the settlement played the part of

partitions, creating a significant visual barrier marking out the living space. The spatial structure of the Late La Tène farmsteads probably aimed to convey the sense of appropriation and belonging their inhabitants experienced whilst reinforcing it at the same time.

It might also be relevant that only people's living space is delimited in this way, and not the whole range of land they farmed. The monumental hedges and banks do not appear to have been used to delineate the boundaries of their farmland and there are few other archaeological remains that can be related to such a purpose. Even where other enclosures or ditches delimited some other parcels, probably for farming purposes, around the farmstead core, they lack the visual impact of the farmstead's hedgerows, with only little evidence of sparse trees and no shrubs, as well as shallower and narrower ditches implying smaller banks. These structures are generally not very extended, creating only a few parcels in the immediate vicinity of the farmhouse and not covering enough land to sustain a household. Most of the time, these small field systems are less than a few hundred metres in length. Thus, farmstead enclosures seem not only to have defined the dwelling space, but also to have expressed the appropriation of the surrounding space by the inhabitants, in a kind of metonymy.

The specific place of the house inside the main enclosure is to be noted, as it was sometimes separated from the rest of the enclosure by internal boundaries. The analysis of the internal organisation of enclosures in north-western Gaul reveals no strict building layout and no specific location for the house. In some cases, however, partitions of the interior space defined several areas, one of them generally dedicated to the main building. In this kind of context, the house was usually built in the innermost place, opposite the entrance (for example Marcé, Hélouine 2 or Pouillé, Le Grand Paisilier, Figure 6.3). There was conceivably a kind of progress from outer space to domestic and then private areas, the organisation of the entrance suggesting a main passageway leading to a working area with granaries, kilns and the like. From there, a way led into the house, sometimes through a specific passageway when it was an enclosed space. At Marcé, Hélouine 2 and at Pouillé, Le Grand Paisilier, a footbridge has been discovered giving access to the main building, in the form of two small foundation trenches designed to support some planks behind the main ditch. This movement from the outside world into the privacy of the house appears therefore to have been constructed to emphasize the notion of access.

Probably for a similar purpose, the farmstead's main entrance was, in some cases, enhanced by specific features. If most Late La Tène enclosures are quite rectangular in plan, some of them appeared to have a trapezoidal layout (for example, Marcé, Hélouine 2 or Oulmes, les Jacquots, Figure 6.3). It is always the entrance side which has been enlarged, so that someone going to the farmstead would have thought it wider than it really was. More often, the ditches are simply dug wider and deeper near the entrance, implying the building of a higher, and thus more impressive bank on this side of the

[1] Caesar, *De Bello Gallico*, VI, 30, 3. '…quod aedificio circumdato silva, ut sunt fere domicilia Gallorum, qui vitandi aestus causa plerumque silvarum atque flminum petunt propinquitates…'

[2] 'La notion de paroi est inhérente à l'idée de l'appropriation de l'espace. L'homme ne conquiert l'espace qu'en le divisant, en l'organisant et en le ramenant à lui-même, en matérialisant ses subdivisions.'

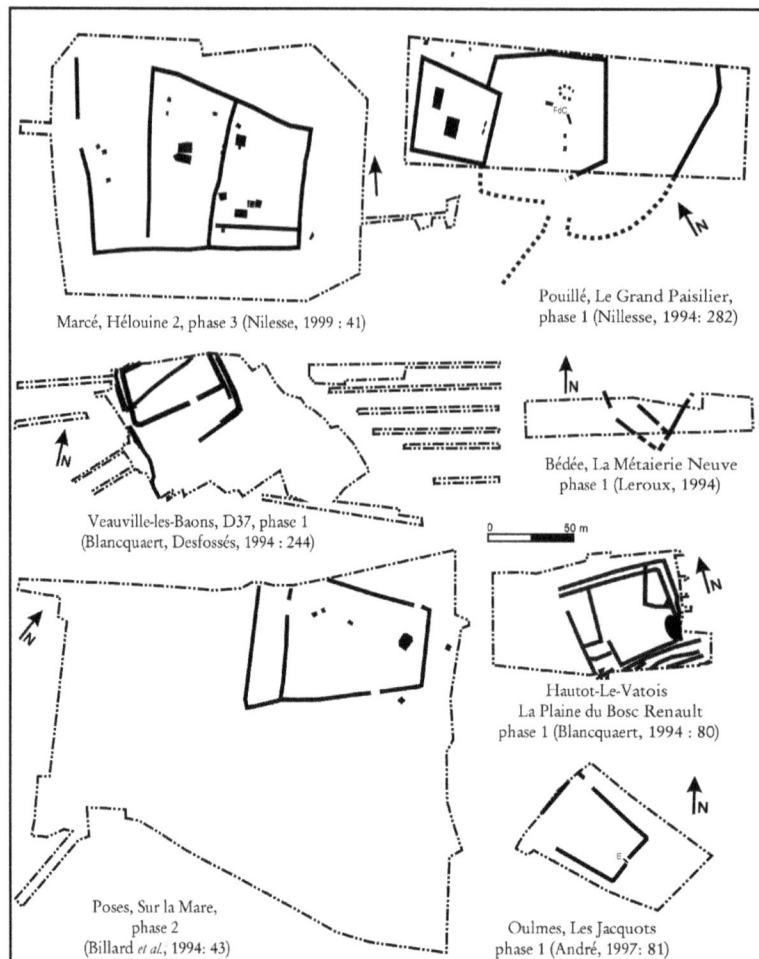

Figure 6.3. Different examples of Late La Tène enclosures from the author's database.

enclosure. In other cases, the same intention is realised by doubling the enclosure's front by another parallel trench (Figure 6.4). In this last case, the double ditches could have been used to erect either a single more important bank or two rows of banks, thereby enlarging the perimeter/boundary and making the entrance more impressive. The modern 'clos masure' are probably a reliable illustration of a Late La Tène farmstead's general form. Their entrance, surrounded by hedgerows on both sides, has a tunnel-like appearance, with trees casting a dark shadow (Figure 6.5). Walking through such an impressive passageway probably reinforced the feeling of leaving the outside world to access a private space, of crossing a boundary.

Hedgerows were not only used as boundaries within the enclosures but also assumed some other functions in farmstead life. The part played by hedges in the agricultural economy is better known for the 'bocage' agriculture in northern France, but 'clos-masure' also provides some interesting parallels. In this last case, for example, part of the hedge consisted of planted trees grown for timber because the farm buildings were traditionally constructed out of daub and timber. The 'clos masure' system has been progressively abandoned since the erection of modern buildings, the timber not being required any longer. Hedges can also provide firewood, something really vital in traditional society. They offer also some shelter to cattle, especially when there was no byre. They can even supply cattle fodder, like foliage, in difficult times. In the Late La Tène period, the enclosure was not only forming a strong boundary but was integral to the farming economy. Planting and then tending to such a hedgerow required a certain continuation in the ownership of place, as timber, for example, can be cut down only several generations after planting. The attachment to place was probably strong enough to imply that the farmstead would still be inhabited by the same group at that time. Late La Tène farmstead enclosures in north-western Gaul were not only built as boundaries but also for practical purposes, conveying with these functions a sense of appropriation and belonging. The repetitive coming and going from the farmstead thus forged and maintained a strong group identity. The management of household refuse expressed, and at the same time reinforced, this division between inner space and outside world. Rubbish seems to have been periodically removed from the enclosed space, maybe after being stored for some time as a midden, and thrown into the enclosure ditch near the house. The structure, organisation and management of the enclosure all came together to create a strong feeling of belonging to the place. Appropriation of farmland was sustained by the visual focal point created by the enclosure, standing out in the rural landscape.

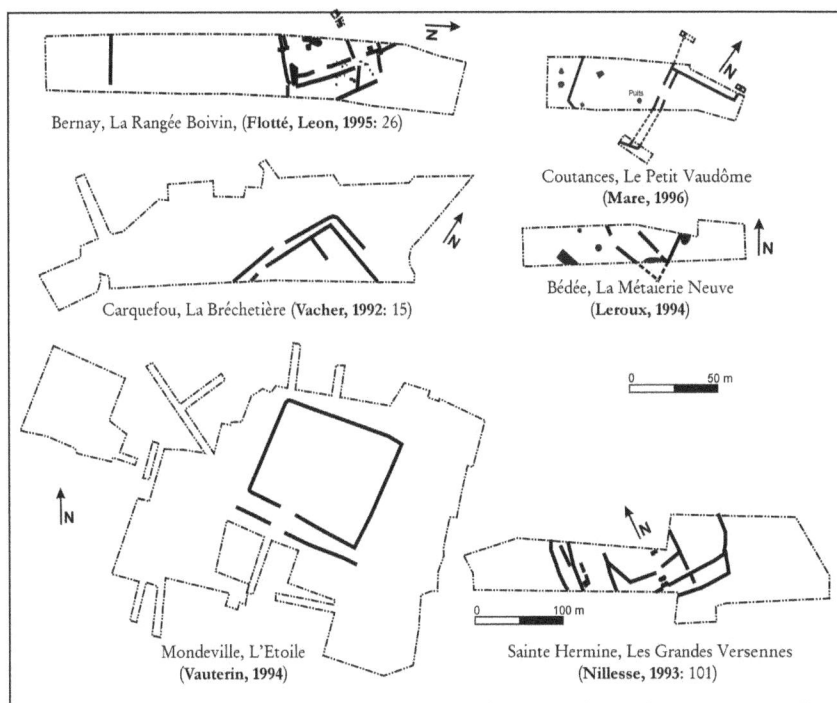

Figure 6.4. Examples of emphasised boundary construction from the author's database.

Enclosures and the management of place in La Tène society

Enclosures can thus be considered as a real architectural component expressing the way their builders related to place and territory. Enclosure is not a unique feature of Late La Tène farmstead structure in northern Gaul, but can also be found on other Iron Age sites. It is, therefore, interesting to point out some other contexts for enclosures and their use.

For instance, late La Tène dwellings appear to be systematically enclosed, not only in rural contexts but also in urban-like *oppida*. With their large enclosures, these settlements had the appearance of fortified sites. Inner and outer space were, in these *oppida*, collectively defined by great earthworks. Fortification is, indeed, one of the main components of their characterisation. What is interesting here is the internal layout of these settlements, specifically in northern France (Fichtl 2000, 75-89). The *oppidum* of Variscourt, Condé-sur-Suippe is organised by streets and plazas. On both sides of the street, rows of household units are easily recognized by the remains of their fences. Each settlement consisted of several buildings, grain silos and wells, enclosed by a picketed fence. The Late Iron Age *oppidum* of Villeneuve-Saint-Germain appears to have been organised by several smaller enclosures, positioned side by side along a street.

Figure 6.5. View of a 'clos-masure' entrance (Photo C.Courbot-Dewerdt).

Figure 6.6. Reconstruction of an internal enclosure at Samara (Picardie), (Photo C.Courbot-Dewerdt).

The life-size reconstruction of a household unit of Villeneuve-Saint-Germain at Samara archaeological park in Picardy shows to what extent these enclosures mirrored the spatial arrangement of farmsteads, but on a smaller scale. The extent of the picket enclosures was quite impressive - around a thousand square metres. The private space thus delimited generally comprised a house, a granary, a cellar and a well, that is a cross-section of the buildings usually found in contemporary farmsteads. The visual impact of the enclosure was probably different, as it was only a division of internal space, conveying the identity of a household inside the group. The monumental earthworks of the *oppidum's* walls would have expressed quite effectively the identity of the group by standing out in the landscape, demarcating urban from rural space. But in this context, too, the appropriation of a space inside the *oppidum* by a household seems to have been conveyed through the enclosure.

In other areas of Late Iron Age life, sites were also carefully enclosed. Sacred places, for example, appear to have been enclosed quite monumentally. In fact, northern Gallic sanctuaries appear to be, first of all, consecrated spaces where specific rites took place. The specific nature of the place was indicated by very large and deep ditches, sometimes doubled, and reinforced by one or two picketed fences (Brunaux 2000b, 271-72). The Gournay-sur-Aronde enclosure, for instance, consisted of two important ditches associated with large banks and picketed fences and a monumental door. The fences created a visual protection for the place of worship inside. Access to the inner space was also generally restricted and the entrances of sanctuaries monumentalised, elaborated by a footbridge and/or porch-like structures. Access to the Gournay-sur-Aronde sanctuary accentuated the notion of crossing a boundary by passing through a porch built on a footbridge that went over the two parallel ditches. Fences and porch were means to control access to the sacred area and therefore had a highly symbolic meaning. In this context, the enclosure itself gave a sacred meaning to the inner space (Van Andringa 2002, 94-95).

There are other occurrences of enclosures giving meaning to specific places in Late Iron Age society. The Ribemont-sur-Ancre ossuary probably represented another kind of ritualised place defined by enclosure. A recent academic study on feasting enclosures in Iron Age Gaul has updated our knowledge of these structures (Poux 2000). Classical writers, like Poseidonius, mentioned these square enclosures as being utilized for ceremonial feasting. Feasting remains such as animal bones, wine amphorae and artefacts associated with the collective preparation and serving of food or drink are found in different contexts from sanctuaries to isolated enclosures, and are sometimes associated with rural settlements. Feasting practice seems strongly related to enclosures and ditches, where important deposits were made. One such enclosure has been discovered next to Fontenay-le-Comte, Les Genâts, an important rural settlement. It comprised a square area, 16m x 17m, surrounded by a ditch and picketed fence. The ditch fills contained an important deposit of deliberately broken amphorae and ovid bone remains. These deposits indicate the ritual aspect of the enclosed area. This is therefore another instance where specific meaning was given to a place by enclosing it, even if it was a short-lived structure for an exceptional use.

Having discussed these various contexts of enclosure use in northern Gaul, it seems important to point out how enclosure appears strongly related to appropriation and identity in different fields of this Late Iron Age society. Boundaries, even if they had functional purposes, also had a symbolic meaning, reinforced most of the time by the visual impact of the boundary and the monumental appearance of the entrance. Enclosure seems to have been an important component of the architectural vocabulary in the Late Iron Age.

Identity in motion: Romanisation of the conception of place

Confronted with another culture, during the integration of northern Gaul as a province of the Roman Empire, this architecture of space underwent some changes. However, enclosures remained a strong feature of different sites, at least in two distinct areas of life: the rural settlement and the sanctuary. The evolution of these two kinds of site shows how the notion of boundary continued, but took on a new form. The evolution of Late La Tène rural settlements into what we call Gallo-Roman *villae* is now archaeologically well documented in northern Gaul. Mostly, the focus has been on the transformation of building architecture and, more recently, the modifications of the farmsteads' layout. From a Roman point of view, the attention directed at the main house appears utterly natural. In his letters, Pliny the Younger had depicted in minute detail his own *villae*, situated in Rome, insisting on two main aspects: the different rooms which constituted the house and the layout of the surrounding countryside (*Letters*, II, 17; V, 6). He thus began one of his letters by describing the scenery surrounding the *villa*: 'The country is beautiful. Imagine a vast amphitheatre like only Nature can create[3]'. He then describes the different vistas of the landscape that were visible from the *villa*. In fact, it appeared that Roman *villae* layout was such that from any part of the house, one could look upon different facets of the countryside: fields, vineyards, woodlands or seashore, depending on the location. The siting of the building thus reflects the importance of having an overview of the landscape for the Roman owner, as the villa is deliberately positioned to include all vistas offered by the location. Therefore, fences and other limits were almost always used for practical farming purposes or to define the confines of the whole estate, and not to delimit the farmstead.

But, in northern Gaul, what is termed Gallo-Roman *villae* has a quite different character. Gauls, in becoming

---

[3] *Ep.* V, 6, 7. 'Regionis forma pulcherrima. Imaginare amphitheatrum aliquod immensum, et quale sola rerum natura possit effingere.'

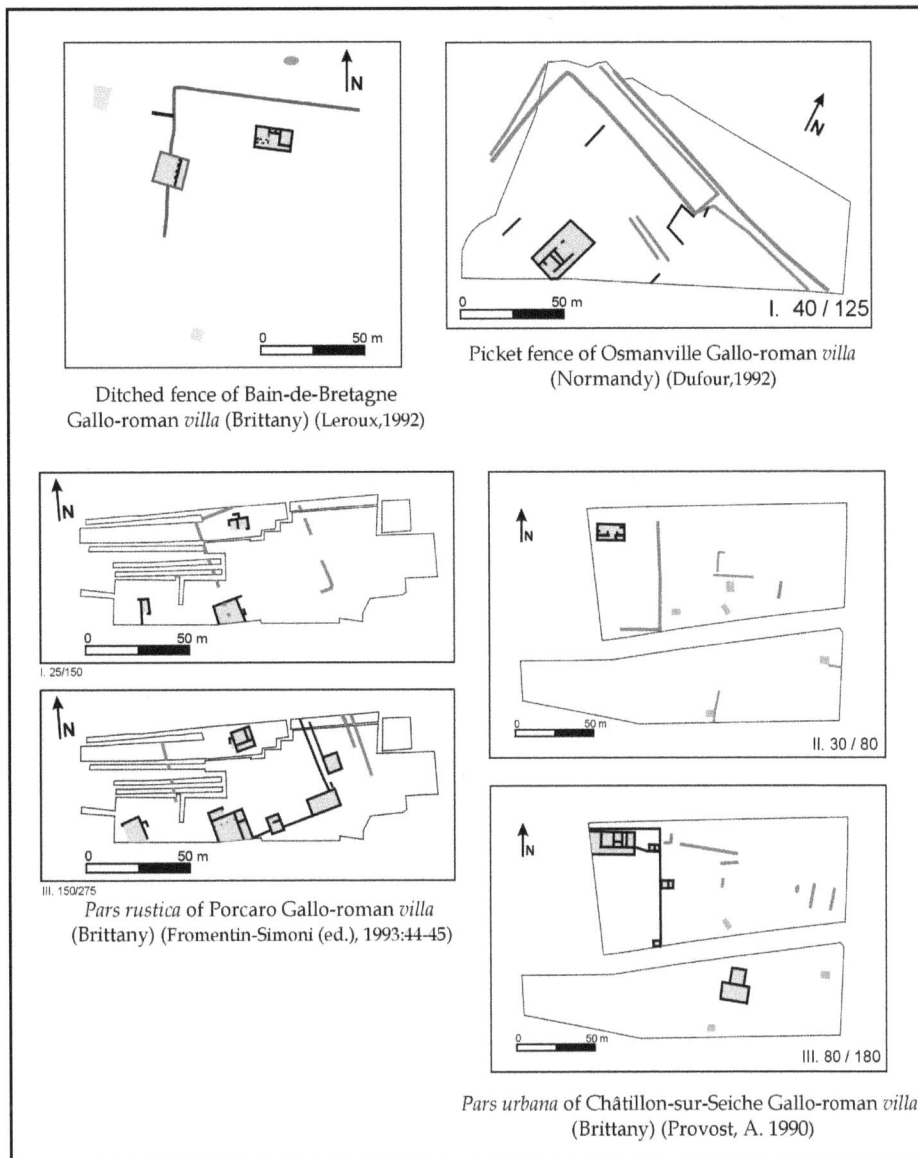

Figure 6.7. Different Gallo - Roman *villae* with their fence enclosures.

Romans, had adopted some Roman architectural principles for their new buildings - like masonry, a tiled roof and a porticus – that make us name their farmsteads *villae*. But the layout and location of the house and buildings appear to be quite different in most northern Gallic early Roman *villae*. One striking difference is the erection of a fence, another is the construction of the main house alongside this limit. This does not fit in well with the Roman idea of having vistas of the surrounding countryside. The *pars urbana* of the sizeable Châtillon-sur-Seiche, La Guyomerais 2 *villa* is very exemplary as the house is set against the enclosure wall (Figure 6.7). It seems that some of the Roman notions linked to the *villa* have not been adopted, as a long-established way to relate to space and place prevailed.

However, enclosures underwent some changes during the evolution from Late La Tène farmsteads to Gallo-Roman *villae*. To begin with, during the first century AD, the hedge and bank system progressively disappeared to be replaced in some cases by a picketed fence. It occurred not only in *villa* settlements like at Osmanville, but also in some farmstead contexts, where ditches were re-used to erect a picketed fence. Such modification may be thought anecdotal, but in fact implied a very different management of rural areas and a distinctive look for the farmstead. Furthermore, the archeobotanical records for the beginning of the early Empire point to an important decline of hedge vegetation. Later, as masonry use became more commonplace, ditches and fences were given up and walls were built in their place. It is important to note that the *villae* affected by these modifications, for example Porcaro, La Demardais or Châtillon-sur-Seiches, La Guyomerais 2, were prosperous settlements with Roman-style buildings. Thus, the enclosure as architectural element persisted, but in a completely new form and within a new set of 'Roman' values. This notion seems to have been so integral to Late Iron Age *mentalité* that it was perpetuated even when a new kind of architecture was slowly adopted.

An analogous phenomenon can be observed at work in the sanctuary context during the early Roman period. Ditched enclosures were the main characteristic of Late La Tène sanctuaries. During the first century AD, in different cities, these enclosures were maintained around the places of worship (Van Andringa 2000, 94-103). In most cases, the ditched enclosures were replaced by picketed fences and, eventually, by walls when the sanctuary became monumental. For example, a picketed fence and a portico took the place of the La Tène quadrangular enclosure of the Bennecourt sanctuary, in the Tiberian/Claudian period. During the second century AD, the sacred space was delineated by a wall, while the Gallo-Roman temple was elaborated with an ambulatory and statues. The site of Ribemont-sur-Ancre underwent a similar development. The persistence of the enclosure was, however, linked to changes in ritual practices, as ditches were used for special deposits. These modifications of the boundaries were paralleled by the transformation of the architecture of the buildings. It is important to note that this layout has no real equivalent in the Italian world. In many ways, the Gallo-Roman sanctuary appears to be an architectural composite of Roman and Gallic elements.

The notion of enclosure remained a significant feature of the architecture of Gallo-Roman *villae* and sanctuaries. The integration of an Iron Age pattern into a basically adopted foreign architecture shows the strength and significance enclosures originally held in La Tène society. It is an ethnological fact that, as A. Leroi-Gourhan wrote: 'People ended up living in their masters' fashion, at least in the accessories[4]' (Leroi-Gourhan 1973, 245; my translation). The interesting fact is thus to be able to point out which "accessories" had been culturally integrated and which misunderstood. The development of fences is also noteworthy, as it implies some changes in practice even if the principle of enclosure survived. The gradual disappearance of the ditches and the hedges suggests fundamental changes in ritual and agricultural practices. Therefore, the motive for such an evolution needs to be elucidated. Part of the explanation is probably linked to the concurrent development of the buildings. The symbolic and monumental meaning of the late La Tène enclosures was formalised afterwards in a new, Roman way, that is by walls.

Conclusion

Enclosures thus seem to have been one way for Gauls to relate to space and to express their feeling of identity and belonging in different aspects of their life. It was so integral to their identity that they maintained this feature through their progressive adoption of a Roman-based culture and society. However, the nature of fences evolved and enclosures were gradually built with imported Roman techniques. Some practices associated with ditches and hedges then fell into disuse, even though the notion of enclosure remained. Repeated patterns in the archaeological record in different contexts of the same period appear therefore to be strong clues to understanding past behaviour. The way similar structures evolved and persisted through major cultural changes thus points out a significant aspect of the *mentalité* of the society under examination.

References

André, M. 1997. Oulmes, Les Jacquots. *Bilan scientifique du SRA Pays de Loire 1995*, 81.

Billard, C. 1994. Poses, Sur La Mare et La Fosse Sulpice. *Bilan scientifique du SRA Haute-Normandie 1993*, 42-43.

Blanquaert, G. 1994. *A29 section Le Havre-Yvetot, rapport de fouille, Hautot-Le-Vatois «La Plaine du Bosc Renault, 76347003 »*. Le Petit Quevilly: SRA Haute-Normandie. Inédit.

Blancquaert, G. & Desfosses, Y. 1994. Les établissements ruraux de l'Âge du Fer sur le tracé de l'autoroute A29 (Le Havre-Yvetot), 227-54. In O. Buchsenchutz & P. Méniel (eds), *Les installations agricoles de l'Âge du Fer en Île-de-France*. Études d'histoire et d'archéologie, vol. IV. Paris: Presses de l'ENS.

Brunaux, J.-L. (ed.), 2000a. Actes de la table ronde sur les enclos celtiques, Ribemont-sur-Ancre, 5 et 6 septembre 1999. *Revue Archéologique de Picardie, 1/2*.

Brunaux, J.-L. 2000b. Propriétés divines, possessions humaines: la fonction symbolique de l'enclos. In J.-L. Brunaux (ed.), Les enclos celtiques, actes de la table ronde de Ribemeont-sur-Ancre (9-10 Décembre 1999, Somme). *Revue Archéologique de Picardie, 1/2*, 271-78

Courbot, C. 1998. Un établissement agricole du Haut-Empire à Pluméliau (Morbihan). *Revue Archéologique de l'Ouest 15*, 127-40.

Courbot-Dewerdt, C. 2004. *Evolution des établissements ruraux de la fin de l''Age du Fer à la mise en place du système des villae dans le quart nord-ouest de la France (Iers. av. J.-C.-IIème s. après J.-C)*. Mémoire de thèse, Université de Paris I Panthéon-Sorbonne. Inédit. 3 vol.

Dufour, M. 1992. *Une occupation Romaine à Osmanville (Calvados), rapport de fouille de sauvetage urgent, avril-octobre 1992*. SRA Basse-Normandie: Caen. Inédit.

Fichtl, S. 2000. *La ville celtique, Les oppida de 150 av. J.-C. à 15 ap. J.-C.* Paris: Errance.

Flotté, P. & Leon, G. 1995. Bernay, Déviation RN 138. *Bilan du SRA Haute-Normandie 1994*, 26.

Fromentin-Simoni F. (ed.), 1993. *Archéologie et grands travaux routiers, Rennes-Saint Malo, Rennes-Lorient, 1993, catalogue d'exposition*, 44-45. Rennes: Porcaro, La Démardais, DRAC Bretagne, SRA Bretagne.

---

[4] 'On finit par se loger à la mode des maîtres, au moins dans les accessoires'.

Hill, J.D. 1995. How should we understand Iron Age Societies and hillforts? A contextual study from Southern Britain, 45-66. In J.D. Hill & C. Cumberpatch (eds), *Different Iron Ages: studies on the Iron Age in temperate Europe*. Oxford: BAR.

Langohr, R. 2000. Creusement, érosion et comblement des fossés, l'approche des sciences de la terre. In J.-L. Brunaux (ed.), Les enclos celtiques, actes de la table ronde de Ribemeont-sur-Ancre (9-10 Décembre 1999, Somme), *Revue Archéologique de Picardie,* 1/2, 57-66.

Leroi-Gourhan, A. 1973. *Milieu et technique.* (1945), Sciences d'aujourd'hui. Paris: Albin Michel.

Leroux, G. 1992. *La fouille du site préhistorique, protohistorique et antiques des Sentes à Bain-de-Bretagne (35), rapport de sauvetage urgent.* Rennes: SRA Bretagne. Inédit.

Leroux, G. 1994. *Bédée, La Métairie Neuve (Ille et Vilaine), DFS de sauvetage urgent.* Rennes: SRA Bretagne. Inédit.

Mare, E. 1996. *Coutances (Manche), Liaison entre la RD. 44 et la RD. 972, Le petit Vaudome 50147057, La Forerie 50147058.* Caen: SRA Basse Normandie. Inédit. 2 vol.

Menez, Y. 1996. *Une ferme de l'Armorique Gauloise, Le Boisanne à Plouër-sur-Rance (Côtes-d'Armor),* DAF 58. Paris: MSH.

Moles, A. & Rohmer, E. 1998. *Psychosociologie de l'espace, textes rassemblés, mis en forme et présentés par Victor Schwach.* Collection 'Villes et entreprises'. Paris: L'Harmattan.

Nillesse, O. 1993. Sainte Hermine, Les Grandes Versennes. *Bilan scientifique du SRA Pays de Loire 1992,* 100-01.

Nillesse, O. 1994. Les établissements ruraux Gaulois dans le sud de la Vendée, 277-93. In O. Buchsenchutz & P. Méniel (eds), *Les installations agricoles de l'Âge du Fer en Île-de-France.* Études d'histoire et d'archéologie, vol. IV. Paris : Presses de l'ENS.

Nillesse, O. 1999. Marcé, Hélouine, *Bilan scientifique du SRA Pays de Loire 1997,* 41.

Poux, M. 2000. Espaces votifs, espaces festifs, banquets et rites de libation en contexte de sanctuaires et d'enclos. In J.-L. Brunaux (ed.), Les enclos celtiques, actes de la table ronde de Ribemeont-sur-Ancre (9-10 Décembre 1999, Somme). *Revue Archéologique de Picardie,* 1/2, 217-231.

Provost, A. 1990. Châtillon-sur-Seiches, La Guyomerais 2. *Gallia Informations 1990* 1/2, 42-46.

Rougier, R. 2000. Les formes d'occupation du territoire à l'Âge du Fer en Pays de Caux (Seine-Maritime) d'après les fouilles sur le tracé de l'autoroute A29. In G. Blancquaert & S. Marion (eds), *Les installations agricoles de l'Âge du Fer en France Septentrionale, Études d'histoire et d'archéologie vol. VI,* 411-27. Paris: Presses de l'ENS.

Vacher, S. 1992. Carquefou, la Bréchetière, *Bilan scientifique du SRA Pays de Loire 1991,* 15.

Van Andringa, W. (ed.), 2000. *Archéologie des sanctuaires en Gaule Romaine,* (Centre Jean Palerne, mémoires XXII). Saint-Étienne: Publications de l'Université de Saint-Étienne.

Van Andringa, W. 2002. La religion en Gaule Romain, Piété et politique (Ier-IIIème s. apr. J.-C.), (Collection des Hespérides). Paris: Éditions Errance.

Vauterin C. 1994. *Mondeville, L'Etoile (Calvados), 14437015 AH, DFS de sauvetage urgent, 15/07/93-31/01/94.* Caen: SRA Basse-Normandie. Inédit.

Fragments of power: LBK figurines and the mortuary record

Daniela Hofmann

Introduction

The Niedereschbach figurine head (Figure 7.2, far right) is an intriguing artefact, but at the same time eludes easy understanding. As depicted here, its most curious characteristics are the strange proportions of the face, the long nose and almost pursed lips, the round eyes which seem astonished or perhaps reproachful, the lush head of curly hair. What a line drawing can not convey is the visual impact of the piece: the smooth, black clay, patiently worked until the surface is almost shiny, the red clay slip covering the hair and making it stand out sharply from the rest of the piece. Is this a human? Why is there only a head? And what can it tell us about the reasons and ideas behind its manufacture?

Searching the published literature for answers is a frustrating exercise. The piece in question belongs to the Linearbandkeramik culture (LBK; 5500-4900 B.C.), one of the best researched prehistoric cultures in Europe found from the Ukraine and western Hungary to the Paris Basin and from the plains of northern Poland to southern Germany (Figure 7.1; Whittle 1996, 146). Considerable effort has been expended discussing its origins, the involvement of colonists from south-east Europe and the role of the indigenous hunter-gatherers (for discussion see Gronenborn 1999; Whittle 1996, 150-52). Individual categories of evidence, such as architecture or burial customs are, however, generally discussed with reference to regionalisation within the LBK, which increases over time (Brink-Kloke 1992, 12-14, 185-89; Coudart 1998, 14; Engelhardt 1981, 37; Jeunesse 1995; 1996; 1997, 101-03; Lüning 2000, 60, 90, 110). Yet despite this accepted trajectory of cultural independence, the discussion of figurines is still almost exclusively based on south-east European material. Even examples from central and southern Germany, on which this paper will focus, are routinely compared to material from other areas, mainly eastern Hungary and Serbia, and often from earlier or later cultures.

Why should this be so and is this an appropriate strategy? I argue that comparison with the south-eastern material has for a long time impeded more creative engagements with LBK clay figurines and other human depictions and has diverted attention from their main characteristics: individuality, abstraction, fragmentation and casual discard. As items of material culture with those characteristics, figurines had to work in the local LBK context and be understood with reference to other experiences in people's lives. Given that most figures depict humans, or human-like creatures, I investigate their relationship with other representations of humans, namely in burial[1]. While this comparison will not result in a specific discursive meaning for each single piece, the

parallels between the two fields reveal parts of a network of metaphor and association in which these items were implicated and possible ways in which the human form was conceptualised. As a result, we might get closer to how people thought about themselves as persons, about what it means to be human, and how this could be expressed in material form. This in turn might explain how figurines, a powerful and emotionally charged artefact, could work in the arena of domestic ritual in the LBK.

The foreign connection: comparisons with south-east Europe

It was Höckmann's 1965 article which launched figurine studies in a systematic way for the western LBK. In it, the author collected and grouped all published material, including human and animal figurines, appliqués (three-dimensional additions on the outside of pots), anthropomorphic and zoomorphic vessels and a few bone and spondylus pieces. At the time, it is not surprising that his interpretation revolved around finding stylistic parallels with those cultures in which the origin of the LBK was supposed to lie (Höckmann 1965, 5-7): after all, this was at the height of the culture-history paradigm.

Yet for a long time, these perceived parallels have remained not only a starting point, but the focus for interpretation. In later articles, some key researchers on LBK religion, like Höckmann (1987, 90) and Kaufmann (1976, 88, 92) point out the stylistic parallels of their figurines to eastern ones, and then proceed to adapt interpretations reached with the aid of eastern material to the LBK. For instance, building on Makkay's (1978) essay on ritual grinding and figurine use in south-east Europe, Höckmann (1985, 106) postulates the existence of very similar practices in the LBK, centring around a general and rather ill-defined fertility cult. The same strategy is adopted by others for material from their own excavations (*cf.* Engelhardt 1992, 368; Kaufmann 1989, 128-34; Lenneis 1995, 43).

More recently, Wunn (2001, 140-43) has surveyed material relating to religious practices from Turkey to Western Europe and criticises the idea of a fertility cult. She believes that figurines were used to re-enact the myth of the first growing of grain by a culture hero and mother goddess. This slightly technical distinction is offset by the extremely generalised interpretation which follows. Wall paintings from Çatal Höyük at one end of Europe, and Irish medieval Sheela-na-gig sculptures, which allegedly originate in Celtic goddess myths, are used to argue that this idea must have travelled via central Europe. Neolithic figurines must be the missing link in this transmission and hence illustrate the same ideas (Wunn 2001, 140-43), although they could also capture the spirits of the dead (Wunn 2002, 47). In the LBK, the mother goddess is also visible in ceramic decoration (Wunn 2002, 49; compare

---

[1] Purely zoomorphic figurines and vessels are excluded from the present discussion.

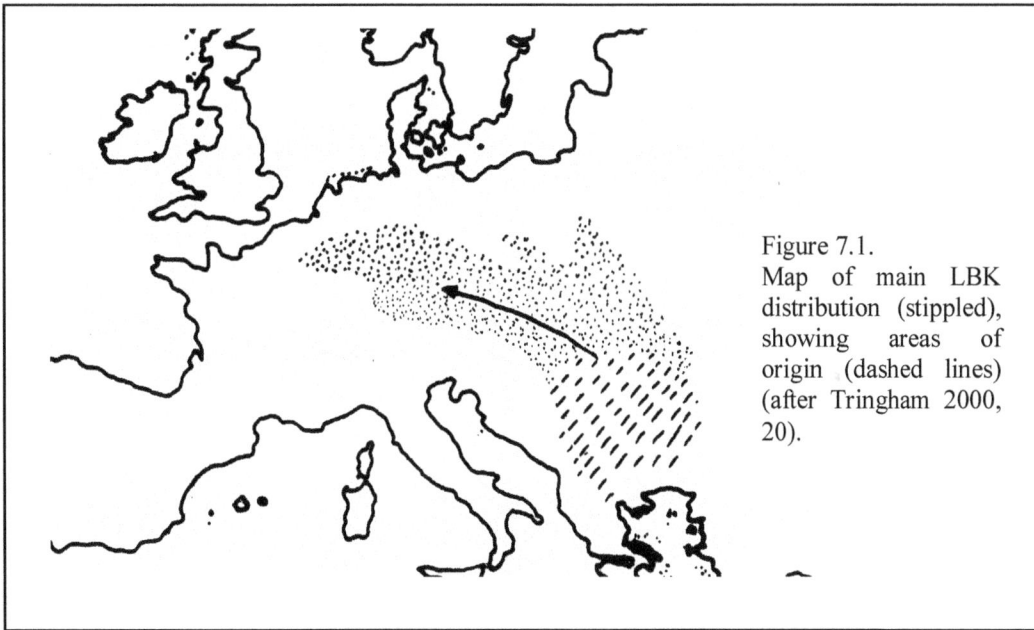

Figure 7.1.
Map of main LBK distribution (stippled), showing areas of origin (dashed lines) (after Tringham 2000, 20).

Stöckl 2002). Supported by a few ethnographic generalisations on the "religion of agriculturalists", Wunn then concludes that reconstructing religion is "relatively easy" (Wunn 2002, 53, my translation).

It thus seems that from standard comparisons follow standard interpretations. It is understandable that people are tempted to flesh out the sometimes scanty LBK material by viewing it in the light of the more plentiful and detailed data from other areas. Yet, even if we accept certain basic similarities, like the shape of some of the heads, or the posture of some of the figurines, does this mean that we have to also subscribe to the accepted reading of these figures as part of a pan-European fertility cult? To arrive at an alternative, the two main problems shared by the approaches above must be overcome; firstly their attempts to ascribe a single, immutable and discursive meaning to the figurines and secondly their treatment of these artefacts as if they were art-historical showpieces.

Whether figurines are seen as mother goddesses, culture heroes (Wunn 2001, 140-43) or indeed animal demons (Lenneis 1995, 43) or even shamanistic equipment (Maurer 1982, 51-55, Höckmann 1985, 98), the explanation apparently so convincing for one context or one type of figurine does not necessarily apply to another. The Rockenberg figurine incorporating flour in its clay may well reinforce links to grain and grinding (Höckmann 1987, 90), but what about the many others which have no such inclusions? The figures with the fir-branch motif (*Tannenzweigmuster*) on their backs may represent skeletons (Maurer 1981, 65; 1982, 51), but this is far from clear (Reinecke 1977, 204f) and most lack these marks.

It is inappropriate to find a single meaning for all the figurines, and moreover to assume that this meaning should have been transmitted alongside a few stylistic criteria from one end of Europe to the other. This idea relies too much on the notion that an exhaustive verbal explanation of its meaning and use was given for each sculpture, allowing people from other areas who never or only occasionally witnessed the appropriate rituals to use it in the correct way (see also Stöckl 2002, 90-94). Yet so far, this is implied in the way most figurines are discussed in relation to south-eastern material, not in terms of how they could actually have functioned in society. Rather than worry whether the head of a figurine is more Körös or more Vinča, should we not be asking about its impact and use? The tendency to neglect these latter aspects no doubt stems from the scholarly tradition of collecting all examples of one kind of material into a corpus and then comparing them divorced from their actual archaeological or social context (Jones 2001a, 217f; 2001b, 340).

Andrew Jones (2001b, 347) has recently criticised this approach as too far removed from the material realities of artefacts, their role in social relations and their mnemonic qualities. He argues that making and using artefacts, and the sensory experiences thereby afforded, create memories of social engagements which the artefacts would later help to recall. Their aesthetic immediacy and importance in ritual and other contexts create memory, which is personal and linked to the experiences of each maker and user. Neither the memory nor the interpretation of the artefact is hence static. Meanings in these circumstances can never be as literal and prescribed as it may appear when the artefacts are presented in a corpus under one heading (Jones 2001b, 348-52). Similarly, Hamilakis (2002, 126-29) argues that the sensory experiences afforded by the use of artefacts in a social situation are what makes them so deeply powerful, as the artefact acts as a reminder of the emotional experiences associated with that situation and the social bonds created.

These suggestions go far beyond the traditional stylistic comparisons and stereotypical interpretations offered for LBK figurines. By investigating their materiality and use, we can establish how they worked as social artefacts. To do this, we must also engage with the main characteristics of the material: its abstraction, individuality and fragmentation, as well as its archaeological context.

Small bits and strange faces: the material characteristics of LBK figurines

Abstraction and Individuality.
Compared to south-east European examples, most of the western LBK depictions are strikingly asexual. In eastern areas, such as lower Austria, researchers have found explicitly female figurines (e.g. Maurer 1982, 26), but even there most examples are ambiguous (Höckmann 1985, 101; Maurer 1982, 61). This trend gets more pronounced further west: the Bavarian material, for example, mostly lacks definite sexual indicators. Even the figurine from Gaukönigshofen, which might show the remains of breasts (Höckmann 1985, 102), can be reconstructed holding a pot instead (Probst 1999, 261), making the breasts practically invisible. In contrast to Romanian Hamangia figurines, which are of ambiguous sex because both male and female traits have been included (Chapman 2000, 76-78), LBK figurines are asexual, as no obvious traits existed at all in most cases.

Instead of femaleness, humanness is depicted, and perhaps only certain traits and qualities of humanness. Occasionally, we cannot even be sure of the straightforward humanity of the depiction, as some figurines and appliqués combine human and animal characteristics. There are combinations of faces with cow horns on some Austrian pottery (Lenneis 1995, 43; Maurer 1981, 69; 1982, 26-43), the "poodle-person" from Niedereschbach near Frankfurt with its animal-like snout (Hampel 1989, 151f), the Zauschwitz appliqué from Saxony (Probst 1999, 258), which is reminiscent of a fox or a sleeping owl, and finally some legs from Bavaria which are more akin to paws (Reinecke 1977, 207; Figure 7.2). Those figurines we recognise as human are hence only one end of a continuum which leads us via the strange hybrids to fully zoomorph depictions, such as cattle and pigs (for examples see Modderman 1977, 130; 1978, 27; Schade-Lindig 2002b, 59).

In addition, each piece is very individualistic, making a unified mother goddess an unlikely explanation (*cf.* Kaufmann 1989, 133). No two figurines found are alike, they each have a unique expression (Figure 7.3) and judging from the different kinds of fragments occurred in a variety of poses. While most of the faces seem very abstract and crudely formed, each piece can easily be recognised and distinguished from others. There are no general rules for facial expressions or postures, although the latter are to an extent more standardised.

Maurer (1981, 70; 1982, 68) argues that this schematic quality is due to a lack of artistic talent on the part of the potters, but this seems unlikely. LBK fine ware, for example, is of very high quality, but also demonstrates a preference for abstract designs as opposed to naturalistic pictures. In fact, figurines are one of the very rare instances when something recognisable is depicted at all, and I believe they deliberately lack detail. In the few instances where human and animal likenesses were produced, they did not aim at an accurate reproduction of nature, but were integral to other social and ritual ideals and practices.

Abstraction and individuality, rather than being limitations, are a vital component.

Yet so far, even those who agree that abstraction is deliberate (e.g. Reinecke 1977, 207) attribute little meaning beyond the aesthetic to this fact. Yet, as Bailey (2005) has shown, abstraction, alongside miniaturism and three-dimensionality, is a powerful visual strategy that charges a figurine with psychological tension, creating an intense experience for the maker and handler. The combination of these traits at once empowers and interests handlers, but also alienates and unsettles them. First, miniaturism means that only certain traits of the full - size object are selected, making the end product a distilled and powerful version of the original. This empowers the handler, who can control and manipulate the object easily, but it is also unsettling: the viewer becomes gigantic in relation to the figurine and is dislocated from normal frames of reference (Bailey 2005, 33).

This unsettling encounter takes place in a very intimate sphere: the object needs to be picked up, turned, maybe brought close to the face and touched to appreciate all the details and changes of texture. This is very different from other objects such as sculptures which can be engaged with casually or from a distance, or a two-dimensional picture which can be taken in at once (Bailey 2005, 36-41). Here, abstraction becomes powerful. As the spectators handle the figurine, abstraction forces them to make their own inferences, of which there can be many depending on the viewers' life history. Abstraction renders the familiar, the human depiction, unfamiliar, simultaneously close to our intimate space and distant from everyday engagements. Understanding figurines is permeated with insecurities and personal associations. While being drawn in and invited to engage with the image, the viewer is at the same time distanced (Bailey 2005, 32f; also Bailey 1996, 292f).

Abstraction, then, emerges as a key component that restores agency to figurines, not simply an artistic deficiency or a static "given" of aesthetics. This sensory and affective engagement is a key to understanding the power of figurines. The abstract, yet individual expression on each piece could be corresponding to the emotional need of the maker in creating it, embodying a particular crisis situation, feeling or need which would then be remembered on subsequent engagements with the piece. Viewers with different backgrounds are affected in different ways, drawn in by the familiar depiction of a human, yet distanced, the haunting image evoking emotions connected to their own experience while leaving them in the dark as to the exact intentions of the maker. It is this tension that makes people react emotionally to a figurine, but also creates the possibility to act upon these tensions and potentials in new ways, or ways impossible in other contexts. For the LBK specifically, the creative tensions between human and animal aspects of the figurine or the ambiguities of gender could express or problematise aspects of LBK personhood and relations with the human and animal world.

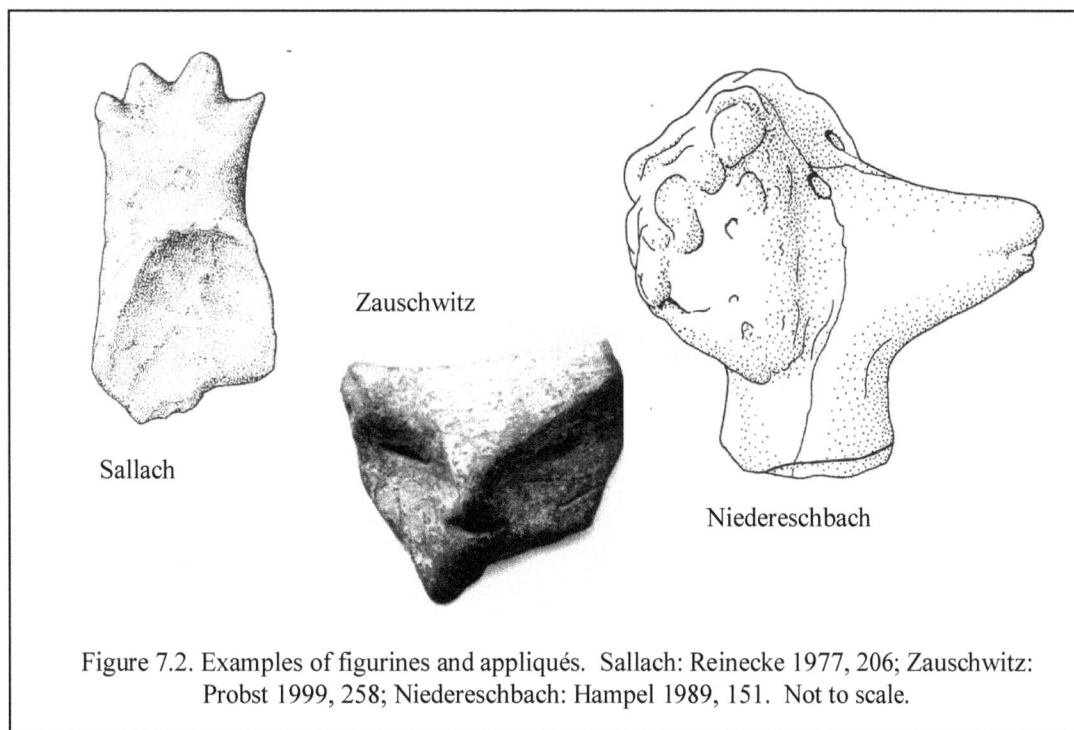

Figure 7.2. Examples of figurines and appliqués. Sallach: Reinecke 1977, 206; Zauschwitz: Probst 1999, 258; Niedereschbach: Hampel 1989, 151. Not to scale.

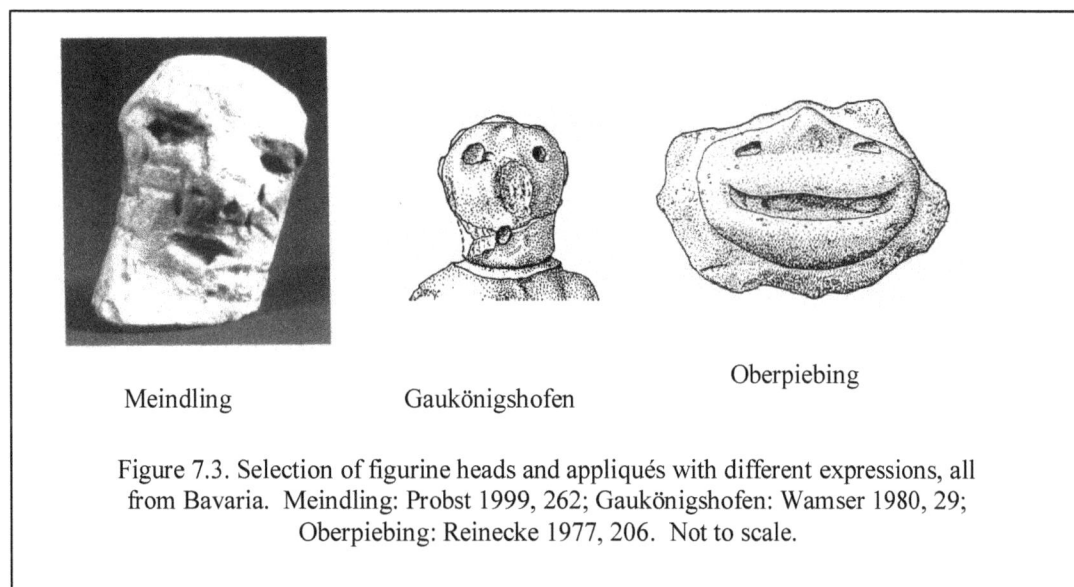

Figure 7.3. Selection of figurine heads and appliqués with different expressions, all from Bavaria. Meindling: Probst 1999, 262; Gaukönigshofen: Wamser 1980, 29; Oberpiebing: Reinecke 1977, 206. Not to scale.

Fragmentation and context

What would persuade people to smash such a powerful object and discard it with everyday settlement rubbish? The majority of figurines have been treated in this way. This applies not only to potentially plough-damaged pieces collected during field-walking, but also to ones found during excavation. Even on sites with many examples, such as Nieder-Mörlen in Hesse, nearly all figures are broken, often into very small pieces and along lines which are not the weakest point in the sculpture (Schade-Lindig 2002b, 52)[2]. In addition, some figurines are poorly fired,

held together by clay or wood pins or assembled from separate parts, so that some researchers believe they were made to be broken (Höckmann 1985, 92f; Kaufmann 1989, 121, 128). For others, use-life did not end with breakage. Breaks were smoothened and polished (Maurer 1982, 57-59) or glue-like substances were applied, pointing to temporary repair before renewed fragmentation (Kaufmann 1976, 90). This is in contrast to ceramic vessels, which are encountered whole on LBK excavations (e.g. Modderman 1986, 24). The fact that these hollow and fragile items occasionally survive intact, while figurines never do, is a further indicator for deliberate fragmentation.

It is also generally true that most figurines occur strewn among other settlement rubbish. Where the quality of

---

[2] At Nieder-Mörlen, the only intact example was a small, bowling-pin or roller-like figurine (Schade-Lindig 2002b, 57).

excavation permits it, a few of them have been recognised as being part of a more structured kind of deposition, such as at Nieder-Mörlen (Schade-Lindig 2002a, 108-10; 2002b, 52) and Baumann (1976, 104-06) points out that many come from pits which are unusually rich in animal bone, plant remains and decorated pottery. But these instances are rare[3], and even then the figures are broken. The majority have been discarded more casually with household waste. There is not even any indication in the literature that figurines should be found in a certain spatial relationship to houses, like decorated pottery and stone tools are (for instance Boelicke 1982; Husty 1999; Last 1998). Therefore, without any more detailed studies on the topic, we must assume that figurines were discarded with no particular thought as to their location, association or future fate.

Chapman (2000, 28-39) has suggested that breaking figurines is part of the social practice of enchainment with which individuals make their relationships materially manifest through breaking valuable objects which embody part of the identity of their makers and each keeping a fragment. But while this approach embeds figurines in the social field, it fails to comment on their visual and emotional powers, so different from the pottery or ornaments which are also "enchained". Moreover, for the LBK material, there is another problem, as enchainment relies very heavily on the evidence of completely excavated tells and other settlements with a large body of figurines (Chapman 2000, 55-64). LBK settlements, however, are rarely completely excavated and produce far fewer pieces. If we take into account that surface middens may have existed, that villages were resettled in some areas, causing disturbance of deposits, and the extensive erosion and plough-damage which have occurred since, we end up with a far more insecure situation than on eastern European tells where assemblages are more often sealed and preserved[4]. Enchainment cannot be proven here and must hence be regarded as peculiar to south-eastern Europe[5].

Figurines and the funerary context

Previous interpretations.
For the LBK, the person who has most explicitly seen fragmentation as an integral part in the way the figurines work symbolically is Höckmann (1985, 97-101), and he has also tried to explain figurine use in terms of indigenous LBK practices. He argues that the "fir-branch design" (*Tannenzweigmuster*) on the back of some LBK figurines is a symbol for the human skeleton (Figure 7.4; see also Maurer 1981, 65; 1982, 51; for criticism see Reinecke 1977, 204f). However, this decoration is quite rare and can hence not be the only important factor. Thus, he proceeds to connect figurines both to the fertility cults of the eastern

European Neolithic and the realm of the dead. The designs make sense as skeletons because LBK people engaged in sacrifices and cannibalistic rights to ensure the fertility of their crops (Höckmann 1985, 101-06, see also Makkay 1978). That is also why figurines always end up fragmented in rubbish pits: they are the unbloody substitute for the victims of cannibalism, which fare similarly (Höckmann 1985, 106; see also Hoffmann 1971, 7-12; Kaufmann 1989, 128; Lenneis 1995, 43).

Figure 7.4. Back of the Gaukönigshofen figurine, showing fir-branch design. From Wamser 1980, 29. Original height: 8.8 cm.

There are indeed instances of probable cannibalism in the LBK (for instance Kneipp and Büttner 1988), although recent re-analyses of bone material have also invalidated many previous claims to that effect, for example at the Jungfernhöhle in northern Bavaria (Orschiedt 1999, 165-78). Yet, Höckmann's approach is limited, as he again tries to find one unified idea behind all figurines, although many do not show the so-called skeleton pattern. Furthermore, the hybrid nature of many depictions and the combinations of vessels and figurines make this class of objects very varied, and not all of them can be substituted for a sacrificial victim. Höckmann also fails to consider the radically different sensory experiences and emotional impact between smashing a small three-dimensional object and killing, mutilating and consuming a human being.

Nevertheless, the LBK funerary record is a useful basis for comparison. Rather than using it to produce a single literal meaning for figurines, however, I will be looking for more general parallels in treatment between the human dead on the one hand and human and human/animal hybrid clay depictions on the other. This will enable me to show whether there is a unified idea about the appropriate treatment of humans and depictions with human characteristics, and if so, what it says about conceptions of personhood and attributes of the person which may also be reflected in figurine use.

LBK funerary practices.
LBK funerary customs comprise three distinct elements: burial in cemeteries, in or on the edge of settlements, and deposition of disarticulated human bones on settlements or

---

[3] This may partially be due to excavation techniques which are not conducive to identifying structured deposition.

[4] Refits generally are rare, but the few from Nieder-Mörlen show different degrees of abrasion, reflecting different possible trajectories for rubbish (Schade-Lindig 2002b, 52).

[5] Although it has been criticised in that context, too (Milisauskas 2002, 889).

```
                    ┌─────────────────────┐
                    │     Dead body       │
                    └─────────────────────┘
              ↙              ↓                ↘
  ┌──────────────┐  ┌──────────────┐  ┌──────────────┐
  │  Cemeteries  │  │  Settlement  │  │  Fragmented  │
  │              │  │   burials    │  │   remains    │
  │ Inhumation   │  │(complete     │  │              │
  │ (single      │  │ bodies)      │  │ in settlements│
  │ or multiple) │  │              │  │ (as          │
  │              │  │ single or    │  │ part of"rubbish"│
  │ Cremation    │  │ multiple     │  │ and with special│
  │              │  │ inhumation   │  │ treatment)   │
  │ Manipulation │  │              │  │              │
  │ (rare)       │  │ in or at     │  │ secondary burial│
  │              │  │ edges of     │  │ (caves, archaeolo-│
  │              │  │ settlement   │  │ gically invisible│
  │              │  │              │  │ locations)   │
  └──────────────┘  └──────────────┘  └──────────────┘
```

Figure 5: Diagram of LBK funerary customs (not including mass graves).

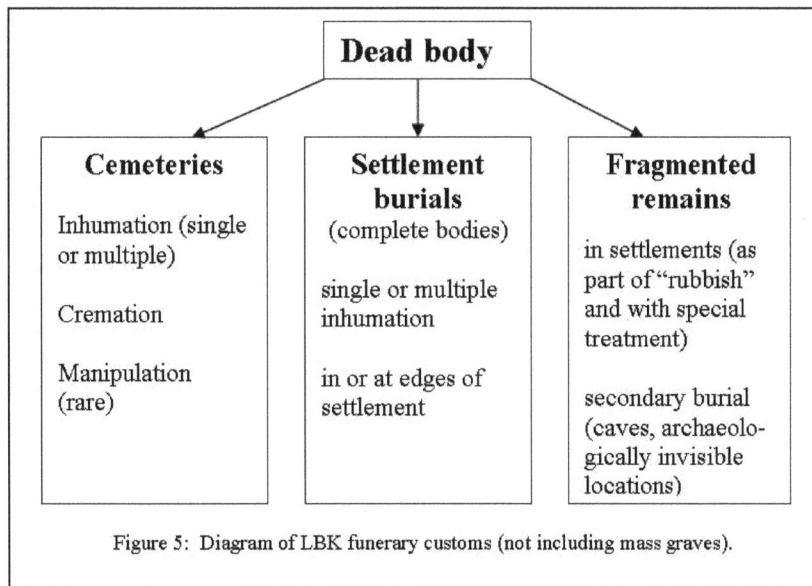

in caves (Figure 7.5; Nieszery 1995, 21- 43; Veit 1996, 77-108). In addition, there may be archaeologically invisible practices, as the total number of graves is still low compared to the total number of known settlements and their estimated duration.

Of these practices, cemetery burial is the one that has yielded most individuals, up to 228 on one site (Nieszery 1995, 54), but cemeteries are restricted chronologically (Nieszery 1995, 23) and form distinct regional clusters (Jeunesse 1997, 26). By comparison, burial in settlements is more ubiquitous (Veit 1996, 110-154, 193). The deposition of disarticulated human bone is so far understudied (but see Veit 1996, 194 - 200). Instances have been linked to cannibalism and head-cults (Hoffmann 1971), but recent re-analysis of cave sites (Orschiedt 1999, 165-78) has revealed that the fragmented state of the bones is most likely due to rites of secondary burial. It thus seems plausible to suggest that equivalent practices may have taken place elsewhere, in regions lacking caves, and that they account for some of the 'missing' LBK dead. Of these funerary practices, settlement burials and secondary burial offer the closest parallels to figurine use and are discussed in more detail, but it should always be borne in mind that a proportion of the LBK dead, at least at certain times in some places, were subjected to different treatments.

As discussed above, fragmentation is a key element of figurine use. Secondary burial, in which the bones of the defleshed dead are gathered up and reburied elsewhere, obviously results in fragmentation, but the trajectory of a normal settlement burial is very similar. When a known individual is buried, the location of the grave is remembered for some time by those who knew the deceased, were emotionally involved or took part in the ceremony. At Mannheim-Vogelstang in south-west Germany, for instance, a burial was deliberately avoided when a loam pit was dug around it (Orschiedt 1998, 5). It is difficult to estimate, however, how long such memories persisted. In time, the exact spot of each burial may have been forgotten. From a specific remembered individual, the interred body would change to a more vague memory in the minds of later generations, a knowledge that the remains of forbears were indeed buried somewhere on the

settlement, but without a precise person and location in mind.

These processes are paralleled by the actual physical decay of the corpse. Gradually, all individual traits are lost as the person turns into a skeleton, anonymous and ready to be imbued with any real or imagined identity by whoever comes across it. The process of decay was no doubt familiar to LBK people, both through the practice of secondary burial at places like the Jungfernhöhle, where select remains of people who decayed elsewhere were introduced (Orschiedt 1999, 176), and through occasional manipulation of remembered burials. One of the dead at Vaihingen (Baden-Württemberg), for example, had his head removed and placed on his belly some time after decay, and similar practices are reported from some Alsatian cemeteries (Jeunesse 1997, 67-70).

In addition to these intended engagements with the decayed and fragmentable dead, there must also have been chance encounters when previous burials were accidentally disturbed during routine settlement activities. Some of these remains, especially body parts easily recognisable as human, were occasionally re-used or re-deposited in a way showing that some importance was still attached to them. There is, for instance, the child skull from Quedlinburg in Sachsen-Anhalt, placed in a bowl and covered with another pot before re-burial (Siemoneit 1997, 130). At Königschaffhausen, in the south-west of Germany, two defleshed skulls with their mandibles missing were carefully placed next to one another, both facing the same way, in the loam pit of a house (Orschiedt 1998, 17).

Both these instances could either be the result of a planned engagement with the decayed dead or the result of chance. The majority of disturbed burials, however, seem to have elicited no such response. Petrasch (2000, 358f) argues that most isolated human bone fragments on LBK settlements are the remains of disturbed settlement burials simply discarded with rubbish, and certainly we cannot assume that each disturbed burial was treated with great ceremony (for ethnographic examples for casual attitudes to disturbed burials, see Oswalt 1999, 181; Wunn 2001, 146f). What we can be sure of, however, is that LBK people were aware of the fate of the human body after death, and that such processes were sometimes actively controlled and elaborated in secondary burial, while at other times skeletonised remains were the focus of further ritual and manipulation.

Partible persons and secondary burial: ethnographic perspectives

Above, I have described the dead as 'partible', a term borrowed from ethnographic discussion on the nature of individuals. The partible person is here contrasted to the individual in the modern Western sense, that is a pre-given, bounded and indivisible biological entity, the basis for our cultural norm of individualism (Rapport 1996, 298). In the Western perspective, relationships remain external to the person; they are, so to speak, grafted onto a pre-existing body during what is called "socialisation" (M. Strathern 1988, 12; 1992, 86-91). The concept of the partible person, on the other hand, has been developed mainly in the context of Melanesian ethnography (Busby 1997; M. Strathern 1988; 1992; see also Fowler 2004, 8f). Here, relationships *within* the body, for instance between flesh – seen as female - and bones – seen as male - are analogous to relationships *between* people. What aspect of his/her personality the individual activates is down to the specific social situation (M. Strathern 1988, 13f).

Discussions on exchange relations and on the nature of objects have been profoundly influenced by this research. It is not only the body of an individual which can objectify relationships (for example between his/her parents), artefacts can operate in a similar manner as a part of their maker's identity becomes embedded in them. In exchange relations, it is not simply things, but parts of people which are extracted and reabsorbed elsewhere, extending the sphere of the individual (Fowler 2004, 53-78; see also Gosden and Marshall 1999). Using and owning certain objects makes relationships and personal identity visible, thus conferring status and also acting as reminder of previous encounters with others (Hoskins 1998).

This parallel conception of objects and people has been used as the basis for several archaeological interpretations involving both artefacts and burials (Brück 2001a; 2001b; Chapman 2000, 28; Fowler 2000; 2001; 2002; 2004, 130-54; Thomas 1996) and could provide a useful metaphor for LBK figurine use. But is there a direct link between conceptions of personhood and burial practice? If we could suggest that fragmentation and dispersal of human remains after death are a sign of partible personhood, then the LBK mortuary record could further strengthen the theory that this conception of the person is the basis for how figurines are used.

There are indications that certain conceptions of personhood predispose to certain kinds of burial custom, but we should not expect a too easy analogy. There is no absolute and strict division between societies in which persons are seen as bounded and individualistic and those where there is more stress on partible, unbounded and relational aspects (Craib 1998, 5-10; Fowler 2001, 137-40; LiPuma 1998); elements of both are usually present. Thus, the Mount Hagen stress partibility, but actions such as marriage and procreation require a unitary person (M.

Strathern 1988, 13-15). In Western society, with its focus on individualism, people are sometimes defined by their relationships with others, for instance when profound loss feels like we have lost part of ourselves (Craib 1998, 4). Therefore, we cannot necessarily expect an unambiguous reflection of mode of personhood in mortuary rites.

With reference to burial, Fowler (2004, 83-85) has pointed out that to an extent, even 'indivisible' Western individuals can fragment after death through organ donation, scattering of their ashes, entry of the soul into an afterlife or redistribution of their possessions among heirs, thereby making those goods part of the survivors' identity. In spite of this, however, it is generally the intact person that is remembered by survivors (Fowler 2004, 96). In contrast, in societies with different ideas of personhood, facets of the person such as different souls are often assumed to split up at death and reside in different places (Fowler 2004, 87-89; Iteanu 1988; 1995, 139-46). In Melanesia, prior to the adoption of more Westernised customs, similar practices of dissolution often focussed on the body: exhumation, disarticulation and the separation of flesh and bones were part of the funerary rites of different peoples, and often some bones of the deceased were kept as mementos (Hirsch 1990, 27; Maschio 1994, 92f; A. Strathern 1982, 117). In parallel, long-drawn cycles of exchange were instituted to redistribute the property of the deceased, thus incorporating their fragmented identity into the networks of the living (Battaglia 1990, 177-81; A. Strathern 1981, 219). Andrew Strathern (1981, 220) could, however, not observe any such practices among the Hagen communities, whose conception of the person also centres on partibility. Fragmentation of the bodies of partible persons after death can hence not be considered essential to this mode of personhood (Fowler 2004, 92).

Instead of a one-to-one correspondence of a conception of personhood with a particular kind of burial, we should envisage tensions between different aspects of the person and choices to be made by the mourners. Different elements of the mortuary ritual could express different facets of personhood. For example, my own research on the Bavarian LBK cemetery of Aiterhofen (Hofmann 2001) has revealed a tension between essential and relational aspects of personhood. While there were stereotypical ideas about the items with which persons of a certain age and sex had to be buried, there was also a lot of variation between individual assemblages in each age/sex category. I believe these were due to the different ties and relationships formed by each individual in life, which became an inextricable part of their identity. As we have seen, at other times more stress may be laid on dividual aspects of the person alone, and thus LBK funerary rites encompass secondary burial and fragmentation alongside the burial of whole bodies.

Alongside ideas of personhood, other aspects, such as the perceived agency of the deceased, can have an impact on fragmentation. This is often important in societies practicing secondary burial, as famously shown by the French sociologist Robert Hertz (1907; English translation 1960, 27-86). He concentrates on the relationship between the corpse, the soul and the mourners to explain the logic behind secondary treatment of human remains (for a fuller treatment of Hertz, see Huntington and Metcalf 1979; Metcalf 1991). For many Bornean tribes, the fate of the soul is analogous to the fate of the body: it is tied to the corpse immediately after death, but progressively released during decomposition. Only when this process is complete can the spirit enter the realm of the dead. This is the logic behind the liminal phase, in which precautions need to be taken to keep the roaming ghost of the dead from harming the living, and also behind secondary burial of the clean bones which marks the final departure of the soul (Hertz 1960, 33-36; Huntington and Metcalf 1979, 67)[6].

Neither Hertz nor his commentators mention whether the Bornean tribes discussed have a more partible or more essential conception of personhood, although according to Metcalf (1991, 52-56), the soul itself has different components. What is most noteworthy here is that the corpse is still imbued with agency until its eventual fragmentation (Huntington and Metcalf 1979, 68-80). The process of decay is conceptualised as beneficial, as negative energies are dispersed through fragmentation. The resulting pure ancestral spirits can, on occasion, positively influence the affairs of the living (Huntington and Metcalf 1979, 87-92).

In conclusion, we can assume that the fragmentation of the body after death is likely to coexist with a conception of the person as partible to a degree, although in some of the Western examples, the personality and soul of the individual are still considered whole. Where fragmentation is at the centre of ritual elaboration, there is a greater chance that persons are conceived as partible, although absence of fragmentation need not denote an ideology of individualism. More generally, secondary burial and fragmentation of the dead involve ideas about how the spiritual energy of the deceased, whether conceived of as fragmented or unitary, must be managed in order to protect or even benefit the survivors and assist the dead on their final journey.

Back to the LBK: interpreting the principles of secondary and settlement burial
We cannot say with certainty whether LBK people believed in a soul, and if so, how exactly it was conceptualised (see discussion between Rinne 2000 and Vosteen 2001). Yet, from the ethnographic material above, the familiarity with processes of decay and their incorporation into funerary practice in the LBK are indicators that the dead were considered active to a degree. The spiritual component of the dead person would slowly leave the body, perhaps to proceed into a different realm, as is the case with the Berawan of Borneo, or to return energy and fertility to the land, like the spirits of the dead in the Andes (Harris 1982; Sillar 1992). It is likely that a conception of the person as partible also informed LBK customs, although it was not foregrounded in all funerary rites. In this light, manipulation of corpses and bones becomes intelligible. It also explains why accidentally unearthing the remains of the dead, whose spirit has left, need not result in elaborate ritual.

---

[6] Note that on Borneo, the relationship between soul and corpse stays close even when secondary burial is not practiced (Gana Ngadi 1998, 51).

The circumstances of their unearthing or interpretation as an omen of some kind may have determined how uncovered human remains were treated, or there might be regional or individual choices involved. Whichever strategy was adopted, the encounter with human bone and its dispersal or re-use powerfully illustrated the message that humans, at least once deceased, are partible and end up dispersed in the very fabric of the settlement. The immediate experience of this fact and its occasional deliberate incorporation into mortuary rites no doubt profoundly engrained this perception. We are hence confronted with a certain way of conceptualising the human form as an individual with powers and abilities, but nevertheless partible after death. Occasionally, these powers remained inherent in some remains, in other instances they would dissipate. It is also important that these reflections are most clearly borne out at a time when humans are at their most abstract, that is when they are merely skeletons.

The ideas of secondary burial and the partibility of persons thus provide us with an insight into how fragmentation can be considered essential to the way living people function, and also to their fate after death, although these aspects need not necessarily be related in a straightforward way. How can this help us to understand the use of figurines?

Fragments of power: the making and use of figurines

Seen in this light, there are obvious parallels between figurines and the treatment of at least some of the LBK dead. The figurine starts out as an abstract artefact, the dead become abstract through decomposition. Both are subsequently fragmented and mostly incorporated into settlement rubbish without much apparent care, although instances of special treatment are also known. From the above discussion we can argue that figurines, through their material and visual qualities, mostly their miniaturisation, three-dimensionality and abstraction, are powerful objects. They could further be charged with energy during their manufacturing process, for instance by incorporating ground grain into the clay (Höckmann 1987, 90), by adding designs or simply through firing. The human person, on the other hand, is imbued with agency, will and spirit, powers and energies which can linger for a longer or shorter period after death.

There is, however, an important distinction between a dead person and a figurine: the agency of the former is difficult if not impossible to control, ghosts and marauding spirits are often feared. These powers dissipate only slowly, through decay. Figurines, on the other hand, condense the powers they are charged with and reduce them to a manageable and controllable form. The smashing of the figurine allows an explosive and directed release of energy towards the goal intended by the maker or user. Once the ceremony is over, the remainder of the figurine is no longer particularly ritually charged in most cases and discarded with other household rubbish, paralleling the treatment of accidentally disturbed burials. Perhaps, the dispersal of the figurine fragments is integral to the success of the ritual, not only creating a strong memory, but making sure that the remainder of this potentially powerful object is properly incorporated into the substance of the settlement.

This is not to suggest that figurines were representations of actual dead individuals or abstract ancestors or were in any way directly connected to funerary practice. Instead, it illustrates how their making and use fits with a conception of personhood visible in other spheres of LBK life. Visualising humans in a partible and fragmentable manner leads to a certain conception of how their inherent powers could be harnessed, directed and released, and this governed the making and use of anthropomorphic figurines, whether they represented other living or dead people or indeed non-human agencies. What is important is that they reinforced a certain way of thinking about persons and other agencies and relied on fragmentation to release their powers. Thus, the actual figures themselves may have served a multiplicity of purpose. Their individuality in expression and degrees of difference from the human form, but also more standard types like the pot-holder, show that each maker embodied her own expectations, emotions and goals into each particular piece, but they still fitted in with more general worldviews.

For example, individual pieces like the Adonis from Zschernitz (Landesamt für Archäologie Sachsen 2003) with its explicit depiction of male sexuality could well be about fertility, figurines with fir branch design might recall ancestors or shamanistic practices, or indeed there may have sinister and harmful purposes in the smashing of a figurine. The existence of human/animal hybrid figurines is also suggestive, as it might afford insights into human-animal relations. People could identify themselves with certain animals in a totemic fashion, or perhaps spiritual qualities or other perceived characteristics of specific animals, such as strength or cunning, were expressed or desired by the figurine maker. We will simply never know. Still, seeing figurines as an embodiment of a conception of personhood augments previous, literal suggestions of unified meanings and explains the basic material characteristics of the figures.

Figurines are fragmented because this is an appropriate way of treating humans in burial, and hence by extension human-like things. They are never found as grave goods because they are emphatically artefacts of the living for a specific goal. Instead, they are incorporated into household rubbish because, like the dead, they have either ceased to matter or their power is allowed to seep into the settlement itself. They are individualistic and not always straightforwardly human because they can serve a variety of individual needs and strategies, rather than just representing imperfect reflections of a goddess. With the idea of the partible person in mind, figurines may even have been considered parts of their makers and could have stood for them in ritual. Furthermore, the power the figurine was imbued with is partly explained through its materiality and its ability to unsettle the user, creating feelings of tension and discomfort, while at the same time its size keeps its handlers seemingly in control.

Outlook: regional and chronological patterns

So far, my discussion has assumed that figurines were used in small-scale domestic ritual involving few people, perhaps only one person. Furthermore, I have written about the makers of figurines as if anybody with enough skill and potting experience could have produced them at will, and implicitly I have assumed that the makers and users, if not actually the same people, had a very intimate relationship to one another. Any prestige or power acquired by making and using those objects would most likely be small-scale, directed and perhaps fleeting. However, there are other possibilities.

The site at Nieder-Mörlen in Hesse, for instance, has yielded a far higher number of figurines than usual, and many more than surrounding settlements in the region (Schade-Lindig 2002b, 75-82). The site is extremely long-lived and also comprises an enclosure, so it is possible that figurine production was the prerogative of central settlements. In Schade-Lindig's (2002b, 83) view, making and using figurines was hedged around with taboos and not everybody was allowed to produce objects of such power[7]. Instead, they were traded to subsidiary settlements from Nieder-Mörlen, thus being directly involved in status relations and the negotiation of ritual supremacy.

This is an exciting new suggestion, but it is not necessarily applicable elsewhere. No figurine finds are reported on Bavarian sites with enclosures, such as Otzing or Stephansposching (Schmotz 1997, 141-54; 2000)[8], and although these are not as long-lived they are larger than most sites around and the prime contenders for being considered central settlements of some sort. Here, it is more appropriate to assume that the power and status of figurine makers would not go far beyond the settlement itself, although the small numbers recovered in the region hint that the ceremonies in which figurines were involved may have been a little more special than other kinds of ritual.

To really answer this question in depth, a new appraisal of figurines on a regional basis is sorely needed. The disparate publication data and the material from at least the most important unpublished excavations must be collected and looked at afresh. For instance, it would be interesting to see whether the figurines from Hesse are really more similar to the south-east than Bavarian ones (see e.g. Schade-Linding 2002a, 105-07; 2002b, 63) or whether Höckmann's (1965, 3) suggestion of regional differences in the body parts of figurines recovered has withstood the test of time.

A new study could also come up with a dating scheme for the material, although the provenance of many pieces from

---

[7] Some (Siemoneit 1997, 82) interpret zoomorphic figurines at least as "just" children's toys, but given that they are so rare (Schade-Lindig 2002b, 58) and form part of a continuum with human depictions rather than being an entirely separate category, this seems unlikely.

[8] There are only interim reports so far, but seeing as figurines are items normally published immediately in an own article, I am confident that no excessive numbers have been found.

surface scatters could make this hard to achieve. In areas with more excavated examples, like Austria, figurines only become common in later phases of the LBK and are extremely rare before (Lenneis 1995, 22, 43). If this pattern is repeated elsewhere, it would open possibilities to investigate figurine use in relation to other social processes. For instance, there are hints that practices of fragmenting the dead and of secondary burial become more common later in the LBK (Krause 1998a, 26; 1998b, 56; Orschiedt 1999, 165; Spatz 1998, 18; 2003, 583). Increased figurine use could be a response to a new kind of interest in the treatment of the dead and a renewed stress on fragmentation. With Nieder-Mörlen in mind, it would also be possible to investigate whether the establishment of larger and ditched settlements and the resulting shift in power structures influenced the production and distribution of figurines in other regions.

Conclusion: LBK figurines in an LBK context

This study has shown how an idea, even if originally introduced from south-east Europe, could begin to make sense in the specific local context of the LBK. Figurines are tied in with a specific cultural conception of personhood, also evident in burial customs, centring on the partibility of the human form and its potential for abstraction and fragmentation. Even though such concepts could be widely shared within the western LBK, there is the further possibility that figurines may have been involved in different ritual and power strategies in different regions, although more research is needed to clarify this. Finally, especially if figurine production was not restricted to a privileged set of people, individual users could have adapted the figurines and surrounding ritual to their specific need, thus making any attempt to find a unified meaning for figurines futile. For each person, making and using figurines recalled their own previous experiences and encounters, while the ritual itself probably resulted in an emotionally charged state of mind and was an occasion to remember. It is because figurines are thus interwoven with individual experiences that they are so powerful.

Several questions have, however, remained unanswered and must be the focus for further research. The connection of figurines with appliqués, anthropomorphic, zoomorphic and simply decorated pottery has not been explored, nor the reasons why clay is an appropriate medium for the production of human depictions. It has, however, become clear that to understand figurines they must be emancipated from their south-east European counterparts. Only by appreciating the material characteristics of figurines, their abstraction, individuality, size and fragmentation, as well as reflecting further on their depositional contexts and comparing them to other areas of LBK life can we come to grips with their social importance. Rather than being passive players in a culture-historical narrative, figurines must become active and powerful objects in our narratives, objects deeply involved in ritual and social processes. Only then are they a key artefact in any study on LBK world view, personhood and lived experience.

Acknowledgements

I would like to thank Alasdair Whittle, Douglass Bailey, Jess Mills and Andrew Cochrane for their criticisms and comments on earlier drafts of this paper. Of course, any remaining mistakes are my own. I must also acknowledge the financial help of the AHRC, which makes my doctoral research possible. Finally, I am grateful to the occupants of the postgrad room for keeping me reasonably sane.

References

Bailey, D.W. 2005. *Prehistoric figurines. Representation and corporeality in the Neolithic.* London: Routledge.

Battaglia, D. 1990. *On the bones of the serpent: person, memory and mortality in Sabarl society.* Chicago: Chicago University Press.

Baumann, W. 1976. Neufunde figürlicher Darstellungen der Bandkeramik aus Sachsen. *Jahresschrift für mitteldeutsche Vorgeschichte* 60, 97-107.

Brink-Kloke, H. 1992. *Drei Siedlungen der Linienbandkeramik in Niederbayern. Studien zu den Befunden und zur Keramik von Alteglofsheim-Köfering, Landshut-Sallmannsberg und Straubing-Lerchenhaid.* Internationale Archäologie 10. Buch am Erlbach: Verlag Marie Leidorf.

Brück, J. 2001a. Body metaphors and technologies of transformation in the English Middle and Late Bronze Age. In J. Brück (ed.), *Bronze Age landscapes. Tradition and transformation*, 149-60. Oxford: Oxbow books.

Brück, J. 2001b. Monuments, power and personhood in the British Neolithic. *Journal of the Royal Anthropological Institute* 7, 649-67.

Boelicke, U. 1982. Gruben und Häuser: Untersuchungen zur Struktur bandkeramischer Hofplätze. In J. Pavúk (ed.), *Siedlungen der Kultur mit Bandkeramik in Europa. Internationales Kolloquium Nové Vozokany 17.-20. November 1981*, 17-28. Nitra: Archäologisches Institut der Slovakischen Akademie der Wissenschaften.

Busby, C. 1997. Permeable and partible persons: a comparative analysis of gender and body in South India and Melanesia. *Journal of the Royal Anthropological Institute* 3, 261-78.

Chapman, J. 2000. *Fragmentation in Archaeology. People, places and broken objects in the prehistory of south eastern Europe.* London: Routledge.

Coudart, A. 1998. *Architecture et société néolithique. L'unité et la variance de la maison danubienne.* Paris: Editions de la Maison des Sciences de l'Homme.

Craib, I. 1998. *Experiencing identity.* London: Sage.

Engelhardt, B. 1981. *Das Neolithikum in Mittelfranken I: Alt- und Mittelneolithikum. Materialhefte zur Bayerischen orgeschichte 41.* Kallmünz: Verlag Michael Lassleben.

Engelhardt, B. 1992. Götteridole der ältesten Bauernkultur (Linienbandkeramik). In M. Hahn and J. Prammer (eds), *Bauern in Bayern. Von den Anfängen bis zur Römerzeit. Katalog des Gäubodenmuseums Straubing Nr. 19*, 367-79. Straubing: Gäubodenmuseum.

Fowler, C. 2000. The individual, the subject and archaeological interpretation. Reading Luce Irigaray and Judith Butler. In C. Holtorf and H. Karlsson (eds), *Philosophy and archaeological practice. Perspectives for the 21st century*, 107-33. Göteborg: Bricoleur Press.

Fowler, C. 2001. Personhood and social relations in the British Neolithic with a study from the Isle of Man. *Journal of Material Culture* 6, 137-63.

Fowler, C. 2002. Body parts. Personhood and materiality in the earlier Manx Neolithic. In Y. Hamilakis, M. Pluciennik and S. Tarlow (eds), *Thinking through the body. Archaeologies of corporeality*, 47-69. New York: Kluwer Academic.

Fowler, C. 2004. *The Archaeology of personhood. An anthropological approach.* London: Routledge.

Gana Ngadi, H. 1998. *Iban rites of passage and some related ritual acts. A description of forms and functions.* Kuala Lumpur: Dewan Bahasa dan Pustaka Kementerian Pendidikan Malaysia.

Gosden, C. and Marshall, Y. 1999. The cultural biography of objects. *World Archaeology* 31, 169-78.

Gronenborn, D. 1999. A variation on a basic theme: the transition to farming in southern central Europe. *Journal of World Prehistory* 13, 123-210.

Hamilakis, Y. 2002. The past as oral history. Towards an archaeology of the senses. In Y. Hamilakis, M. Pluciennik and S. Tarlow (eds), *Thinking through the body. Archaeologies of corporeality*, 121-36. New York: Kluwer Academic.

Hampel, A. 1989. Bemerkenswerte Fundstücke aus der linienbandkeramischen Siedlung in Frankfurt a. M. – Niedereschbach. *Germania* 67, 149-57.

Harris, O. 1982. The dead and the devils among the Bolivian Laymi. In M. Bloch and J. Parry (eds), *Death and the regeneration of life.* Cambridge: Cambridge University Press.

Hertz, R. 1907. Contribution à une étude sur la représentation collective de la mort. *Année sociologique* 10, 48-137.

Hertz, R. 1960. A contribution to the study of the collective representation of death. In R. Hertz (ed.), *Death and the right hand*, 27-86. London: Cohen and West.

Hirsch, E. 1990. From bones to betelnuts: processes of ritual transformation and the development of "national culture" in Papua New Guinea. *Man* 25, 18-35.

Höckmann, O. 1965. Menschliche Darstellungen in der bandkeramischen Kultur. *Jahrbuch des Römisch-Germanischen Zentralmuseums Mainz* 12, 1-34.

Höckmann, O. 1985. Ein ungewöhnlicher neolithischer Statuettenkopf aus Rockenberg, Wetteraukreis. *Jahrbuch des Römisch-Germanischen Zentralmuseums Mainz* 32, 92-107.

Höckmann, O. 1987. Gemeinsamkeiten in der Plastik der Linearkeramik und der Cucuteni-Kultur. In: M. Petrescu-Dîmbouiţa (ed.), *La civilisation de Cucuteni en contexte Européen. Session Scientifique Iaşi-Piatra Neamţ 1984*, 89-97. Iaşi: Université Al. I. Cuza.

Hoffmann, E. 1971. Spuren anthropophager Riten und von Schädelkult in Freilandsiedlungen der sächsisch-thüringischen Bandkeramik. Ein Beitrag zur Geschichte der Anthropophagie und ihrer Motivation. *Ethnographisch-Archäologische Zeitschrift* 12, 1-27.

Hofmann, D. 2001. The representation of personal identity in the mortuary record of Early Neolithic Bavaria. Unpublished M.A. dissertation, Cardiff University.

Hoskins, J. 1998. *Biographical objects: how things tell the story of people's lives.* London: Routledge.

Huntington, R. and Metcalf, P. 1979. *Celebrations of death. The anthropology of mortuary ritual.* Cambridge: Cambridge University Press.

Husty, L. 1999. Ein aussergewöhnliches Steinbeildepot aus der linearbandkeramischen Siedlung von Adldorf-Kreuzäcker, Gemeinde Eichendorf, Landkreis Dingolfing-Landau. *Historischer Verein für Straubing und Umgebung, Jahresbericht. No. 101*, 27-109.

Iteanu, A. 1988. The concept of the person and the ritual system: an Orokaiva view. *Man* 25, 35-53.

Iteanu, A. 1995. Rituals and ancestors. In D. de Coppet and A. Iteanu (eds), *Cosmos and society in Oceania*, 135-63. Oxford: Berg.

Jeunesse, C. 1995. Les groupes régionaux occidentaux du Rubané (Rhin et Bassin Parisien) à travers les pratiques funéraires. *Gallia Préhistoire* 37, 115-54.

Jeunesse, C. 1996. Variabilité des pratiques funéraires et differenciation sociale dans le néolithique ancien danubien. *Gallia Préhistoire* 38, 249-86.

Jeunesse, C. 1997. *Pratiques funéraires au Néolithique ancien. Sépultures et nécropoles danubiennes 5500-4900 av. J.-C.* Paris: Editions Errance.

Jones, A. 2001a. Enduring images? Image production and memory in Earlier Bronze Age Scotland. In J. Brück (ed.), *Bronze Age landscapes. Tradition and transformation*, 217-28. Oxford: Oxbow books.

Jones, A. 2001b. Drawn from memory: the archaeology of aesthetics and the aesthetics of archaeology in Earlier Bronze Age Britain and the present. *World Archaeology* 33, 334-56.

Kaufmann, D. 1976. Linienbandkeramische Kultgegenstände aus dem Elbe-Saale Gebiet. *Jahresschrift für mitteldeutsche Vorgeschichte* 60, 61-96.

Kaufmann, D. 1989. Kultische Äußerungen im Frühneolithikum des Elbe-Saale Gebietes. In F. Schlette and D. Kaufmann (eds), *Religion und Kult in ur- und frühgeschichtlicher Zeit*, 111-39. Berlin: Akademie-Verlag.

Kneipp, J. and Büttner, H. 1988. Anthropophagie in der jüngsten Bandkeramik der Wetterau. *Germania* 66, 489-97.

Krause, R. 1998a. Die bandkeramischen Siedlungsspuren bei Vaihingen an der Enz, Kreis Ludwigsburg (Baden-Württemberg). Ein Vorbericht zu den Ausgrabungen von 1994-1997. *Berichte der Römisch-Germanischen Komission* 79, 5-105.

Krause, R. 1998b. Archäologische Denkmalpflege und interdisziplinäre Forschung in Vaihingen an der Enz, Kreis Ludwigsburg. *Archäologische Ausgrabungen in Baden-Württemberg 1998*, 53-56.

Landesamt für Archölogie Sachsen. 2003. Der "Adonis von Zschernitz". Die älteste männliche Tonfigur Europas.

http://www.archsax.sachsen.de/aktuelles/21082003.html

Last, J. 1998. The residue of yesterday's existence: settlement space and discard at Miskovice and Bylany. In I. Pavlů (ed.), *Bylany. Varia 1*, 17-46. Prague: Studio Press.

Lenneis, E. 1995. Beschreibung der Kulturgruppen. In E. Lenneis, C. Neugebauer-Maresch and E. Ruttkay (eds), *Jungsteinzeit im Osten Österreichs*, 11-56. St. Pölten: Verlag Niederösterreichisches Pressehaus.

LiPuma, E. 1998. Modernity and forms of personhood in Melanesia. In M. Lambek and A. Strathern (eds), *Bodies and persons: comparative views from Africa and Melanesia*, 53-79. Cambridge: Cambridge University Press.

Lüning, J. 2000. *Steinzeitliche Bauern in Deutschland. Die Landwirtschaft im Neolithikum.* Universitätsforschungen zur prähistorischen Archäologie Band 58. Bonn: Rudolf Habelt.

Makkay, J. 1978. Mahlstein und das rituelle Mahlen in den prähistorischen Opferzeremonien. *Acta Archaeologica Academiae Scientiarum Hungaricae* 30, 13-36.

Maschio, T. 1994. *To remember the faces of the dead: the plenitude of memory in Southeastern New Britain.* Madison: University of Wisconsin Press.

Maurer, H. 1981. Linearkeramische Kultobjekte aus Niederösterreich. *Fundberichte aus Österreich* 20, 57-94.

Maurer, H. 1982. *Neolithische Kultobjekte aus dem niederösterreichischen Manhartsbergbereich. Ein Beitrag zur jungsteinzeitlichen Geistesgeschichte. Mannus-Bibliothek Band 19.* Hückeswagen.

Metcalf, P. 1991. *A Borneo journey into death. Berawan eschatology from its rituals.* Kuala Lumpur: S. Abdul Majeed & Co.

Milisauskas, S. 2002. Interpretations and narratives of the Neolithic of southeastern Europe. *Antiquity* 76, 887-89.

Modderman, P. 1977. *Die neolithische Besiedlung bei Hienheim, Ldkr. Kehlheim I: Die Ausgrabungen am Weinberg 1965 bis 1970. Materialhefte zur Bayerischen Vorgeschichte 33.* Kallmünz: Verlag Michael Lassleben.

Modderman, P. 1986. Die neolithische Besiedlung bei Hienheim, Ldkr. Kehlheim. *Analecta Praehistorica Leidensia* 19, 1-187.

Modderman, P. 1978. Eine jungsteinzeitliche Siedlung aus Meindling, Gemeinde Oberschneiding, Landkreis Straubing-Bogen. *Beiträge zur Geschichte Niederbayerns während der Jungsteinzeit I. Beilage zum amtlichen Schul-Anzeiger für den Regierungsbezirk Niederbayern Nr. 1*, 21-27.

Nieszery, N. 1995. *Linearbandkeramische Gräberfelder in Bayern. Internationale Archäologie 16.* Espelkamp: Marie Leidorf.

Orschiedt, J. 1998. *Bandkeramische Siedlungsbestattungen in Südwestdeutschland. Archäologische und anthropologische Befunde. Internationale Archäologie 43.* Rahden: Marie Leidorf.

Orschiedt, J. 1999. *Manipulationen an menschlichen Skelettresten. Taphonomische Prozesse, Sekundärbestattungen oder Kannibalismus?* Tübingen: Mo Vince Verlag.

Oswalt, W. 1999. *Eskimos & explorers. Second edition.* Novato: Chandler & Sharp.

Petrasch, J. 2000. Menschenknochen in neolithischen Siedlungen. Spuren sepulkraler Riten oder Abfall? *Archäologisches Korrespondenzblatt* 30, 353-68.

Probst, E. 1999. *Deutschland in der Steinzeit. Jäger, Fischer und Bauern zwischen Nordseeküste und Alpenraum.* München: Orbis.

Rapport, N. 1996. Individualism. In A. Barnard and J. Spencer (eds), *Encyclopedia of social and cultural Anthropology*, 298-302. London: Routledge.

Reinecke, K. 1977. Neue Funde der Linearbandkeramik aus Niederbayern. *Archäologisches Korrespondenzblatt* 7, 201-10.

Rinne, C. 2000. Vom Leben mit dem Tod- Ein Graben zwischen Diesseits und Jenseits? www.jungsteinsite.de

Schade-Lindig, S. 2002a. Idole und sonderbar verfüllte Gruben aus der bandkeramischen Siedlung "Hempler" in Bad Nauheim – Nieder-Mörlen. In H.-J. Beier (ed.) *Varia Neolithica II. Beiträge zur Ur- und Frühgeschichte Mitteleuropas 32*, 99-115. Weissbach: Beier & Beran.

Schade-Lindig, S. 2002b. Idol- und Sonderfunde der bandkeramischen Siedlung von Bad Nauheim – Nieder-Mörlen "Auf dem Hempler" (wetteraukreis). *Germania* 80, 47-114.

Schmotz, K. 1997. Altneolithische Grabenwerke in Niederbayern. Zum Stand der Kenntnis aufgrund Luftbildarchäologie, Magnetometerprospektion und archäologischer Ausgrabung. In K. Schmotz (ed.), *Vorträge des 15. Niederbayerischen Archäologentages*, 119-60. Espelkamp: Marie Leidorf.

Schmotz, K. 2000. Die altneolithische Siedlung von Otzing, Landkreis Deggendorf, Niederbayern. *Das Archäologische Jahr in Bayern 2000*, 14-17.

Siemoneit, B. 1997. *Das Kind in der Linienbandkeramik. Befunde aus Gräberfeldern und Siedlungen in Mitteleuropa. Internationale Archäologie 42.* Rahden: Marie Leidorf.

Sillar, B. 1992. The social life of the Andean dead. *Archaeological Review from Cambridge* 11, 107-23.

Spatz, H. 1998. Krisen, Gewalt, Tod – zum Ende der ersten Ackerbauernkultur Mitteleuropas. In A. Häußler (ed.), *Krieg oder Frieden? Herxheim vor 7000 Jahren*, 10-19. Speyer: Landesamt für Denkmalpflege.

Spatz, H. 2003. Hinkelstein: eine Sekte als Initiator des Mittelneolithikums? In J. Eckert, U. Eisenhauer and A. Zimmermann (eds), *Archäologische Perspektiven. Analysen und Interpretationen im Wandel. Festschrift für Jens Lüning zum 65. Geburtstag*, 575-87. Rahden: Marie Leidorf.

Stöckl, H. 2002. Hatten bandkeramische Gefäßverzierungen eine symbolische Bedeutung im Bereich des Kultes? In H.-J. Beier (ed.) *Varia Neolithica II. Beiträge zur Ur- und Frühgeschichte Mitteleuropas 32*, 63-97. Weissbach: Beier & Beran.

Strathern, A. 1981. Death as exchange: two Melanesian cases. In S. Humphries and H. King (eds), *Mortality and immortality: the Archaeology and*

Anthropology of death, 205-23. London: Academic Press.

Strathern, A. 1982. Witchcraft, greed, cannibalism and death: some related themes for the New Guinea Highlands. In M. Bloch and J. Parry (eds), *Death and the regeneration of life*, 111-33. Cambridge: Cambridge University Press.

Strathern, M. 1988. *The gender of the gift. Problems with women and problems with society in Melanesia.* Berkeley: University of California Press.

Strathern, M. 1992. Parts and wholes. Refiguring relationships in a post-plural world. In A. Kuper (ed.), *Conceptualizing society*, 75-104. London: Routledge.

Thomas, J. 1996. *Time, culture and identity: an interpretive archaeology.* London: Routledge.

Tringham, R. 2000. Southeastern Europe in the transition to agriculture in Europe: bridge, buffer, or mosaic. In T. D. Price (ed.) *Europe's first farmers*, 19-56. Cambridge: Cambridge University Press.

Veit, U. 1996. *Studien zum Problem der Siedlungsbestattung im europäischen Neolithikum.* Tübinger Schriften zur ur- und frühgeschichtlichen Archäologie. Münster: Waxmann.

Vosteen, M. 2001. Der Graben zwischen Diesseits und Jenseits – eine Erwiederung zu "Vom Leben mit dem Tod" von Christoph Rinne. www. jungsteinsite.de

Wamser, L. 1980. Eine gefäßhaltende Idolfigur der frühen Linearbandkeramik aus Mainfranken. *Jahresbericht der Bayerischen Bodendenkmalpflege* 21, 26-38.

Whittle, A. 1996. *Europe in the Neolithic. The creation of new worlds.* Cambridge: Cambridge University Press.

Wunn, I. 2001. *Götter, Mütter, Ahnenkult. Religionsentwicklung in der Jungsteinzeit. Beiheft der Archäologischen Mitteilungen aus Nordwestdeutschland Nr. 36.* Rahden: Marie Leidorf.

Wunn, I. 2002. Religiöse Symbole im Neolithikum – ihre Entschlüsselung und Bedeutung. In H.-J. Beier (ed.) *Varia Neolithica II. Beiträge zur Ur- und Frühgeschichte Mitteleuropas 32,* 35-54. Weissbach: Beier & Beran.

'What the Romans did for us.' A question of identity in the Broekpolder.

Marjolijn Kok

Abstract

In this paper, I try to show how we as archaeologists form past identities on the basis of artefacts and how a sudden change in the composition of archaeological evidence must be evaluated carefully. Within Roman Iron Age contexts, Roman imports seem to lead to extreme excitement in a lot of archaeologists, as is shown by the description of every piece of Roman material and the meagre description, if any, of local artefacts. We need to evaluate if the local inhabitants shared the same reverence for Roman (material) culture during the Iron Age, or if they incorporated Roman artefacts in their own way.

Introduction

The Broekpolder is situated in the centre of the Oer-IJ estuary (Figure 8.1). It is a tidal area which was closed off from the sea around the beginning of the Christian era. From this period onwards, the area was flooded by the sea only under extreme circumstances. The landscape was still dominated by water, but direct access to the sea had shifted from west to east. The area has been extensively researched by the University of Amsterdam and found to contain sites/landscapes ranging from the Bronze Age to the Medieval Period, of which the Assendelver Polder is the best known.

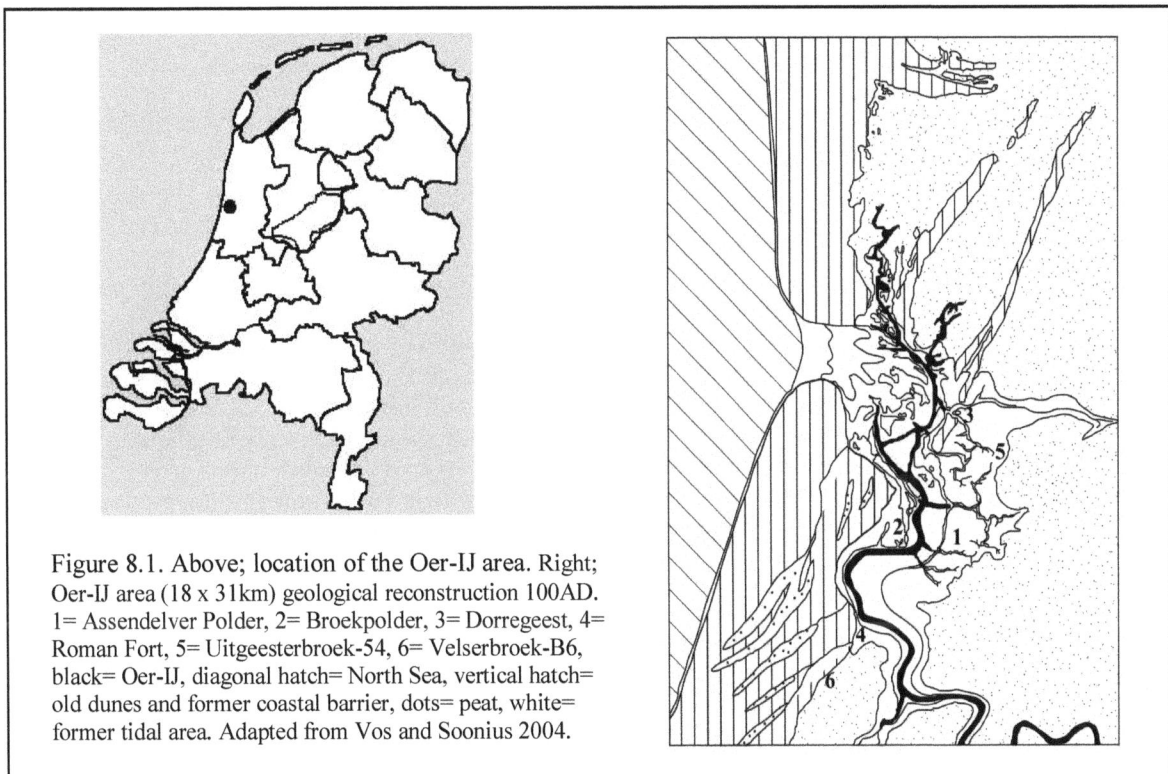

Figure 8.1. Above; location of the Oer-IJ area. Right; Oer-IJ area (18 x 31km) geological reconstruction 100AD. 1= Assendelver Polder, 2= Broekpolder, 3= Dorregeest, 4= Roman Fort, 5= Uitgeesterbroek-54, 6= Velserbroek-B6, black= Oer-IJ, diagonal hatch= North Sea, vertical hatch= old dunes and former coastal barrier, dots= peat, white= former tidal area. Adapted from Vos and Soonius 2004.

Because the area is bordered by peat, natural coastal barriers and sea, the Oer-IJ area has been traditionally seen as a unified social, cultural and economic unit by archaeologists (Brandt 1983, 132). This assumption is supported by the distinctive type of pottery (van Heeringen 1992), a type of wall-ditch house to the north of Oer-IJ that is only known in this area or much further abroad (Therkorn 1987, 206, 209), and the continuation of the settlement tradition of single farmsteads throughout the Roman Iron Age. This does, however, not mean that this area was totally isolated from the rest of the world. Although the pottery has a distinctive style of its own, it has many affiliations with the Frisian area to the northeast and in a lesser way to the area south (van Heeringen 1992). Certain resources, like stone and bronze, do not occur naturally in this area and therefore have to be imported. This could take place through exchange with neighbouring areas or through forays outside of the local area. Lastly, the main type of house in this area is of the general northern European type of a three-aisled farmhouse, with the byre and living quarters under one roof. The proposed unity of the area appears also to correlate with the research programs that focus on a specific area.

The old dunes and coastal barriers were inhabited from the Late Neolithic onwards, and evidence for land use, like loose sherds and axes, has been found. The first evidence for housing dates from the Middle Bronze Age (1400-1200 BC). In the Early Iron Age (final part of the 7th century BC), people moved into the adjacent areas and built houses on peat, after initial use for summer grazing and other means of exploitation such as reed cutting. At the end of the Middle Iron Age, around 300 BC, conditions became drier as the influence of the sea started to weaken. For several centuries, until the Late Roman Iron Age, the tidal areas, marshes and peat were inhabited and used. The main type of building was the post structured three-aisled farm with a northeast-southwest orientation. This gave the built environment a uniform appearance in which the path of the sun could be followed from each house in a similar manner.

The inhabitants of the Oer-IJ are generally considered to be part of the Frisian/Germanic world. The settlement pattern consisted of single farmsteads instead of aggregated settlements as in other parts of the Netherlands. Religious practices involved the deposition of artefacts in wet places, houses and pits. Sometimes the pits were filled with specific artefacts, and these have been interpreted as practices associated with the economy as bound to the seasonal cycle (Therkorn 2004). The practices associated with the dead are elusive. From the Iron Age only one inhumation (Jelgersma *et al.* 1970, 141) is known, as well as the deposition of single human bones in specific contexts (Kok forthcoming). In the later part of the Roman Iron Age, inhumations and cremations are again archaeologically visible, but limited in number. Generally speaking, until the end of the Late Iron Age, the region can be characterised as stable, with people connecting with their neighbours, interacting with their ever-changing environment and practicing rituals connected with the more stable passing of the seasons.

Roman and native inhabitants

Around the year 15 AD, the people of the Oer-IJ region were confronted directly with a totally new way of life. A Roman harbour complex was built on the south bank of the Oer-IJ. Not only was this a new type of building, it also involved a new way of living, with different eating habits, material culture, laws, social and political rules, taxation and regulations.

The relationship between the local inhabitants and the Romans in the first century AD has been a puzzle for some time. From the written sources, it becomes clear that the locals had to pay tax in the form of hides, as a revolt in 28 AD is documented that involved a fight around a fort called Flevum, and possibly at the site of the Roman harbour works.

Local Iron Age pottery has been found inside the Roman fort, indicating some form of exchange with the local inhabitants (Bosman 1997, 87). Strangely enough, little Roman material culture appears to have entered into the Oer-IJ area. Until recently, only occasional small Roman sherds were found in settlements there. At first, these sherds were interpreted as some sort of primitive money (Brandt 1983). However, they never form complete objects and cannot be refitted to other sherds in the same settlement, but sometimes they do fit to sherds in other settlements. On the basis of this evidence, the so-called 'pick-up theory' was seen as more probable. This theory proposes that the local inhabitants had no access to Roman objects through exchange, but picked up the sherds after the Romans were partly defeated in 28 AD and/or left definitely, after abandoning the rebuilt fort, around 48AD (Vons & Bosman 1988, Meffert 1998).

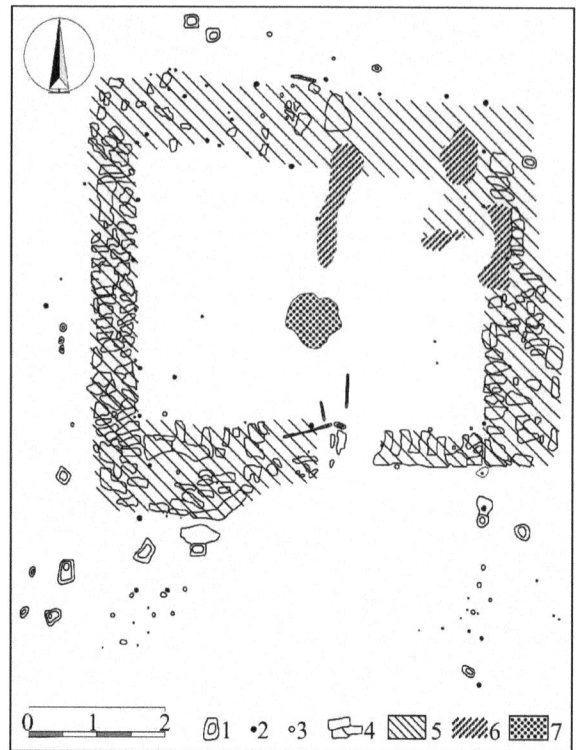

Figure 8.2. Uitgeesterbroekpolder-54, sod/turf wall house. 1-3= post(holes), 4=sod/turf, 5= probable wall, 6= burnt layer, 7= hearth. After Therkorn et al. 1986.

The only marked change in the material culture of the local inhabitants at this time was the construction of the new type of house mentioned earlier, a wall-ditch house that is unknown from any other area in the Netherlands (Figure 8.2). Twenty-two wall-ditch houses were excavated during the Assendelver Polder project and they all date to the first century AD and are located in the remnants of tidal marshes, an area previously uninhabited. This new form of house breaks with the tradition in which livestock were stalled under the same roof as the human inhabitants. Now livestock were being stalled in outside cattle enclosures. Importantly, this type of house is restricted to a specific area that was good for grazing, but not as good for agriculture, due to the somewhat brackish conditions. The normal three-aisled houses continued to be used in all the other geo-ecological zones. The wall-ditch house is seen as a reaction to Roman taxes that had to be paid in hides (Therkorn 1987, 209). This could have led to an intensification of cattle breeding with outdoor stalling. This appears plausible, because these structures do not seem to have been a mode of housing after the first century AD. Another possible explanation for the wall-ditch houses is that they are a local adaptation to the progressively wetter environmental conditions. The houses could have been seasonally occupied by the persons who looked after the cattle grazing in the former tidal area. But in winter, people returned to the three-aisled houses, where the cattle were stalled indoors (Meffert 1998). However, the distance between the two types of houses does appear to be too small (a few hundred metres) for the need of seasonal housing and they have the same quality and range of finds as the three-aisled farmhouses, which suggests similar use.

Another indication that these houses should be connected to a Roman influence is that in Uitgeesterbroekpolder-54 a sod/turf wall house (Figure 8.2) contained some Roman imports and possibly produced hemp, a plant which in the Netherlands is only known in Roman contexts (Therkorn *et al.* 1986). The inhabitants, however, were locals, as there were no other Roman artefacts and this house is seen as the only one in the region with signs of acculturation (Therkorn *et al.* 1986).

To summarize, a small region in the area underwent some change in the construction, orientation and appearance of the houses, the way livestock was stalled, and therefore the view of the landscape. The other parts of the Oer-IJ remained the same, showing no clear signs of Roman influence beyond some picked-up sherds. Changes concentrated in the newly inhabited area with the wall-ditch houses, perhaps thereby neutralizing the Roman influence away from the traditional settlements. By the end of the first century, when the Romans had departed, this new type of house disappeared again and the inhabitants returned to building only three-aisled farms. With the Romans gone, the need for this specific type of building seems to diminish, as the emphasis on cattle-breeding for taxes was no longer necessary.

Offering sites

This lack of first century Roman material culture in the major parts of the Oer-IJ in the first century AD would have remained unchanged if excavation of a different type of context had not taken place in the last few years. Different excavation strategies were employed, so that not only the settlements, but also the surrounding areas and lower-lying wet areas were excavated. This has led to the discovery of two offering sites (Velserbroek B6 and Broekpolder), a phenomenon unrecognised before in the western Netherlands. And it led to the re-consideration of a possible third offering site (Dorregeest) that had always been viewed as a rubbish dump (de Koning 2002). The sites are not yet published in full, but this is expected within a few years.

I will now focus on one of these sites: Heemskerk-Broekpolder, where a large area of 12 hectares was excavated, containing all kinds of archaeological features and giving a general insight into the region from the Bronze Age onwards (Therkorn *et al.* forthcoming; Offenberg 2003). I will concentrate on two areas. The first is characterized by house plans and associated features dating to the 1st-3rd centuries AD. The other is a low-lying, watery place with deposits which were primarily made in the 6th/7th century AD. These excavated areas were 250 m apart and separated by an archaeological monument (AMK 9209). It consists of an area in which archaeological traces from the Bronze Age to the Medieval Period are expected and which is preserved for future generations.

The settlement

The settlement consisted of at least six three-aisled farmhouses that were not contemporary. These farmhouses were built in an area of about 7000m². In connection to the houses, a number of gullies filled with mainly pottery were recovered, but the layout of the individual farmyards could not be fully established due to many inter-cutting features. The remains of fields were indicated by gullies with few artefacts. A number of pits with special deposits, such as small animals, pots, bones and wood, lay within the settlement area. The settlement lies on the same bank as the Roman harbour, less than 5km to the south. The amount of Roman imports does not exceed 0.5 percent of the total of artefacts. It is a typical settlement for the Oer-IJ area with no traces of Roman influence (Kok forthcoming).

The offering site

The offering site consisted of a small freshwater pool at the outlet of a creek which ran through the major former tidal ridge, on which the settlement was also situated, towards the Oer-IJ channel depression in the east. A low-lying area of over 9000m² has been excavated. The deposits date to the first century AD, but the main body of artefacts was deposited during the 6-7th century AD. Along the edge of the water, shallow access channels were dug and redug. Furthermore, separate rows of stakes were placed in the water. They all have a somewhat similar orientation towards the southeast. Deposits of a range of artefacts made from stone, wood, bone, pottery and metal were made. The most distinctive feature of the site was the deposition of unworked stone and iron nails in several clusters. Worked wood and branches are found in the entire wet area. Although some of the wood may have drifted in to the pool naturally, the diversity (26 species), combination and positioning point towards intentional deposition. For example, although they are distributed throughout the offering site, all six pieces of cornel (*cornus*) are found in combination with birch (*betula*). Several single human bones have also been deposited. A concentration of bones of a small infant (3-7 months) gives the earliest C-14 date of the offering site in the first or second century (KIA14282 2σ: 68-164 AD). An unusually large amount of Roman artefacts were deposited in the pool, such as fibulae, coins, pottery and roof tiles, thereby setting it apart from the typical settlement evidence in the Oer-IJ area. Considering the placement and chronology of deposits (Therkorn et al. forthcoming), it becomes evident that most of the Roman finds were deposited during the 6th/7th century.

Comparison of deposits

The excavated parts of the settlement and the offering site are of fairly similar size, which makes comparison between the two areas a reasonable enterprise. Both sites are the result of long-term use. As a starting point, a general overview of the different finds categories is made in the different contexts of the settlement and the offering site (Figure 8.3). These contexts contain different kinds of features, but these are not taken into consideration here.

If we look at the sheer number of artefacts, there is a striking difference. The settlement context contains 13,249 artefacts and the offering site a mere third of that – 4,356. If we take into consideration that due to time-pressure and research choices not all the pottery from the gullies was collected in the settlement, it becomes clear that the settlement contained much more material culture then the offering site. This may sound a bit strange, as for us archaeologists the votive site is almost completely defined by artefacts instead of features, but it makes us aware that people actually engaged with more objects in the settlement. The inhabitants did not think of the offering site as an area with an overwhelming amount of objects,

especially because most of them disappeared into the pool and went out of sight. It was a place for the memories of the repeated depositions of artefacts at the place where a small creek joined the remnants of the Oer-IJ.

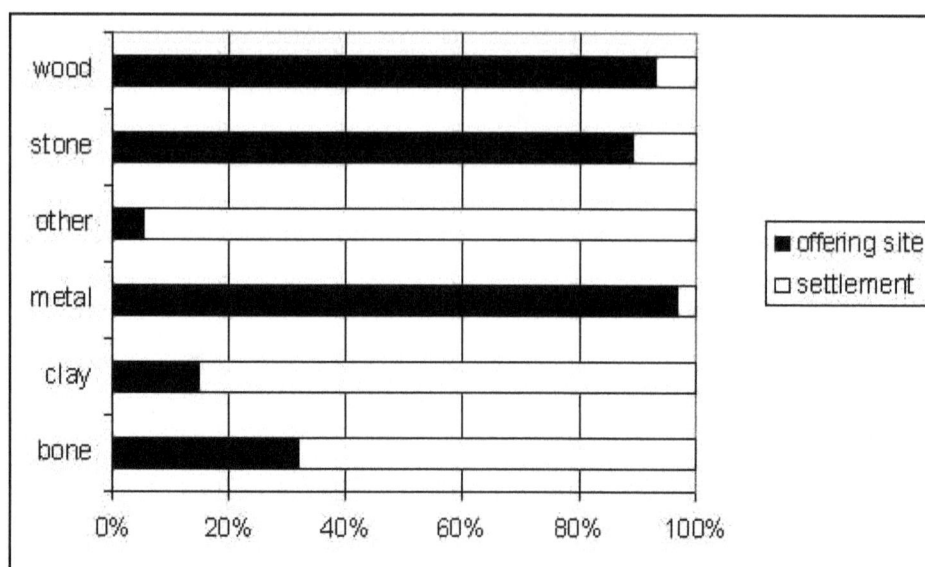

Figure 8.3. Distribution of the different artefact categories in relation to their context. The artefact category 'other' mainly comprises cinders.

If we separate the artefacts from the offering site and the settlement into categories of material, it becomes clear that not only does the amount of artefacts differ, but also their distribution. The settlement has more bone, clay/pottery and slag/cinders. The offering site contains more wood, stone and metal artefacts. In addition, the different categories are also not evenly distributed within the different contexts. If we look at the kind of clay objects, it becomes clear that all spindle whorls, loom weights and oven material of local production come from the settlement. In contrast, all but four fragments of the 39 bricks and 35 roof tiles with a Roman background occur at the offering site. And when we look at the Roman pottery, 140 sherds are found at the offering site, compared to only 22 in the settlement. This may look like a small difference, but if we take the amount of sherds into consideration, the pattern becomes clearer. 7.5 percent of the pottery at the offering site is Roman, while it is only 0.2 percent in the settlement. Your chances of finding a Roman sherd are 37 times greater at the votive site than in the settlement. If we look at other settlements in the area, the same picture emerges, with less than a half percent of the pottery having a Roman origin. The lack of (near) complete Roman pottery at these sites places the Roman sherds within the pick-up theory.

The over-representation of Roman objects becomes even clearer when we look at metal objects. 97% of the metal was found at the offering site. A third of it consisted of nails of a probably local origin. Looking at other artefact types, five of the six coins and 27 of the 28 fibula of Roman origin are found at the offering site. Furthermore, there are some small pins and fittings of Roman origin at the offering site.

The native inhabitants' selection of artefacts

The real question is: what do these figures mean? Why does the amount of Roman imports differ so markedly at the offering sites compared to other contexts, and why were they deposited so late - after the fall of the Roman Empire, and centuries after the Roman presence in the area ceased. I have not described the other two sites (Velserbroek B6 and Dorregeest), but they also have an over-representation of Roman imports, albeit of a slightly different kind.

There is a tendency to date indigenous sites with Roman material to the Roman period. However, Roman sherds also appear in later contexts, even as late as the Medieval period. Bradley (2002, 53) has pointed out that the use of the chronology of a certain type of artefact can be problematic when dating deposits. We have to be aware that a deposit could be reopened and new material added and/or that the assemblage could be made up of material of different ages. These are not just theoretical possibilities, there are many examples of the use of old artefacts in new contexts. This phenomenon of Roman sherds appearing in younger contexts is quite widespread north of the Roman border. Vons and Bosman (1988) established fairly early on for the Oer-IJ area that Roman sherds appear in Medieval settlements. This has not led to the expected questioning of the validity of dating native settlements with Roman imports. However, on sites where the contexts in which the artefacts are found can be dated more accurately, it has become clear that Roman sherds often appear in younger contexts. Examples of this can be found in Schagen (Diederik 1982) and Wijnaldum (Volkers 1999). A one-to-one relation between Roman objects and direct contact with Romans can therefore be seen as flawed. It rather appears to be the case that at the time of the Roman presence, the local inhabitants purposefully avoided Roman artefacts. There are no signs whatsoever of any interest in acquiring these new goods. The admiration many modern archaeologists have for Roman objects can certainly not be projected back to the period of contact in the Oer-IJ. Although they were in sight of one another, contact must have been limited to the absolutely essential. The local inhabitants did not associate themselves with the Roman identity through the use of their material culture. In the local inhabitants' everyday practices, the Romans were silenced. Only after the Romans departed was their material culture gradually seen in a manner disconnected from their direct conquest. Connotations of Roman overbearance, taxation, domination and land appropriation could be left unconsidered. They had become a thing of the past; and their things of the past could become new artefacts and could acquire new meanings. Hence a reworking of their old meanings by the local inhabitants took place. These meanings had more to do with opening up the local landscape to foreign contact in a more general sense.

In addition, not just any Roman artefact was deposited at the offering site at the Broekpolder. We must assume that a selection had taken place in the type of Roman objects that were available in the vicinity. Fragmented pottery and brick/tiles were preferred to military objects. This becomes clear when we look at the other two possible offering sites (Velserbroek B6 and Dorregeest) in the area. They both contain military objects like spear points and helmet parts, something lacking from the Broekpolder. The content differs between the offering sites, although they would have had roughly equal access to the same material culture. At the Roman fort itself, there were military objects left, which could have been taken. Furthermore, wooden objects like tent pegs are not taken from the fort, although wood, in the form of branches and sticks, is over-represented in the deposits.

Lastly, the pick-up theory indicates that the local inhabitants did not have complete pottery objects in the first century, but evidently valued the sherds enough to take them along. This could be due to the material qualities of the sherds instead of their use-qualities. Appearance seems to be more important than functionality. The Roman objects deposited were probably never used in a purely utilitarian way as, for example, either pots or roofs. As shown above, the connotations of the Romans as conquerors may have diminished over time. It may seem a bit strange, but in the Oer-IJ estuary hard objects do not naturally occur and even the pottery is of a relatively soft quality. Metal and stone had to be imported. If we look at the different artefacts at the offering site, it becomes obvious that just as imported artefacts are over-represented, these so are hard objects and local wood. This is especially clear with the 399 stones that all had to be brought from at least 50 kilometres distance. The predominantly grey and white stones seem to be complemented by the fragments of red Roman bricks and roof tiles. Gerritsen (2000) argued for the importance of colour in the selection of artefacts for depositions in the Oer-IJ area. For example, in the southern part of the

Broekpolder (700metres south of the offering sites), the combination of a red/brownish and a yellow/whitish sherd are found several times (Gerritsen 2000). Their major qualities can therefore be described as hard, red and foreign instead of just Roman. This possible preference for terra sigillata sherds because of their colour and sheen has also been noticed by Volkers (1999). This may suggest a magic/religious connotation similar to amulets.

The material quality of objects seems to be a major influence when offerings are chosen in the Broekpolder. This becomes especially clear because large parts of the offering site are formed after the first century AD. At this time, complete Roman objects appear in the Oer-IJ area, but not in the offering site. It was not the Roman objects in themselves that the locals were interested in. There seems to be a preference for hard foreign objects, like stone, pottery and tiles, and local wood.

Conclusion

To conclude, it seems that the relatively large amount of Roman imports at the offering site of the Broekpolder does not reflect the appropriation of Roman ideas. Local inhabitants chose objects that had specific qualities which were both absent and present in their natural environment. A new place was created and represented by many local objects in the form of pieces of wood complemented by foreign hard objects. In this way, qualities of the local and the foreign were combined. This indicates that the people of the Oer-IJ saw themselves not just as a group turned inward in the way that they are portrayed by modern researchers. We have to reconsider the meaning of the Oer-IJ area as a separate cultural unit when we realise that the offering site in the Broekpolder seems to adhere to a worldview in which the local inhabitants place themselves within the context of both local and foreign elements, deposited near what was once the main line of communication, the Oer-IJ.

Acknowledgements

This paper is part of my PhD thesis which is funded by the Netherlands Organisation for Scientific Research and the University of Amsterdam. I thank Linda Therkorn for her comments and Erik van Rossenberg for discussions. Figure 8.2 drawn by Line Kramer. All errors are mine.

References

Bosman, A.V.A.J. 1997. *Het culturele vondstmateriaal van de vroeg-Romeinse versterking Velsen 1.* Unpublished PhD Thesis. University of Amsterdam.

Bradley, R. 2002. *The past in prehistoric societies.* London: Routledge.

Brandt, R.W. 1983. A brief encounter along the Northern frontier. In R.W. Brandt and J. Slofstra (eds), *Roman and native in the Low Countries*, 129-45. Oxford: BAR.

Diederik, F. 1982. Molenweg, Waldervaart. Een vroeg-middeleeuwse nederzetting the Schagen. *Westerheem* 31, 53-68.

Gerritsen, S. 2000. *De archeologische context van Romeins importmateriaal, een aanzet tot patroon-analyse in Noord-Holland.* Unpublished MA Thesis. University of Amsterdam.

Jelgersma, S.J., de Jong, J., Zagwijn, W.H. and van Regteren Altena, J.F. 1970. The coastal dunes in the Western Netherlands; Geology, vegetational history and archaeology. *Mededelingen Rijks Geologische Dienst, Nieuwe Serie* 21, 93-167.

Heeringen, R.M. van. 1992. *The Iron Age in the Western Netherlands.* Amersfoort: ROB.

Kok, M.S.M. forthcoming. *The homecoming of religious practice.* Unpublished PhD Thesis. University of Amsterdam.

Koning, J. de 2002. Why did they leave? Why did they stay? On continuity versus discontinuity from Roman times to the Early Middle Ages in the western coastal area of the Netherlands. In T. Grünewald and S. Seibel (eds.), *Kontinuität und Diskontinuität: Germania inferior am Beginn und am Ende der römischen Herrschaft, 53-82.* Berlin: Walter de Gruyter.

Meffert, M. 1998. *Ruimtelijke relaties in het Oer-IJ estuarium in de Romeinse ijzertijd met nadruk op de Assendelver polders.* Unpublished PhD Thesis. University of Amsterdam.

Offenberg, G.A.M. 2003. *Broekpolder: Een archeologisch monument op een VINEX-locatie.* Haarlem: Provincie Noord-Holland.

Therkorn, L.L. 1987. The structures, mechanics and some aspects of inhabitants' behaviour. In R.W. Brandt, W. Groenman-van Waateringe and S.E. van der Leeuw (eds), *Assendelver Polder Papers 1,* 177-224. Amsterdam: University of Amsterdam Press.

Therkorn, L.L. 2004. *Landscaping the powers of darkness & light. 600 BC-350 AD settlement concerns of Noord-Holland in wider perspective.* Unpublished PhD Thesis. University of Amsterdam.

Therkorn, L.L., Diepeveen-Jansen, M., Gerritsen, S., Kaarsemaker, J., Kok, M.S.M., Kubiak-Martens, L., Slopsma, J. and Vos, P. forthcoming. *Landscapes in the Broekpolder: excavations around a monument with aspects of the Bronze Age to the Modern.* Amsterdam.

Therkorn, L.L., van Rijn, P. And Verhagen, M. 1986. Uitgeest. *Holland* 18, 284-88.

Volkers, T.B. 1999. The terra sigillata from Wijnaldum-Tjitsma in regional perspective. In: J.C. Besteman, J.M. Bos, D.A. Gerrets, H.A. Heidinga and J. de Koning (eds), *The excavation at Wijnaldum: reports on Frisia in Roman and Medieval times,* 151-56. Rotterdam: A.A. Balkema.

Vons, P. and Bosman, A.V.A.J. 1988. Inheemse boeren bezochten de verlaten Romeinse versterkingen Velsen I en II. *Westerheem* 37 (1), 1-16.

Vos, P. and Soonius, C. 2004. Oude landschappen. In S. Lange, E.A. Besselsen and H. van Londen (eds), *Het Oer-IJ estuarium: Archeologische KennisInventarisatie (AKI),* 30-40. Amsterdam: AAC-projectenbureau.

War and domestic peace in the Bronze Age and Early Iron Age of Abruzzo (Central Italy).
Social reproduction and cultural landscapes as a starting-point for the construction of *mentalités*

Erik van Rossenberg

Abstract

This paper starts from the notion that social reproduction entails the construction of identities on several levels, which can be studied archaeologically through the material conditions provided by the interrelationships between places within cultural landscapes. In the Bronze Age cultural landscape of the Abruzzo region (Central Italy), the tensions between layers of social life were reconciled through movements between permanent sites of ritualized practice and periodically shifting sites of routine practice. The fact that ritualisation in the Early Bronze Age predominantly referred to the routines of everyday life and included collective burial practices suggests a *mentalité* rooted in the social reproduction of households and local communities. In the Middle Bronze Age, another ritualized field of practice related to martiality and wider social interaction was introduced into ritual praxis. Until the Final Bronze Age, the latter sites of ritualized practice were kept apart in the cultural landscape from the ones related to domesticity, and thus may have referred to a layer of social life beyond the local community. The generally accepted idea of social transformation through increased individuality in the Final Bronze Age and Early Iron Age does not stand up to close scrutiny of the funerary evidence. Although seemingly related to individuals and part of a changing set of material conditions, these funerary contexts were still tied in with the construction of collective identities. In the selection of objects we can recognize the Early Iron Age burial as a locale which incorporated the movements of the Bronze Age cultural landscape into a microcosm. As such, it became a site of conflicting interest in itself and a site of reproduction for a new *mentalité*.

Introduction: cultural landscapes, material conditions and social reproduction

In the course of the history of archaeological thought, the culture concept has gradually lost prominence to the notion of landscape. As discursive objects, archaeological cultures and landscapes share a high degree of abstraction and as such provide a framework for archaeological synthesis. Nowadays, relational approaches to archaeological landscapes situate cultural practices at particular places within cultural landscapes (*cf.* Thomas 2001). Moreover, archaeological applications of praxis theory have suggested that places should be regarded as locales within social networks. Situating cultural practices, locales provide the material conditions for the reproduction of social identities. Following the archaeological project outlined by Barrett (2001, 158-161), our understanding of transformation has to be situated in the reconstruction of 'material structural conditions'. Transformation is not so much situated in the place itself, as in the material conditions which constitute it as a locale. This theoretical and methodological stance has the potential to rephrase the genre of archaeological synthesis: from rather abstract narratives, aimed at closure, into open-ended narratives which explore the structuring principles of material conditions.

The emphasis on material conditions opens up the possibility to make a methodological connection with *Annaliste* approaches or structural history. In archaeological *Annaliste* approaches, the emphasis normally lies on the tripartite model of Braudelian timescales (*cf.* Bintliff 1991), bracketing off the history of events from structural history. Traditionally, the archaeological record is thought to be most suitable for the study of the latter, i.e. questions of social and cultural change in the long- and medium-term, but with the adoption of praxis theory attention has been redirected to the short-term (e.g. Foxhall 2000). Although archaeologists tend to conceptualize archaeological evidence as a record which keeps track of transformation in the long- and medium-term, it rather represents instances of reproducing material conditions (*cf.* Barrett 2001). Nonetheless, the idea that the creation of the archaeological record was punctuated and often most pronounced in terms of modifications when there was a change in the use of particular places (Olivier 2001, 191) suggests that archaeological evidence, although short-term in nature, may still be taken to represent significant changes in the medium- and long-term. In its multi-scalar properties, archaeological evidence seems to show congruity with the interconnected timescales of structural history. This leaves us with the challenge of exploring the structural properties of the archaeological record in the context of a multi-scalar approach to the reproduction of material conditions (*cf.* Olivier 1999).

The cross-over between praxis theory and *Annaliste* approaches highlights the structuring principles of material conditions for social reproduction. Material conditions were inhabited by particular fields of social practice (Barrett 2001, 158) and as such constituted the locales for the reproduction of social identities on several levels. Analytically, one could distinguish between fields "which were often reproduced through routine practice and those fields which were more formally and discursively organized" (*ibid.*) through ritualized practice. Practically, however, this distinction should not be taken at face-value as a binary opposition between ritual and non-ritual places. Routine practices normally associated with sites of routine practice could be incorporated as ritualized practices at sites of ritualized practice, and ritualized practices could be incorporated at sites of routine practice. Social reproduction was situated in the interrelationships between places within cultural landscapes, which constituted the material conditions inhabited by lifeworlds or *mentalités*. Starting from an archaeological perspective that regards places as sites of social reproduction within cultural landscapes, the construction of collective identities, such as households and communities, can be studied in relation to particular locales and fields of practice. This makes changes in material conditions, situated in the interrelationships between settlement, funerary and other ritual contexts, a good starting-point for the study of transformation in the materiality of social reproduction and *mentalités* (Van Rossenberg, in prep.).

Structural properties of the archaeological record: routine and ritualized practices

Taking up the challenge of exploring the structural properties of archaeological evidence in the context of a multi-scalar approach to the reproduction of material conditions, one can go beyond the general statement that the archaeological record is fragmentary. In terms of the structure of the archaeological record, it seems that culturally specific practices result in specific structural properties of archaeological evidence. Following the analytical distinction between routine and ritualized fields of practice, routine and ritualized practices can be recognized archaeologically. Both these types of practice leave distinctive traces in the archaeological record, but there seems to be a paradox in this relationship. Generally, routine practices will have occurred most frequently and at the same location, which makes it harder for archaeologists to recognize these in any detail (*cf.* Smith 1992, 29-31); on the other hand, ritualized practices can often be recognized in far more detail in the archaeological record, because these occurred less frequently and often in the form of structured depositions at specific places. However, this analytical distinction in terms of practices should not be stretched so far as to distinguish between sites of routine practice and sites of ritualized practice. In fact, recognizing acts of structured deposition at sites of predominantly routine practice has become accepted as an interpretive strategy within archaeology (Bradley 2003).

The fact that acts of structured deposition are archaeologically highly visible leaves us with the impression that the archaeological record is punctuated rather than continuous (*cf.* Olivier 2001). Moreover, there seems to exist congruity between the structural properties of archaeological evidence and the punctuated character of social life. The lifecycles of people, households and local communities have a material counterpart in the use of settlements, cemeteries and cult places. Acts of structured deposition – in the lifecycle of houses, in the act of burial or other events within ritual praxis – are recursively related to the rhythms of social life (*cf.* Foxhall 2000) and seem to mark events in social reproduction. In these fragments of detailed archaeological evidence one can recognize instances of reproducing material conditions. It is tempting to regard these punctuated properties of archaeological evidence as the locus of transformation. However, transformation of material conditions is not instantaneous; it is dictated by the rate of social reproduction. Social and cultural change is archaeologically punctuated in the sense

that, for instance, one had to wait for someone to die before one could adopt a new kind of burial practice – or even longer if burial was selective and only open to people with a particular social status, or one was dependent on the periodicity of wider social interaction to acquire a copy of a new non-local class of object before one could introduce it in funerary or other ritual practices. In the end, transformation of material conditions is a long-term process and thus archaeologically visible.

Transformation in the materiality of social reproduction can be recognized as changes in interrelationships between places within cultural landscapes, which correlate with changes in the structure of the archaeological record. In a very generalizing manner, the Bronze Age-Iron Age transition in Central Italy can be characterized by two significant changes in both material conditions and specific structural properties of archaeological evidence (*cf.* Guidi 1992). On the one hand, funerary practices changed from selective and collective to non-selective and individual; on the other, modes of settlement changed from periodically shifting villages or single houses, changing place every one or several generations, to more permanent villages or even larger settlements, lasting at least several generations. Apart from differences in the structure of archaeological evidence, this suggests significant differences in the material conditions of social reproduction. Whereas in the case of selective burial – as far as funerary practices are archaeologically visible – particular people were singled out and came to represent a larger social group in the production of a collective identity; in the case of non-selective burial everyone seems to have been buried, often individually, which gave rise to larger cemeteries in which collective identities could be reproduced on several levels simultaneously. In correlation, the greater permanency and increasing size of settlements would have changed the focus in social reproduction on a day-to-day basis from the collective identity of the household to the collective identity of the local community. Such changes in material conditions can often be related to the reorganization of cultural landscapes, abandoning particular types of place and creating new ones. In the following case-study of the Abruzzo region in Central Italy, an attempt will be made to situate fields of practice in the interrelationships between places within cultural landscapes, in order to define places in terms of scales of interaction within social networks, thus situating the materiality of social reproduction in these interrelationship.

Case-study: social reproduction and cultural landscapes in the Bronze Age and Early Iron Age of the Abruzzo region (Central Italy)

The case-study of the Bronze Age and Early Iron Age in the Central Italian Abruzzo region (Figure 9.1) starts from a contextual analysis of depositional practices involving metal objects (Table 9.1). Initially, this places the emphasis on ritualized fields of practice and the question of selective deposition, i.e. to what extent depositional practices were related exclusively to particular contexts (*cf.* Fontijn 2001/2002). The fact that metal objects are generally regarded as 'special' finds and described in contextual detail opens up the possibility to extend the contextual analysis to interrelationships between ritualized and

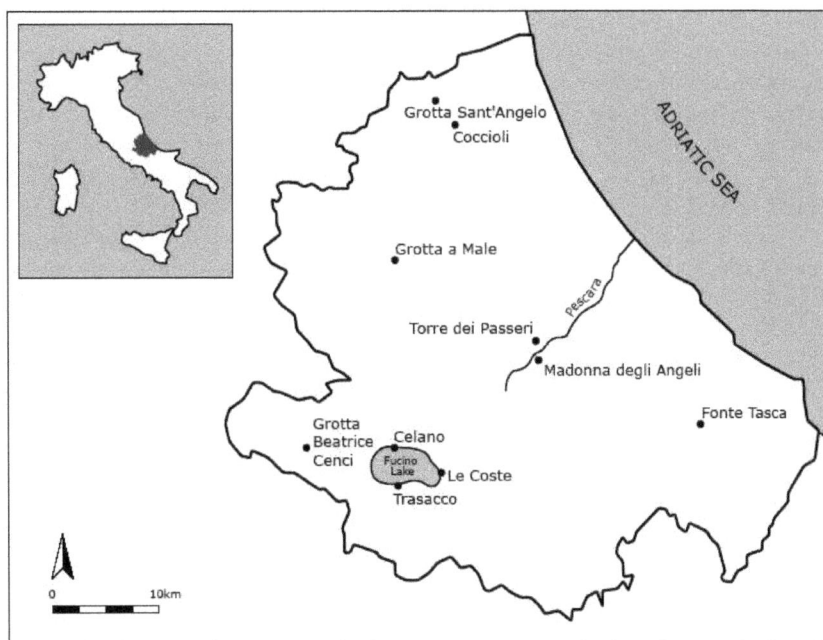

Figure 9.1. Map of the Abruzzo region (Central Italy), showing Bronze Age sites mentioned in the text (drawing by D.E. Smal).

Abruzzo	Early Bronze Age	Middle Bronze Age	Late Bronze Age	Final Bronze Age	Early Iron Age
sickle				wetland	?
axe	hoard wetland	wetland (cave)	wetland	hoard wetland	hoard
sword		wetland	wetland	wetland	wetland
					burial
spearhead			?	wetland	burial
dagger	hoard wetland	wetland (cave)	?		
	burial	settlement			
knife			wetland	settlement	burial
razor			?	burial	burial
fibula			wetland	settlement	settlement
				burial	burial
				hoard	
dress-pin			settlement	settlement	burial
					(settlement)

Table 9.1. Contextual analysis of depositional practices involving metalwork in the Bronze Age and Early Iron Age of Abruzzo.

79

routine fields of practice (*cf.* Van Rossenberg 2003). Moreover, the ways in which local communities dealt with non-local objects – such as classes of metal objects at the time of their introduction in the region – can shed light on material conditions related to wider social interaction.

Early Bronze Age (*c.* 2200-1700 BC)

Archaeological evidence for the Early Bronze Age in the Abruzzo is limited (Cocchi Genick 1998) and slightly biased towards ritualized practices. A small number of 'multiple' hoards, consisting of several daggers or axes, and a higher number of 'isolated', single depositions of daggers and axes are known (Bietti Sestieri and Giardino 2003). Wetland is the preferred context of deposition (rivers, lakes, bogs); only a small number of daggers have been found in individual inhumation burials. The multiple hoards are interpreted as acts of marking territorial boundaries (Cocchi Genick 1998, 348), for instance in the context of the Pescara river, and are thus implicated in social reproduction on the level of a wider community. On the other hand, the rare and isolated individual burials and the more frequent single depositions of metalwork seem to be related to the social reproduction of local communities. Ritualized practices in caves referred to routine practices in domestic contexts, in the form of acts of deposition involving complete ceramic vessels and foodstuffs (Miari 1995). As in the preceding periods, this field of practice was connected with – selective, collective and predominantly secondary – funerary practices (e.g. *Grotta Sant'Angelo*, Di Fraia and Grifoni Cremonesi 1996). Because ritualized practices were connected with natural places (caves and wetland), the social reproduction of collective identities entailed movements within the cultural landscape between settlements – periodically shifting sites of routine practice – and permanent sites of ritual practice. The fact that depositional practices involving metalwork were not incorporated in the ritualized field of practice in caves, existing since the Neolithic, suggests that a new locale had emerged for the construction of collective identities in wetland contexts. In general, the Early Bronze Age *mentalité* was rooted in the social reproduction of households and local communities.

Middle Bronze Age (*c.* 1700-1350 BC)

Archaeological evidence for the Middle Bronze Age is more balanced, in the sense that houses are known and the interrelationships between sites of routine practice and sites of ritual practice can be assessed in more detail. Depositional practices involving metalwork still had a preference for wetland contexts, but no longer in the form of multiple depositions. Hoards – in terms of rarity and context of deposition – were replaced by the sword, known from acts of deposition in the Pescara river and the Fucino Lake basin. It is not surprising that the swords, as newly introduced objects of non-local origin, became situated in the previously created locale constituted by wetland depositions of metalwork. Through selective deposition, they would have been given their proper place within the cultural landscape of the Middle Bronze Age, resolving the ambiguity of both the social status of their owner in the context of an elitist warrior ideology and social interaction beyond the local community (*cf.* Fontijn 2001/2002, 221-

37). Axes and daggers, on the other hand, were more evenly distributed throughout the region, seem to have been produced locally, and were sporadically involved in acts of deposition in the context of settlements and caves (Bietti Sestieri and Giardino 2003, 415-18). These objects became incorporated in the ritualized field of practice that had previously been restricted to caves, but was extended in this period. Acts of deposition involving complete ceramic vessels and foodstuffs have not only been found in caves (Miari 1995), but also in the context of settlements (e.g. *Le Coste*, Radi 1995). The range of objects in assemblages from caves was extended to include other objects with a domestic connotation, such as quernstones and spindlewhorls (Table 9.2). Similarities in composition can be found in the assemblages from structure B in the settlement at *Torre dei Passeri* (Recchia 2003) and the caves of *Grotta Sant'Angelo* (Di Fraia and Grifoni Cremonesi 1996), *Grotta a Male* (Pannuti 1969) and *Grotta Beatrice Cenci* (Agostini *et al.* 1991) in particular. Explicitly domestic symbolism in ritual praxis is represented by miniature vessels (Table 9.2), spindlewhorls made from human and animal bones (*Grotta a Male* and *Trasacco 1*), and disarticulated human remains (*Torre dei Passeri, Grotta Sant'Angelo, Grotta a Male* and *Grotta Beatrice Cenci*). To sum up, the Middle Bronze Age *mentalité* remained rooted in the social reproduction of households and local communities, but another ritualized field of practice, related to martiality and wider social interaction, had found its place within the region. This coincided with the extension of the ritualized field of practice related to domesticity from caves to settlement contexts, and the elaboration of domestic ritualized practices. Thus, the materiality of social reproduction still entailed movement between periodically shifting sites of routine practice and permanent sites of ritual practice at natural places, but the fact that the ritualized fields of practice related to domesticity and martiality were kept apart within the cultural landscape suggests that distinct collective identities were reproduced in the respective locales.

Late Bronze Age (*c.* 1350-1200 BC)

Archaeological evidence for the Late Bronze Age is limited (Di Fraia 2004), which makes it difficult to assess the interrelationships between sites of routine practice and sites of ritual practice. Both the scarcity of funerary evidence and the decline in the use of caves suggest that the ritualized field of practice related to domesticity became less pronounced. The ritualized field of practice involving depositions of metalwork still had a preference for wetland contexts; again, these were the proper place within the cultural landscape for the introduction of new classes of objects such as knives and fibulae (Table 9.1). The Fucino Lake basin in particular was not only a central place for local production of metalwork (Peroni 1961), but also for its ritual consumption. Although the Fucino bronzes (knives, fibulae, swords) have been interpreted as grave goods in association with the rare occurrence of (disarticulated) human remains, they seem to have been more generally related to ritual praxis. Some of the knives show traces of fire, which could be related specifically to a burial practice involving cremation, but also more generally to the ritual use of fire. The fibulae are

site	structure	pottery	other ceramics	flint	stone	bone/ antler	other
Torre dei Passeri (PE)	settlement (structure A)	fragments, miniature vessels	spindle-whorls, loom-weight	artefacts		awl	tuyère
Torre dei Passeri (PE)	settlement (structure B)	fragments, miniature vessels	spindle-whorls	arrow-heads	'hammer-stone', pendant	awl, plaque (boar tusk)	human remains, tuyères
Madonna degli Angeli (PE)	settlement	fragments	cooking-stands		quern-stones		
Grotta Sant'Angelo (TE)	cave	fragments, miniature vessels	spindle-whorls	artefacts	quern-stone		human remains
Coccioli (TE)	settlement	fragments, miniature vessels	spindle-whorls	arrow-head, artefacts	quern-stones	awls	bronze dagger, fragment of mould (axe), smelting remains
Casale di Fossa (AQ)	settlement	fragments, miniature vessels	cooking-stands, spindle-whorls & spool	arrow-head, artefact	small axe		
Grotta a Male (AQ)	cave with burials and a sequence of hearths	fragments, complete smaller vessels	spindle-whorls		quern-stones, whet-stones, pendant	awl, spindle-whorl (human bone)	human remains, bronze dagger and arrow-heads?, mould (axe), smelting remains
Grotta Beatrice Cenci (AQ)	cave	fragments	cooking-stands, spindle-whorls		quern-stone, whet-stones	(wool) comb	human remains
Trasacco 1 (AQ)	settlement (lakeside)	fragments, miniature vessels, complete vessels?	spindle-whorls, spoons, perforated disks	arrow-head, artefact		awl, arrow-head, spindle-whorls (animal bone)	

Table 9.2. Archaeological assemblages with most variation from settlements and caves in the Middle Bronze Age of Abruzzo. Abbreviations (PE=Pescara, TE=Teramo, AQ=L'Aquila) refer to provinces within the region. [Sources: Torre dei Passeri (Fratini 1997a), Madonna degli Angeli (Fratini 1997a), Grotta Sant'Angelo (Di Fraia and Grifoni Cremonesi 1996), Coccioli (D'Ercole and Pellegrini 1990), Casale di Fossa (Cosentino, D'Ercole and Mieli 2001), Grotta a Male (Pannuti 1969; Damiani *et al.* 2003), Grotta Beatrice Cenci (Agostini *et al.* 1991), Trasacco 1 (Radi 1986).]

unfinished objects of non-functional size and should therefore probably not be considered as grave goods. Finally, the sword is unknown as grave good in the Bronze Age of Abruzzo, with the exception of the only cremation burial known in the region (Nino 1892). In particular, it is striking that the large fibulae, as ostentatious objects, were introduced in the locale constituted by the deposition of swords, thereby highlighting the element of display in the ritualized field of practice related to martiality. On the other hand, the dress-pin found at the settlement of *Badia di Schiavi* (Di Fraia 2004) is the first act of structured deposition involving ornaments in the ritualized field of practice related to domesticity, which would be elaborated upon in the ensuing period. To sum up, the ritualized fields of practice related to domesticity and martiality were still kept apart within the cultural landscape. However, the decline in the use of caves in the Late Bronze Age suggests that changes took place in the movements between periodically shifting sites of routine practice and permanent sites of ritual practice at natural places, and that the material conditions for social reproduction were in a process of redefinition.

Final Bronze Age (*c.* 1200-950 BC)

Archaeological evidence for the Final Bronze Age is so balanced again that the interrelationships between sites of routine practice and sites of ritual practice can be assessed in more detail. Most significantly, caves were abandoned as locales for ritualized practice; their funerary function was taken over by individual inhumations under barrows (Cosentino, D'Ercole and Mieli 2003). Although burial was still selective and the outline of the barrows was marked with stones, there is not much evidence for display in the selection of grave goods, i.e. fibulae, needles and a wooden comb for women and razors for men (D'Ercole 2001; Cosentino, D'Ercole and Mieli 2003). It is striking that only razors were included in this field of practice, not weaponry, although both categories are normally associated in the supposedly European-wide warrior ideology (*cf.* Treherne 1995). This shows that the ritualized fields of practice related to martiality and domesticity were also kept apart at this new locale within the cultural landscape. In addition to swords, spearheads were included in depositional practices of weaponry in wetland contexts, which were also the proper place for the introduction of the sickle as a new class of metal object in the region. Acts of deposition of complete ceramic vessels and foodstuffs disappeared from caves, but were prominent elements in settlements at lake-sides (e.g. *Celano*, D'Ercole 1990) and other places around the Fucino Lake (Peroni 1961, 145).

In addition, ornaments were included in the ritualized field of practice related to domesticity: dress-pins are predominantly known from settlement contexts (*cf.* the Late Bronze Age one at *Badia di Schiavi*), for example the structured deposition of a dress-pin at the centre of a house at *Madonna degli Angeli* (Fratini 1997b). Moreover, hoards – consisting of fibulae and rings and to a lesser extent tweezers, dress-pins and wheel-shaped pendants – have been found at the lake-side settlement of *Trasacco* (Radi 1986) and near *Goriano Sicoli* at the source of a stream flowing into the Fucino Lake (Peroni 1961, 168-71). A similar range of ornaments was included in acts of deposition in settlement contexts, for instance shown by the assemblage from the settlement of *Fonte Tasca*, which apart from ornaments consisted of loomweights, quernstones, fragments of axes, several hundred spindle-whorls and disarticulated human remains (Di Fraia 1995). Compared with other settlements, which – in addition to the wide range of objects including ornaments – have yielded symbolic elements with a domestic connotation, such as miniature vessels and zoomorphic figurines, *Fonte Tasca* is unique in the sheer number of objects and the presence of human remains. The similarity of this particular assemblage with those from caves and settlements in the Middle Bronze Age (Table 9.2) suggests that settlements – in combination with individual burials under barrows (e.g. *Celano*) – took over the ritualized field of practice previously related to both caves and settlements. This seems to be related to the material condition that settlements became more permanent (*cf.* Bietti Sestieri 2001), i.e. with a life span of more than one or two generations. To sum up, the considerable changes in the material conditions for social reproduction in the Final Bronze Age are epitomized by the abandonment of caves. The demise of this significant locale entailed a reorganization in the cultural landscape with increasingly permanent sites of routine practice and the creation of a new locale for ritualized practice in the form of cemeteries. Nonetheless, the ritualized fields of practice related to domesticity and martiality were still kept apart.

Early Iron Age (*c.* 950-750 BC)

Archaeological evidence for the Early Iron Age is biased towards burials; hardly any detailed evidence is known from settlement contexts. This seems to be related to further reorganization within the cultural landscape, which is suggested by the fact that funerary contexts became the preferred depositional context of metalwork (Table 9.1). Hoards of bronze axes and a small number of swords, still placed within wetland contexts (Fratini 1997b), were the exceptions to this new regime of selective deposition. The ritualized field of practice related to martiality and the one related to domesticity were united in the context of cemeteries consisting of individual inhumation burials under barrows. There seems to have been an emphasis on display in the act of burial, given the ostentatious appearance of the people buried. A distinction can be made between, on the one hand, the idealized male identity of the warrior, with the paraphernalia of several items of weaponry and a razor, and on the other hand the idealized female identity, adorned with ornaments, among which decorated belts stand out (Cosentino, D'Ercole and Mieli 2001; 2003). Although gendered, the standardized and idealized character of these identities suggests that they did not reflect daily life, but were connected to special occasions. In this respect, these burials seem to have taken over the role of structured depositions of weaponry and hoards of ornaments respectively.

The cemeteries, which emerged throughout the region, are normally considered as territorial markers because of their inherent monumentality (D'Ercole 2000), but should also be regarded as a locale for ritualized fields of practice, related to both display and domesticity. The latter was expressed by acts of deposition of complete ceramic vessels and foodstuffs – previously related to wetland and settlement contexts – situated both within graves and in the vicinity of barrows (Cosentino, D'Ercole and Mieli 2001). The combination of ritualized fields of practice made these cemeteries a locale for the reproduction of social identities on several levels simultaneously, thus incorporating the movements within the Bronze Age cultural landscape into a microcosm. As such, the Early Iron Age burial became a site of conflicting interest in itself and a site of reproduction for a new *mentalité*. It constituted a new setting for the materiality of social reproduction, in combination with the material condition that settlements ceased to be appropriate places for ritualized practices, probably due to their greater permanence (*cf.* D'Ercole 2000; Bietti Sestieri 2001).

War and domestic peace: material conditions and *mentalités*

The trajectory of emerging social complexity in the course of later prehistory and protohistory in Central Italy is normally taken for granted (e.g. D'Ercole 2000; Bietti Sestieri 2001; 2003), so that the specific material conditions that constituted this process of social transformation are seldom studied in detail. The case-study of the Bronze Age and Early Iron Age in Abruzzo presented here is an attempt to analyze these historically specific conditions archaeologically, through the study of changes in the interrelationships between places within cultural landscapes. It has been argued that the ritualized fields of practice related to martiality and domesticity were kept apart within the Bronze Age cultural landscape, although changes did occur in the movements between periodically shifting sites of routine practice and permanent sites of ritual practice. This goes to show that transformation of material conditions is not instantaneous, but was in this case constituted by a series of changes that resulted in a significantly changed set of material conditions for social reproduction in the Early Iron Age.

It is tempting to link the ritualized field of practice related to domesticity with the social reproduction of households and local communities, and the ritualized field of practice related to martiality and display with the social reproduction of local communities in the context of wider social interaction. If one would accept this hypothesis, the combination of both these ritualized fields of practice in Early Iron Age cemeteries would make these a locale for the social reproduction of identities on several levels simultaneously. Here, the element of display involved in the deposition of metalwork became linked to the end of the lifecycle of people in the act of burial. In combination with the creation of more permanent settlements, this constituted the material conditions for the emergence of pronounced differences in social rank that had to be dealt with on a day-to-day basis, one of the key elements in social complexity. Unlike the Bronze Age situation, in which the social reproduction of collective identities was dispersed throughout the cultural landscape and intimate knowledge of the sites of ritual practice was probably restricted to a small group of people within the community, in the Early Iron Age spatial proximity between settlements and cemeteries allowed for first-hand knowledge among a wider group of people. This provided the material conditions for the creation of a new *mentalité* in which the focus was on social status of individuals and households rather than local communities. The standardized character of idealized male and female gender identities in the context of non-selective burial practices in the Early Iron Age (*cf.* Whitehouse 2001) shows, however, that ritualized practices at local cemeteries were still linked to social reproduction of collective identities on a regional scale. In the Abruzzo region, pronounced differences in social rank between individuals and households, i.e. élites, would emerge only later in the Iron Age, albeit in the locale provided by Early Iron Age cemeteries, some of which would remain in use for almost a thousand years (Cosentino, D'Ercole and Mieli 2003).

In due course, the historically and culturally specific character of this reconstruction of transformation in material conditions during the Bronze Age and Early Iron Age in the Abruzzo region will be assessed through a comparison with the course of structural history in the adjacent region of Lazio (*cf.* Van Rossenberg in press; in prep.).

Acknowledgements

First, I'd like to thank the organizers of the TAG session and editors of this volume for accepting my contribution on both occasions, and for their editorial efforts which have improved this paper considerably. Marjolijn Kok, Peter van Dommelen and David Fontijn are thanked for commenting on earlier versions of this paper; and my supervisors prof. J.L. Bintliff and prof. H. Fokkens (Leiden University) for their support and advice. All mistakes are my own. Finally, the research on which this publication has been based was funded partly by the Royal Dutch Institute at Rome, in the form of two scholarships (December 2002-January 2003 and June 2004).

References

Agostini, S., Coubray, S., De Grossi Mazzorin, J., D'Ercole, V. and Remotti, E. 1991. Cappadocia (L'Aquila). Località Oveto. Indagini preliminari nella Grotta Beatrice Cenci. *Bollettino di Archeologia* 8, 61-71.

Barrett, J.C. 2001. Agency, the duality of structure, and the problem of the archaeological record. In I. Hodder (ed.), *Archaeological theory today*, 141-64. Cambridge: Polity Press.

Bietti Sestieri, A.M. 2001. La tarda età del bronzo nell'area adriatica centrale. In G. Colonna (ed.), *Eroi e regine: Piceni popolo d'Europa*, 36-42. Roma: Edizioni De Luca.

Bietti Sestieri, A.M. 2003. L'età del bronzo in Abruzzo. In S. Cosentino (ed.), *Atti della XXXVI Riunione Scientifica. Preistoria e protostoria dell'Abruzzo. Chieti-Celano 27-30 settembre 2001*, 293-315. Firenze: Istituto Italiano di Preistoria e Protostoria.

Bietti Sestieri, A.M. and Giardino, C. 2003. Alcuni dati sull'industria metallurgica in Abruzzo. In S. Cosentino (ed.), *Atti della XXXVI Riunione Scientifica. Preistoria e protostoria dell'Abruzzo. Chieti-Celano 27-30 settembre 2001*, 411-30. Firenze: Istituto Italiano di Preistoria e Protostoria.

Bintliff, J. 1991. The contribution of an *Annaliste*/structural history approach to archaeology. In J. Bintliff (ed.), *The Annales School and archaeology*, 1-33. London: Leicester University Press.

Bradley, R. 2003. A life less ordinary: the ritualization of the domestic sphere in later prehistoric Europe. *Cambridge Archaeological Journal* 13(1), 5-23.

Cocchi Genick, D. 1998. *L'antica età del bronzo nell'Italia centrale. Profilo di un'epoca e di un'appropriata strategia metodologica*. Firenze: Octavo/Franco Cantini Editore.

Cosentino, S., D'Ercole, V. and Mieli, G. 2001. *La necropoli di Fossa. Volume I. Le testimonianze più antiche. Documenti dell'Abruzzo Antico*. Pescara: CARSA Edizioni.

Cosentino, S, D'Ercole, V. and Mieli, G. 2003. Costumi funerari in Abruzzo tra l'età del bronzo finale e la prima età del ferro. In *I Piceni e l'Italia medio-adriatica. Atti del XXII Convegno di Studi Etruschi ed Italici. Ascoli Piceno – Teramo – Ancona. 9-13 aprile 2000*, 423-50 Pisa-Roma: Istituti Editoriali e Poligrafici Internazionali.

Damiani, I., D'Ercole, V., Festuccia, S. and Remotti, E. 2003. Le nuove ricerche alla Grotta a Male di Assergi (AQ). In S. Cosentino (ed.), *Atti della XXXVI Riunione Scientifica. Preistoria e protostoria dell'Abruzzo. Chieti-Celano 27-30 settembre 2001*, 317-28. Firenze: Istituto Italiano di Preistoria e Protostoria.

D'Ercole, V. 1990. Celano (L'Aquila). Loc. Paludi. Insediamenti protostorici e villa romana. *Bollettino di Archeologia* 1-2, 225-28.

D'Ercole, V. 2000. I «paesaggi di potere» dell'Abruzzo protostorico. In G. Camassa, A. De Guio and F. Veronese (eds), *Paesaggi di potere: problemi e prospettive. Atti del Seminario Udine 16-17 maggio 1996*, 121-52. Roma: Edizioni Quasar.

D'Ercole, V. 2001. La necropoli delle Paludi di Celano nel Fucino. In G. Colonna (ed.), *Eroi e regine: Piceni popolo d'Europa*, 43-44. Roma: Edizioni De Luca.

D'Ercole, V. and Pellegrini, W. 1990. *Il Museo Archeologico di Campli*. Teramo: Soprintendenza Archeologica dell'Abruzzo-Comune di Campli.

Di Fraia, T. 1995. L'abitato dell'età del Bronzo Finale di Fonte Tasca (comune di Archi, Chieti). Studio preliminare su alcune classi di manufatti. *Origini* 19, 447-77.

Di Fraia, T. 2004. Badia di Schiavi e il Subappenninnico in Abruzzo: una riconsiderazione della facies. In D. Cocchi Genick (ed.), *L'età del bronzo recente in Italia. Atti del Congresso Nazionale di Lido di Camaiore, 26-29 ottobre 2000*, 475-80. Viareggio-Lucca: Mauro Baroni editore.

Di Fraia, T. and Grifoni Cremonesi, R. (eds) 1996. *La Grotta Sant'Angelo sulla Montagna dei Fiori (Teramo). Le testimonianze dal Neolitico all'Età del Bronzo e il problema delle frequentazioni cultuali in grotta. Collana di Studi Paletnologici 6*. Pisa-Roma: Istituti Editoriali e Poligrafici Internazionali.

Fontijn, D.R. 2001/2002 *Sacrificial landscapes. Cultural biographies of persons, objects and 'natural' places in the Bronze Age of the southern Netherlands, c. 2300-600 BC. Analecta Praehistorica Leidensia 33/34*. Leiden: Faculty of Archaeology, Leiden University.

Foxhall, L. 2000. The running sands of time: archaeology and the short-term. *World Archaeology* 31(3), 484-98.

Fratini, T. 1997a. *La protostoria nella Valle del Pescara. 1. Bronzo antico e Bronzo medio-recente. Museo delle Genti d'Abruzzo. Quaderno 24*. Pescara: Comune di Pescara-Archeoclub di Pescara-ASTRA.

Fratini, T. 1997b. *La protostoria nella Valle del Pescara. 2. Bronzo finale e prima età del ferro. Museo delle Genti d'Abruzzo. Quaderno 25*. Pescara: Comune di Pescara-Archeoclub di Pescara-ASTRA.

Guidi, A. 1992. Le età dei metalli nell'Italia centrale e in Sardegna. In A. Guidi and M. Piperno (eds), *Italia preistorica. Manuali Laterza 34*, 420-70. Roma/Bari: Laterza.

Miari, M. 1995. Offerte votive legate al mondo vegetale e animale nelle cavità naturali dell'Italia protostorica. In L. Quilici and S. Quilici Gigli (eds), *Agricoltura e commerci nell'Italia antica. Atlante tematico di tipografia antica. Supplemento 1*, 11-29. Roma: L'Erma di Bretschneider.

Nino, A.D. 1892. S. Benedetto in Perillis. *Notizie degli Scavi di Antichità*, 484-85.

Olivier, L. 1999. The Hochdorf 'princely' grave and the question of the nature of archaeological funerary assemblages. In T. Murray (ed.), *Time and archaeology. One World Archaeology 37*, 109-38. London: Routledge.

Olivier, L. 2001. Temps de l'histoire et temporalités des matériaux archéologiques: à propos de la nature chronologique des vestiges matériels. *Antiquités Nationales* 33, 189-201.

Pannuti, S. 1969. Gli scavi di Grotta a Male presso L'Aquila. *Bullettino di Paletnologia Italiana* 78 (N.S. 20), 147-247.

Peroni, R. 1961. Bronzi dal territorio del Fucino nei Musei Preistorici di Roma e Perugia. *Rivista di Scienze Preistoriche* 16, 125-205.

Radi, G. 1986. Le ricerche nel Fucino: notizie preliminari sull'insediamento di Trasacco. In G.L. Carancini (ed.), *Atti dell'incontro di Acquasparta 1985 "Gli insediamenti perilacustri dell'età del bronzo e della prima età del ferro: il caso dell'antico Lacus Velinus". Palazzo Cesi, 15-17 Novembre 1985. Quaderni di Protostoria 1*, 301-16. Perugia: Cattedra di Protostoria Europea, Istituto di Archeologia Università di Perugia.

Radi, G. 1995. Le Coste: stazioni dell'eneolitico e della media età del bronzo nel Fucino (Pescina, L'Aquila). *Origini* 19, 415-45.

Recchia, G. 2003. Una riconsiderazione sull'uso delle strutture protoappenniniche di Torre dei Passeri, Pescara. In S. Cosentino (ed.), *Atti della XXXVI Riunione Scientifica. Preistoria e protostoria dell'Abruzzo. Chieti-Celano 27-30 settembre 2001*, 329-42. Firenze: Istituto Italiano di Preistoria e Protostoria.

Smith, M.E. 1992. Braudel's temporal rhythms and chronology theory in archaeology. In A.B. Knapp (ed.), *Archaeology, Annales, and ethnohistory*, 23-34. Cambridge: Cambridge University Press.

Thomas, J. 2001. Archaeologies of place and landscape. In I. Hodder (ed.), *Archaeological theory today*, 165-86. Cambridge: Polity Press.

Treherne, P. 1995. The warrior's beauty: the masculine body and self-identity in Bronze-Age Europe. *Journal of European Archaeology* 3, 105-44.

Van Rossenberg, E. 2003. Embedding material culture in perceptions of landscape. A contextual analysis of the deposition of bronzes in Northern Italy. In A. Brysbaert, N. de Bruijn, E. Gibson, A. Michael and M. Monaghan (eds), *SOMA 2002. Symposium On Mediterranean Archaeology Proceedings of the Sixth Annual Meeting of Postgraduate Researchers. University of Glasgow, Department of Archaeology, 15-17 February, 2002, Glasgow*, 157-64. Oxford: BAR.

Van Rossenberg, E. (in press). Between households and communities. Layers of social life in the later Bronze Age and Early Iron Age of Central Italy. In *Proceedings of the 6th international Conference on Italian Archaeology, 15-17 April 2003 at Groningen University.*

Van Rossenberg, E. (in prep.). *Between households and communities. Layers of social life in the Bronze Age and Early Iron Age of Central Italy.* PhD thesis, Faculty of Archaeology, University Leiden.

Whitehouse, R.D. 2001. Exploring gender in prehistoric Italy. *Papers of the British School at Rome* 69, 49-96.

Identity and change: the inception of the Bell Beaker phenomenon in the central Mediterranean Sea area

Marc Vander Linden

Introduction

Since those good old days when archaeological cultures meant something, identity has been central to archaeological discourse. For the past twenty years or so it has become subject to enthralling and cruel debates in the struggle that opposes so-called processualist and post-processualist scholars. Likewise, the question of change has led to manifold pages and volumes written by archaeologists, specialists as we are of diachrony. However, it is far less easy to articulate both concepts in a single narrative. Obviously, traditions and identities are by nature processes and not given realities; yet, the effective constant 'negotiation' (following Wenger 1998) of these processes appears to be very difficult to describe and analyse, especially when coping with long time-spans and 'indirect traces in bad samples', as Clarke (1973, 6) once described the archaeological record.

If these statements might look like some kind of truism, they still remain crucial for archaeology and social sciences in general, as shown by recent evaluations of the internal contradictions of Bourdieu's sociology (see contributions in Lahire 2001a, especially Favereau 2001 and Lahire 2001b), or recent work on the insertion of the individual in a nebular - but coherent - matrix of social relationships (e.g. Kaufmann 1995; Lahire 2004). Drawing, among others, on Norbert Elias' sociology (e.g. Elias 1991), several social scientists indeed demonstrate how dualities such as 'society vs. individual' or 'structure vs. agency' should not be apprehended as antagonisms, but rather as complementary extremes, from which articulation solely allows progression (after Kaufmann 1995, 10). In this perspective, identity, being at individual or group level, can no longer be taken either as a static idea or as a mere abstract construction (Poutignat & Streiff-Feinart 1995). Quite to the contrary, identity is the outcome of a complex process of negotiation and thus ineluctably tied to the notion of change.

However caricatured and schematic this sketch of these fundamental ideas remains, it nevertheless provides us with the underlying framework for this paper. My point is not to consider that sociologists have reached such a level of discernment that we, poor archaeologists, can now draw upon their thought to explore undiscovered fields (see for instance Conkey & Gero 1991). Instead, they simply allow us to re-consider basic issues from a divergent point of view, for instance the heuristic and anthropological value of archaeological cultures, the nature of change, in brief, the history of the people behind the artefacts.

Such concepts or grand ideas may be very tentative, shining like crazy diamonds, but they nevertheless remain empty boxes if they are not tested against data. So, if we wish to open the box and not to be disillusioned, we need appropriate methods to articulate what we plan to do with what can be done. Here, another old traditional archaeological concept appears as a valuable tool in order to delineate the necessary complex web of relations exemplified by past situations: polythetism. For David Clarke, 'a polythetic group is a group of entities such that each entity possesses a large number of attributes of the group, each attribute is shared by large numbers of entities and no single attribute is both sufficient and necessary to the group membership' (Clarke 1968, 36). Although the nearly mathematical formulation now sounds a little bit obsolete, polythetism still allows to set forth, in a unique coherent framework, readings of several facets of the archaeological record, where too often specialisation forces us to concentrate on a particular type of data, and therefore on a given social and cultural trajectory (on this dynamic perception of polythetism, see also Pétrequin *et al.* 1987-1988).

Yet, one has to admit that, in its initial formulation, polythetism as such lacks integrative capacities in order to reach historical interpretation. Actually, to become truly useful, the results of polythetic analysis must not simply be juxtaposed, but actually confronted and articulated together (see for instance Vander Linden 2001; 2004). Here, the concept of *mentalité*, in the general sense of a system of relations, is welcome, as it forces us to explicitly focus on the potential and multiform connexions that may, or may not, have existed and been significant for past social actors. This results neither, from a strict archaeological perspective, in a mere comeback to the absolutely coherent Childean archaeological culture, nor, in a more sociological perspective, in the almighty holism favoured by Durkheim, but rather leads us to adopt a relational perspective, from which the modalities of combining elements appear as the prime determinant of a given 'cultural tradition'.

The potential value of these theoretical statements will be tested against a particular case-study, the inception of the Bell Beaker culture in the central Mediterranean area. Although this phenomenon is characterized by an impressive geographical distribution and by congruent factual variability (Vander Linden 2001; 2004), mainstream interpretations tend to apprehend this period either as some kind of cultural *tabula rasa*, elements of continuity being mere anecdotes compared to the extent of change, or as a local continuous development, characterized however by ineluctable process of growing social hierarchy. Both readings are of course extreme, as they fail to account in satisfactory terms for the subtle variety of local situations and historical trajectories that the Bell Beaker phenomenon manifests throughout Europe. In this perspective, there is much to gain by looking at the way the local people dealt with social life before and whether they accepted or rejected one or several traits that compose the abstract Bell Beaker phenomenon.

Before Bell Beakers: the end of the Neolithic in the central Mediterranean area (3600/3500-2600/2500 cal. BC)

Being at the same time a Continental cul-de-sac and an opening to the almost closed world of the Mediterranean Sea, the Italian Peninsula naturally represents a crossroads. This geographical and cultural position is particularly patent during the Copper Age (3600/3500-2600/2500 cal. BC), indeed shaped by several interwoven cultural influences.

From this perspective, one of the most significant events is the rise of the Remedello culture (3200-2600 cal. BC), closely associated with copper metallurgy, deriving from the Hungarian basin (Balaton group: Matuschik 1997). Remedello cemeteries, our sole source of information, are found in the Po Basin and were for the most part excavated during the 19th century (for example the sites of Remedello, Cumarola, Fontanella, Volongo and Mantono: Barfield 1971, 55-59; Whittle 1996, 317). Funerary practices are characterized by primary individual burials. The body is generally laid in a flexed position on the left side and in only a few cases either on the right side, or on the back. Rare instances of disarticulated skeletons are also known, suggesting secondary deposits and/or reopening of graves (Bagolini et al. 1998, 273). On the eponymous site, some of the graves were aligned in parallel rows.

The selection of grave goods seems to be related to age, rather than gender, categories: flint knives are sometimes associated with children, while triangular copper or flint daggers, arrowheads, halberds, and copper flat axes, as well as stone axes, awls, ornaments or ceramics are more systematically placed with adult women and men (Barfield 1971, 55-59; Bagolini et al. 1998, 273). Daggers are often placed close to the right hand, arrowheads to the shoulder, positions that evoke a functional equipment, as the one associated with the 'Iceman' found some fifteen years ago in the Alps (Spindler 1997). The variety of raw materials used (jadeite, marble, steatite, copper and silver) attests to the multiplicity of contacts that this culture shared with other Alpine regions (Bagolini et al. 1998, 273). It is noteworthy that closely related funerary practices characterize the Spilamberto group, dated to the first half of the 3rd millennium cal. BC, in the region of Modena (Bagolini et al. 1998, 269-71).

Thus, not only is the funerary significance of weapons obvious, but actually all the components of the Remedello funerary system are coherent. Individual burial, grave good associations according to age classes, strict rules regarding the deposition of the dead and spatial distribution of the deceased in the necropolis demonstrate a deliberate intention to assign given identities to the deceased. Here, dealing with the dead runs through well-defined practices of recurrent application.

At the periphery of the two former groups, the funerary practices of the remaining Italian Alpine and peri-Alpine zones are clearly dominated by collective burial (e.g. Vecchiano group in northern Tuscany: Cocchi-Genick 1989; Civate group: Barfield 1971, 60-62; Barfield 1982; 1983). One of the best examples of these collective burials remains the rock shelter of Manerba del Garda, excavated by Lawrence Barfield (1983). This shelter comprised four funeral chambers, of which three were furnished with wooden walls. At least two of them show traces of burning, also observable on the human remains. Unfortunately, because of later Roman disturbance, taphonomic processes are difficult to outline. However, several elements, like the presence of hand and foot bones as well as the over-representation of jawbones, suggest that some burials, if not all, were primary and that, afterwards, skeletal remains were intentionally redeposited (Barfield 1983, 122). In the Trento and Venice areas, the variety of funeral practices is quite pronounced, with individual burials in caves (Nogarole, La Cosina), cist burials (Le Scalucce, Acquaviva, Dos della Forca) and secondary deposits (Vela Valbusa: Bagolini et al. 1998, 268). Finally, if weapons were quite rare in a funerary context, they nevertheless appear as significant elements on several carved rock panels and statue-menhirs, commonly found in most of northern Italy (De Marinis 1995a, 1995b; van Berg & Cauwe 1995).

Actually, this complex ever-changing mosaic of weapons, contained within both individual and collective burials, is to be found throughout the Copper Age Italian Peninsula. For instance, in north-western Tuscany, collective burials deposited in natural and artificial caves show traces of secondary deposits and post-depositional selection of bones (for instance the site of Fondineto: Cremonesi et al. 1998, 189, 191). Copper metallurgy is documented by numerous weapons, including arrowheads and daggers. Further south, the Rinaldone culture is also exclusively known through its funerary practices (Cremonesi et al. 1998). Weapons frequently occur (such as daggers, battle-axes, arrowheads, and mace heads), as well as carefully made metal artefacts (awls and ornaments). Funerary structures are classified into three main categories: on the one hand caves and rock-cut tombs (tombe a forno) gathered in necropoleis, which are associated with collective burials, and, on the other hand, individual burials in pits (tombe a fossa). The deceased are generally placed in a flexed position (Whittle 1996, 338-43). For example, in the cemetery of Fontenoce di Recanati, 21 individuals were found in two individual and ten collective graves (Silvestrini & Piagnocchi 1997). Apart from one adult female, they were all placed on their right side on a north-east/south-west axis. In the collective burials, the remains of the primary inhumations were pushed aside in order to free physical space for the secondary interments.

On the Tyrrhenian coast of central Italy (which covers Campania and Latium), the Gaudo culture is dated to between 3600/3400 and 2500 cal. BC (Cipolloni Sampo et al. 1998, 58-63). Ornaments were rare, as is metallurgy, which was mostly dedicated to the production of awls and weapons (triangular daggers and halberds). Funerary practices are rather diversified and include pits, megaliths, and often rock-cut tombs. The latter are sometimes grouped into cemeteries and comprise individual, multiple and collective burials. The dead are placed either in a flexed position or lying on their back, with few grave goods (ceramics and weapons for men, rare spindle-whorls for women: Whittle 1996, 338-43). Anthropological evidence suggests that the dead may be grouped according to kin relations. However, there is no strict relationship between the number of the deceased, their sex and their age. For instance, in Buccino, tomb 8 comprised two men, seven women and twelve juveniles, while in tomb 7, there were twelve men, six women and seven juveniles (Whittle 1996, 338-43).

The archaeology of the Adriatic Sea coast is less well-documented for this period. I will, however, mention the presence of metal weapons as grave goods within individual and collective burials in the Conelle and Ortocchio cultures (Cremonesi *et al.* 1998, 183-85).

Off the Continent, the picture slightly changes on the islands of Corsica, Sardinia and Sicily. In the latter, the Eneolithic - this label being favoured to the Copper Age in the local taxonomy - begins during the second half of the 4th millennium cal. BC (for example the sites of San Cono-Piano Notaro, Conzo, Calafarina, Conca d'Oro I and Spaterella: Tine & Tine 1998, 143-45). Not only does it correspond to the inception of metal artefacts, but also to the gradual replacement of individual burials by collective ones. These are generally located in rock-cut tombs, sometimes grouped in small cemeteries. This period also yielded small anthropomorphic figurines, which testify to some cultural difference with the Continent (Tine & Tine 1998, 144). During the final stage of the Eneolithic, partly synchronous with the Bell Beaker phenomenon (Tine & Tine 1998, 147-49), collective burial in rock-cut tombs appears as the norm. These are now real masterpieces of architecture as exemplified by the carving of rock-cut tombs with several linked levels (Guilaine 1994, 211-13). Collective burials are also deposited in caves (e.g. Grotta del Fico). In contrast to the Continent, weapons are very rarely present (for instance battle-axes in San Cusumano and Uditore: Leighton 1999, 96).

The cultural situation of the Late Neolithic in Corsica is not very well known. Copper metallurgy is attested on the site of Terrina, while megalithic structures are scattered over the landscape of the entire island (Lewthwaite 1983, Ambert & Carozza 1998, Weiss 1998).

In north-western Sardinia, the Filigosa culture (4th and 3rd millennium cal. BC) marks a new popularity of weapons, especially displayed in graves (Depalmas *et al.* 1998, 357-60). Funeral architecture is dominated by rock-cut tombs (*domus de jana*) containing collective deposits. These monuments were sometimes decorated with bull representations, horn-shaped motifs as well as anthropomorphic steles (Depalmas *et al.* 1998, 356). Collective burials in rock-cut tombs or megalithic structures, occasionally ornamented with engraved or painted representations, were also frequent in the Abealzu culture (first half of the 3rd millennium cal. BC: Depalmas *et al.* 1998, 360-63). In the Monte Claro culture (3rd millennium cal. BC), copper metallurgy was well developed, and focused on the production of awls and

daggers, which were generally discovered in tombs (Depalmas *et al.* 1998, 363-67). Here, both individual and collective burials occur in a variety of architectural surroundings (caves, pits, cists, pit tombs, urned cremations).

On this basis, it is possible to identify several cultural dynamics. The first one, of which the initial impetus is given by the Remedello culture, seems to derive from central Europe. This tradition is defined by a specific configuration of cultural traits, namely individual burial and weaponry, and expresses itself mainly in the funerary domain, while social reality is difficult to outline because of the absence of domestic data. It must be noted that this fashion for weapons, and especially metal ones, can also be discerned in the neighbouring French Midi, where physical violence is revealed by the wounds on skeletal remains found in collective burials (Guilaine & Zammit 2001, 198-201). Interestingly, metallurgical prototypes for the first French metal weapons (e.g. daggers) are to be found in northern Italy (Ambert & Carozza 1998), and not in eastern Spain where copper metallurgy is much older (Ruiz-Taboada & Montero-Ruiz 1999).

A second cultural dynamic is exemplified by collective burials and rock-cut tombs. Although local Neolithic prototypes are known in Continental Italy (Malone 2003), both are subject to a fast-growing development, especially on the islands. From this point of view, the Italian Peninsula and surrounding areas were embarked upon a larger Western Mediterranean process of secondary development of megalithism (Guilaine 2004). Statue-menhirs obviously belong to this sphere of interaction (Barfield 1995; van Berg & Cauwe 1995). Yet, at the same time, their decoration, concentrating on weapons, attests to the new ideological significance granted to military imagery.

Do things really change? Bell Beakers in the central Mediterranean area

The Bell Beaker phenomenon is unevenly distributed over the Italian peninsula (Figure 10.1), (Nicolis & Mottes 1998, 14). The main site concentrations are recorded in northern Italy, particularly in the former Remedello area (Bagolini *et al.* 1998, 275; Nicolis 1998; 2001). In central Italy, Bell Beaker sites are mostly located on the Tyrrhenian coast, between Tuscany and Latium (Sarti 1998). To the south, the Bell Beaker phenomenon is restricted to scattered surface finds (e.g. potsherds and daggers), found throughout the territory, with the exception of the Adriatic coast (Fuggazola Delpino & Pellegrini 1998). On the contrary, in Sicily Bell Beaker sites are numerous, but once again concentrated on the western coast (Leighton 1999, 110-12). The cultural situation on the eastern coast rather recalls the Aegean Sea (Tusa 1998a; 1998b; 2001). While nearly absent in Corsica (Weiss 1998), some 40 Bell Beaker sites are known so far in the whole of Sardinia, with the notable exception of the south-eastern part of the island (Depalmas *et al.* 1998, 368).

Figure 10.1. Distribution of the Bell Beaker sites in continental Italy, Sicily and Sardinia (after Nicolis & Mottes 1998, 14).

The radiocarbon evidence for the Bell Beaker phenomenon in Italy is rather poor (compared with neighbouring southern France: Guilaine *et al.* 2001). Some dozen dates suggest the phenomenon should be dated to the second half of the 3rd millennium cal. BC, any further precision being precluded by the large standard deviations of several dates (Vander Linden 2001, chap. 2).

If the Bell Beaker phenomenon is often associated with a new climax of individual burial, especially with reference to the central European and British sequence (but see Gibson 2004), in the Italian case only the northern part of the area has yielded more or less extensive records of this practice. Modalities of disposal of the deceased are rather fluctuating: in Santa Cristina, two individuals were placed in a left flexed position, head to the east, while in Roccolo Bresciani, one of the two graves contained an individual buried in a left flexed position, but on a north-south axis. Ceramics and weapons were associated with several graves (Santa Cristina, Ca' di Marco: Barfield 1977), evoking the Spilamberto group (Nicolis 1998). In Ca' di Marco (Tirabassi 2001), the presence of postholes at the four corners of the pit suggests the existence of a mortuary structure. A similar structure found in Santa Cristina probably covered two juxtaposed graves. According to Barfield (1971, 62-63), this practice testifies to links with central Europe. The recently excavated funeral pit in Castellari suggests similar influences (Odetti 1998; Del Lucchese & Odetti 2001). Some megalithic sites have yielded Bell Beaker elements (e.g. Velturno-Tanzgasse: Tecchiati 1998).

In central Italy, Bell Beaker artefacts are found in collective burials in caves (for instance Grotta della Scaletta; Spacco delle Monete: Cremonesi *et al.* 1998, 194), although the long-standing use of these caves from the early Neolithic onwards (Malone 2003), as well as later disturbances, makes it difficult to be certain of the exact nature of the Bell Beaker levels (for instance Grotta del Fontino: Vigliardi 1998). Further south, the main chamber of the Fosso Conicchio rock-cut tomb (Fugazzola Delpino and Pellegrini 1998) has also yielded several Bell Beaker elements, including nearly complete ceramics and four stone wrist guards, but associated human remains were scarce. In the Firenze Plain, rich in Bell Beaker domestic sites (Sarti 2004), only one putative funerary site is known, the mound of Via Bruschi (Sarti & Martini 1998). However, because of the acidity of the soil, no organic remains were discovered. If the funerary character of this site has thus still to be demonstrated, its morphology indicates central European influences, as does the finding of an ox burial in the settlement of Querciola (Sarti & Anastasio 2001).

Not surprisingly, countless pages are dedicated to ceramic typology and its potential for the identification of affinities of northern and central Italy with other regions of the Bell Beaker phenomenon. In this sense, the new preference for horizontal bands in ceramic decoration - the Bell Beaker typological trait *par excellence* - actually is not really useful from the perspective adopted here since it just recalls the incorporation of the Italian Peninsula into the Bell Beaker network, but without any further precise geographical indication. Instead, morphological analysis provides us with some more interesting results. Indeed, recent investigation of several domestic assemblages from northern and central Italy demonstrates the heavy influence of central European morphological traits and types, while elements of continuity change from one area to the next (Leonini 2004). Furthermore, typological comparisons

with southern France, although less clear (Strahm 2004), should not be underestimated (Besse 2004).

If some of the aforementioned elements express, in one way or another, some privileged interaction between the northern and central regions of the Italian Peninsula with central Europe, lithics, on the contrary, exhibit strong local continuity (Barfield 2001). For instance, bifacially flaked daggers, contrary to traditional conceptions, are no longer a good typological and chronological marker of the Copper Age/Bell Beaker differentiation, but rather occur in both periods (Mottes 2001). Likewise, although the literature is still patchy, elements of lithic continuity are also attested in central Italy (for instance arrowhead morphology: Vigliardi 1998).

In Sicily, collective burial was still an undisputed rule, as was the building of complex multi-roomed rock-cut tombs. This process reached its climax during the Early Bronze Age Castelluccio culture (Leighton 1999, 93-99, 121-32). Some 30 funerary sites are known on the western coast (e.g. Torre Cusa: Campobello di Mazara, Trapani; caves of Buffa I, Buffa II and Porcospina: Villafrati, Palermo; Torrebiggini: Partanna, Trapani: Tusa 1998a, 1998b). These generally contain disarticulated skeletal remains (mostly skulls and long bones) with, in a few cases, one or two complete skeletons, probably placed in the grave last. Some rock-cut tombs only yielded skull deposits. Simpler tombs are also attested, such as the pits found in Piano Vento (Tusa 1998a). The first inhumations in jars, also a later characteristic of the Early Bronze Age (Leighton 1999, 162), are dated to the Bell Beaker period (sites of Marianopoli and Camaro: Leighton 1999, 96). From the point of view of ceramic decoration, Sicily stands out in the entire Bell Beaker phenomenon as it is the sole area where painted pottery occurs (with the exception of a few painted potsherds found at the southern French site of Le Mourral: Vaquer 1998; Vaquer *et al.* 2000). If the use of this technique evidently stems from local Neolithic traditions (Veneroso 1991), it must however be noted that the decoration so produced often exhibits the classical Bell Beaker horizontal zoned pattern, with alternated red and black stripes. Pots with radial decoration centred on the base are also comparable to assemblages from the Iberian Peninsula (Harrison 1977) and the so-called 'local styles' of the French Midi (*style languedocien* and *style provençal*: Giligny & Salanova 1997; Guilaine *et al.* 2001).

Sardinian funerary practices closely recall their Sicilian counterparts. Rock-cut tombs (*domus de jana*; for instance Anghelu Ruju-Alghero, Locci-Santus-San Giovanni Suergiu, Pranu Narbonis-San Vito: Contu 1998; Demartis 1998; Canino 2001) are also the dominant architectural type, alongside other structures: a cist with an individual lying on its back in Santa Vittoria di Nuraxinieddu (Usai 2001), natural caves in Volpe-Iglesias, Corongiu de Mari-Iglesias and Corongu Acca-Villamassargia, rare megalithic structures (presence of a stone wrist guard in Motorra-Dorgali: Depalmas *et al.* 1998, 369-70). The main funerary practice is the secondary collective burial, few primary individual burials being also known. For instance, in the Bingia 'e Monti rock-cut tomb, the remains of some 150 dead were gathered in the first archaeological level, dated to the Bell Beaker period. Indications of post-depositional manipulation of the bones were plentiful (Atzeni 1998b). However, three individual burials were also excavated, all placed in a left flexed position on a north-south axis. In another part of the tomb, a deposit comprising some 50 adult skulls was discovered (see also the contemporary hypogeum of Padru Jossu: Ugas 1998).

As for Sicily, the co-occurrence of horizontal bands and radial designs in ceramic decoration recalls the western Mediterranean region of the Bell Beaker phenomenon (Vander Linden 2004). At the same time, the morphology of several ceramic types, like small polypod pots, strongly recalls central European influences (Atzeni 1998a).

Discussion

At first sight, this brief review of the evidence regarding the Italian Copper Age and Bell Beaker phenomenon may leave the impression that both periods are shaped by similar processes, marked by similar foreign influences. On the one hand, the central European impact is highly relevant in northern Italy, but progressively fades away further south to become invisible in Sicily. On the other hand, the southern half of Continental Italy, as well as Sardinia and Sicily, present more points of convergence with the cultural dynamics of the western Mediterranean, most importantly the joint development of collective burial and megalithism, especially under the form of rock-cut tomb architecture.

Nevertheless, as far as the fate of the Bell Beaker phenomenon is concerned, it is insufficient to point to macroscopic similarities and then to consider that the former Copper Age paved the way for the inception of that pan-European cultural process. In order to produce historical sense, we need to re-consider each region as a coherent unit according to the various cultural elements at stake, before eventually comparing all local results.

In this view, the cultural sequence of northern Italy is remarkable. This region exhibits an intimate geographical proximity between the Remedello culture and the local manifestation of the Bell Beaker phenomenon, which, at the same time, are the two groups that present the most salient links with central Europe. This last point, however, cannot simply be explained as the outcome of the restricted distances between these regions. Indeed, for the Remedello culture, links with central Europe are obvious as far as copper metallurgy is concerned (Matuschik 1997). Although funerary affinities are less easy to argue, satisfactory potential prototypes exist in the Hungarian Plain in the form of cemeteries with flat graves (for example the site of Budakalász: Chapman 2000, 128) and the long-standing insertion of weapons into tombs in the Hungarian Plain (since the mid-fifth millennium cal. BC within Tiszapolgár-Bodrogkeresztur culture: Bognar-Kutzian 1963, 1972). For the Bell Beaker phenomenon, funerary propinquity is more salient, but points to Austria or southern Germany rather than Hungary, where the local Bell Beaker group, the Csepel group, is characterized by cremation, with few instances of inhumations (Kalicz-

Schreiber & Kalicz 1998). The other points of convergence, concerning domestic ceramics, tell a more complicated story. First, not only are central European influences recorded, but similarities with southern French examples are also possible. Second, the Bell Beaker domestic assemblage in central Europe eventually derives from the Early Bronze Age cultures of the Carpathian basin (especially the Makó-Kosihy-Čaka culture: Machnik 1991; see also Strahm 2004). However, because of the large-scale diffusion of this assemblage amongst the central European Bell Beaker groups, it is impossible to determine with precision if its presence in northern Italy derives from Hungary or elsewhere. The last argument also holds true for ceramic decoration.

In central Italy, the Copper Age and the Bell Beaker phenomenon tell the same story, with the gradual incorporation of streams of northern influences. Conversely, the importance of local and of western Mediterranean traits becomes more and more discernable further south. Much like weapons, which, in contrast to individual burial, only reached southern Italy during the Copper Age, only few diagnostic Bell Beaker artefacts are known in the area.

Points of divergence particularly stand out in the neighbouring islands. During the Copper Age, Continental elements were rare in Sardinia and in Sicily. Keeping a certain cultural individuality, as exemplified respectively by internal decoration of megaliths and feminine representations, they were at the same time well incorporated into the wider western Mediterranean development of megalithism. During the Bell Beaker phenomenon however, they embark on distinctive historical trajectories. Despite the quantity of Bell Beaker sites on its western coast, one cannot speak of a true Bell Beaker culture in Sicily, in both the anthropological and the archaeological sense. First, the contiguous development of megalithic architecture and collective burial reveals an independence from the changes on the Continent. Second, technological continuity in the making of the pottery decoration strongly suggest that local potters only imitated foreign prototypes, without altering the very nature of their production. In this sense, it is tempting to conceive of the Bell Beaker presence as a matter of ceramic fashion.

In Sardinia, on the contrary, not only does ceramic decoration attest to the adoption of Bell Beaker traits, but so does ceramic morphology, as well as, in a restricted way, funerary practices, with the co-occurrence of collective and individual burials in the same megalithic structures. Still profoundly shaped by the western Mediterranean area, Sardinia thus seems more receptive to change than Sicily, not to mention Corsica, for which the lack of available documentation prevents any in-depth analysis.

It is thus no longer possible to apprehend the Bell Beaker phenomenon solely as the introduction of new artefacts (see Cocchi-Genick 1998). Likewise, beyond similarities in their general direction, the scale and diversity of influences sharply differs between the Italian Copper Age and the Bell Beaker phenomenon. On the one hand, the Copper Age saw the introduction of elements ultimately deriving from northern Europe and their gradual acceptance throughout the Continent, as well as traits shared with the western Mediterranean basin; yet, interaction exclusively involved either socially valuable items (copper artefacts, especially weapons), or ideological matters (funerary practices and architecture). On the other hand, if the Bell Beaker phenomenon exhibited the same scope of regional influences, it must be noted that these covered a wider range of material culture and associated behaviour. From one region to the next, the modalities of change differ sharply. In northern and central Italy, as well as in Sardinia, we are faced with a real cultural package, expressed by funerary practices but also by domestic ceramics. Further south in Sicily, the Bell Beaker phenomenon is a mere fashion, perceptible in ceramic decoration only: this, however, is not surprising since we are here at the extreme periphery of this pan-European process.

This last case left aside, it is significant that, during the Bell Beaker period, the cultural integration of the investigated regions concerned the domestic sphere. In this sense, although ideology surely played a driving role in this process, the creation and maintenance of the Bell Beaker 'sphere of integration' throughout Europe was possible and effective because, contrary to mainstream theories, it largely exceeded the sole level of the élites and dominant ideologies, but rather actively involved people and their everyday practices (for a larger, complementary, perspective, see Vander Linden 2001; 2004).

Conclusion

I have tried here to show how a quite formal polythetic analysis can lead to the recognition of complex interwoven webs of influences. The crucial point was not merely to pay particular attention to a given class of artefacts, but rather to recognise the variety of situations described and to try to articulate them in a single coherent narrative. Whilst funerary practices were more particularly studied for the Italian Copper Age, this method was explicitly followed in order to account for the Bell Beaker phenomenon in the central Mediterranean area. So, both periods tell to some extent similar stories, since we are in each case faced with general processes of progressive assimilation and congruent resistance to several new traits, originating from central Europe and the western Mediterranean area. Yet, we can note that the scope of integration, as well as its geographical scale, is by far larger within the Bell Beaker phenomenon. Besides changes in the ideological domain (especially funerary practices), it is noteworthy that this last archaeological culture also marks changes discernible in the domestic sphere of activities (ceramic decoration and morphology).

If from a certain point of view this paper is utterly classical in essence, my approach sensibly differs from culture-history, as the driving idea, borrowed and adapted from modern sociology, remains that identity is always a work in progress, constantly shaped and negotiated by individuals and communities. From this point of view,

'archaeological cultures' or 'cultural influences' do not only exist in workbooks or as taxonomical units, but have an effective anthropological significance as they crystallize, in given areas and time-spans, various fields of human experience documented by the archaeological record.

Throughout this paper, I deliberately remained silent about the way people acted, and thus left the discourse full of abstract terms like 'influence' or 'interaction'. Indeed, however crucial the role of agency might have been in the historical development of these phenomena, it is not that easy to point out the motivations which led past people to accept or reject foreign artefacts, like metal weapons or bell beakers, and their accompanying practices, like metallurgy or funerary ideology. Of course, it is tempting to move one step further, for instance by resorting to sociologically and anthropologically derived theories and/or concepts. Interesting as these questions are, I nevertheless think that, given the nature and somewhat restricted amount of available data, such an approach would only poorly mimic the invoked analogical models. The 'why?' may well be more appealing, although eventually remaining out of reach, but the accurate description of the 'how?' is as central, if not more so, to the conduct of any social science as archaeology.

References

Ambert, P. & Carozza, L. 1998. Origine(s) et développement de la première métallurgie française. Etat de la question. In B. Fritsch, M. Maute, I. Matuschik, J. Müller & C. Wolf (eds), *Tradition und Innovation. Prähistorische Archäologie als historische Wissenschaft. Festschrift für Christian Strahm*, 149-73. Rahden: Verlag Marie Leidorf (Internationale Archäologie. Studia Honoraria Band 3).

Atzeni, E. 1998a. La cultura del bicchiere campaniforme in Sardegna. In F. Nicolis & E. Mottes (eds), *Simbolo ed enigma. Il bicchiere campaniforme e l'Italia nella preistoria Europea del III millennio a.C.*, 243-53. Trento: Ufficio Beni Archeologici.

Atzeni, E. 1998b. La tomba ipogeico-megalitica di Bingia 'e Monti. In F. Nicolis & E. Mottes (eds), *Simbolo ed enigma. Il bicchiere campaniforme e l'Italia nella preistoria Europea del III millennio a.C.*, 254-60. Trento: Ufficio Beni Archeologici.

Bagolini, B., Pedrotti, A. & Barfield, L. 1998. L'Italie septentrionale. In J. Guilaine (ed.), *Atlas du Néolithique Européen II. L'Europe occidentale*, 233-341. Liège: Université de Liège (E.R.A.U.L. 46).

Barfield, L.H. 1971. *Northern Italy before Rome*. London: Thames & Hudson.

Barfield, L.H. 1977. The Beaker culture in Italy. In R. Mercer (ed.), *Beakers in Britain and Europe*, 27-49. Oxford: BAR.

Barfield, L.H. 1982. The Chalcolithic of northern Italy in the context of third millennium Europe: questions of basic theory. In J.G.P. Best & N.M.W. de Vreies (eds), *Interaction and acculturation in the Mediterranean vol. II*, 19-31. Amsterdam: Grüner.

Barfield, L.H. 1983. The Chalcolithic cemetery at Manerba del Garda. *Antiquity* 57, 116-23.

Barfield, L.H. 1995. The context of statue-menhirs. *Notizie Archeologiche Bergomensi* 3, 11-20.

Barfield, L.H. 2001. Beaker lithics in northern Italy. In F. Nicolis (ed.), Bell Beakers today. Pottery, people, culture, symbols in prehistoric Europe. Proceedings of the international colloquium Riva del Garda (Trento, Italy) 11-16 May 1998, 507-18. Trento: Ufficio Beni Archeologici.

Besse, M. 2004. Bell Beaker common ware during the third millennium BC in Europe. In J. Czebreszuk (ed.), *Similar but different. Bell Beakers in Europe*, 148-227. Poznań Adam Mickiewicz University.

Bognár-Kutzián, I. 1963. *The Copper Age cemetery of Tiszapolgár-Basatanya*. Budapest: Akadémiai Kiadó (Archaeologica hungarica 42).

Bognár-Kutzián, I. 1972. *The early Copper Age Tiszapolgár culture in the Carpathian Basin.* Budapest: Akadémiai Kiadó (Archaeologica Hungarica 48).

Canino, G. 2001. Le culture campaniforme e Bonnanaro nella necropoli ipogeica di Pranu Narbonis-San Vito (Cagliari). In F. Nicolis (ed.), *Bell Beakers today. Pottery, people, culture, symbols in prehistoric Europe. Proceedings of the international colloquium Riva del Garda (Trento, Italy) 11-16 May 1998*, 677-79. Trento: Ufficio Beni Archeologici.

Chapman, J. 2000. *Tensions at funerals. Micro-tradition analysis in later Hungarian prehistory.* Budapest: Archaeolingua (Series Minor 14).

Cipolloni Sampo, M., Calattini, M., Palma di Cesnola, A., Cassano, S., Radina, F., Bianco, S., Marino, D.A., Gorgoglione, M.A., Bailo Modesti, G. & Grifoni Cremonensi, R. 1998. L'Italie du sud. In J. Guilaine (ed.), *Atlas du Néolithique Européen II. L'Europe occidentale,* 9-112. Liège: Université de Liège (E.R.A.U.L. 46).

Clarke, D. 1968. *Analytical archaeology*. London: Methuen.

Clarke, D. 1973. Archaeology: the loss of innocence. *Antiquity* 47, 6-18.

Cocchi-Genick, D. 1989. The Chalcolithic and Early Bronze Age cultures of Northern Tuscany. In *Das Äneolithikum und die früheste Bronzezeit (C¹⁴ 3000-2000 b.c.) in Mitteleuropa: kulturelle und chronologische Beziehungen. Acta des XIV. internationalen Symposiums Prag – Liblice 20-24. 10. 1986. Praehistorica* XV, 263-67.

Cocchi-Genick, D. 1998. Il campaniforme nella Toscana nord-occidentale. In F. Nicolis & E. Mottes (eds), *Simbolo ed enigma. Il bicchiere campaniforme e l'Italia nella preistoria Europea del III millennio a.C.,* 161-63. Trento: Ufficio Beni Archeologici.

Conkey, M. & Gero, J. 1991. Tensions, pluralities and engendering archaeology: an introduction to women in *prehistory*. In J. Gero & M. Conkey (eds), *Engendering archaeology. Women in prehistory*, 3-30. Oxford: Basil Blackwell.

Contu, E. 1998. La cultura del vaso campaniforme in un ipogeo di Marinaru (Sassari). In F. Nicolis & E. Mottes (eds), *Simbolo ed enigma. Il bicchiere campaniforme e l'Italia nella preistoria Europea del III millennio a.C.,* 286-91. Trento: Ufficio Beni Archeologici.

Cremonesi, G., Grifoni Cremonesi, R., Radi, G., Tozzi, C. & Nicolis, F. 1998. L'Italie centrale. In J. Guilaine (ed.), *Atlas du Néolithique Européen II. L'Europe occidentale*, 165-231. Liège: Université de Liège (E.R.A.U.L. 46).

Del Lucchese, A. & Odetti, G. 2001. I vasi campaniformi in Liguria. In F. Nicolis (ed.), *Bell Beakers today. Pottery, people, culture, symbols in prehistoric Europe. Proceedings of the international colloquium Riva del Garda (Trento, Italy) 11-16 May 1998*, 625-27. Trento: Ufficio Beni Archeologici.

De Marinis, R.C. 1995a. Le statue-stele della Lunigiana. *Notizie Archeologiche Bergomensi* 3, 195-212.

De Marinis, R.C. 1995b. Le stele antropomorfe di Aosta. *Notizie Archeologiche Bergomensi* 3, 213-20.

Demartis, G.M. 1998. La cultura del vaso campaniforme ad Anghelu ruju – Alhero (Sassari). In F. Nicolis & E. Mottes (eds), *Simbolo ed enigma. Il bicchiere campaniforme e l'Italia nella preistoria Europea del III millennio a.C.,* 281-85. Trento: Ufficio Beni Archeologici.

Depalmas, A., Melis, M.G. & Tanda, G. 1998. La Sardaigne. In J. Guilaine (ed.), *Atlas du Néolithique Européen II. L'Europe occidentale*, 343-94. Liège: Université de Liège (E.R.A.U.L. 46).

Elias, N. 1991. *La société des individus.* Paris: Fayard.

Favereau, O. 2001. L'économie du sociologue ou penser (l'orthodoxie) à partir de Pierre Bourdieu. In B. Lahire (ed.), *Le travail sociologique de Pierre Bourdieu. Dettes et critiques,* 231-314. Paris: La Découverte (La Découverte/ Poche Sciences humaines et sociales 110).

Fugazzola Delpino, M. & Pellegrini, E. 1998. La struttura ipogeica di Fosso Conicchio (Viterbo). In F. Nicolis & E. Mottes (eds), *Simbolo ed enigma. Il bicchiere campaniforme e l'Italia nella preistoria Europea del III millennio a.C.,* 181-85. Trento: Ufficio Beni Archeologici.

Gibson, A. 2004. Burials and beakers: seeing beneath the veneer in Late Neolithic Britain. In J. Czebreszuk (ed.), *Similar but different. Bell Beakers in Europe,* 173-92. Poznań Adam Mickiewicz University.

Giligny, F. & Salanova, L., David, C., Dechezleprêtre, T., Durand, S., Grouber, P., Peake, R., Perrin, T., Pierrat, J.-M., Théron. V., Timsit, D. & Weller O. 1997. La variabilité des corpus céramiques méridionaux au Néolithique final - Chalcolithique. *Bulletin de la Société Préhistorique Française* 94, 237-58.

Guilaine, J. 1994. *La mer partagée. La Méditerranée avant l'écriture. 7000-2000 avant Jésus-Christ.* Paris: Hachette.

Guilaine, J. 2004. Les Campaniformes et la Méditerranée. *Bulletin de la Société Préhistorique Française*, **101** : 239-252.

Guilaine, J., Claustre, F., Lemercier, O. & Sabatier, P. 2001. Campaniformes et environnement culturel en France Méditerranéenne. In F. Nicolis (ed.), *Bell Beakers today. Pottery, people, culture, symbols in prehistoric Europe. Proceedings of the international colloquium, Riva del Garda (Trento, Italy), 11-16 May 1998*, 229-75. Trento: Ufficio Beni Archeologici.

Guilaine, J. & Zammit, J. 2001. *Le sentier de la guerre. Visages de la violence préhistorique.* Paris: Seuil.

Harrison, R.J. 1977. *The Bell Beaker cultures of Spain and Portugal.* Harvard: Peabody Museum.

Kalicz-Schreiber, R. & Kalicz, N. 1998. Die Somogývar-Vinkovci-Kultur und die Glockenbecher in Ungarn. In B. Fritsch, M. Maute, I. Matuschik, J. Müller & C. Wolf (eds), *Tradition und Innovation. Prähistorische Archäologie als historische Wissenschaft. Festschrift für Christian Strahm,* 325-47. Rahden: Verlag Marie Leidorf (Internationale Archäologie. Studia Honoraria Band 3).

Kaufmann, J.-C. 1995. *Corps de femmes, regards d'hommes. Sociologie des seins nus.* Paris: Nathan (Essais & Recherches).

Lahire, B. (ed.) 2001a. *Le travail sociologique de Pierre Bourdieu. Dettes et critiques.* Paris: La Découverte (La Découverte/ Poche Sciences humaines et sociales 110).

Lahire, B. 2001b. Champ, hors-champ, contre-champ. In B. Lahire (ed.), *Le travail sociologique de Pierre Bourdieu. Dettes et critiques,* 23-57. Paris: La Découverte (La Découverte/ Poche Sciences humaines et sociales 110).

Lahire, B. 2004. *La culture des individus. Dissonances culturelles et distinction de soi.* Paris : La Découverte (Textes à l'appui / Laboratoire des sciences sociales).

Leighton, R. 1999. *Sicily before history. An archaeological survey from the Palaeolithic to the Iron Age.* London: Duckworth.

Leonini, V. 2004. La céramique domestique du campaniforme de l'Italie centrale et septentrionale. In J. Czebreszuk (ed.), *Similar but different. Bell Beakers in Europe,* 149-70. Poznań Adam Mickiewicz University.

Lewthwaite, J. 1983. The Neolithic of Corsica. In C. Scarre (ed.), *Ancient France. 6000-2000 bc,* 146-83. Edinburgh: Edinburgh University Press.

Machnik, J. 1991. *The earliest Bronze Age in the Carpathian basin.* Bradford: Department of Archaeological Sciences.

Malone, C. 2003. The Italian Neolithic: a synthesis of research. *Journal of World Prehistory* 17(3), 235-312.

Matuschik, I. 1997. Der neue Werkstoff - Metall. In *Goldene Jahrhunderte. Die Bronzezeit in Südwestdeutschland,* 16-25. Stuttgart: Theiss (Almanach 2 hrsg. vom Archäologischen Landesmuseum Baden-Württemberg).

Mottes, E. 2001. Bell Beakers and beyond: flint daggers of northern Italy between technology and typology. In F. Nicolis (ed.), *Bell Beakers today. Pottery, people, culture, symbols in prehistoric Europe. Proceedings of the international colloquium Riva del Garda (Trento, Italy) 11-16 May 1998,* 519-45. Trento: Ufficio Beni Archeologici.

Nicolis, F. 1998. Alla periferia dell'impero: il bicchiere campaniforme nell'Italia settentrionale. In F. Nicolis & E. Mottes (eds), *Simbolo ed enigma. Il bicchiere campaniforme e l'Italia nella preistoria Europea del III millennio a.C.,* 47-68. Trento: Ufficio Beni Archeologici.

Nicolis, F. 2001. Some observations on the cultural setting of the Bell Bakers of northern Italy. In F. Nicolis (ed.), *Bell Beakers today. Pottery, people, culture, symbols in prehistoric Europe. Proceedings of the international colloquium, Riva del Garda (Trento, Italy), 11-16 May 1998,* 207-227. Trento: Ufficio Beni Archeologici.

Nicolis, F. & Mottes, E. (ed.) 1998. *Simbolo ed enigma. Il bicchiere campaniforme e l'Italia nella preistoria Europea dell III millennio a.C.* Trento : Ufficio Beni Archeologici.

Odetti, G. 1998. Tomba campaniforme di località Castellari. In F. Nicolis & E. Mottes (eds), *Simbolo ed enigma. Il bicchiere campaniforme e l'Italia nella preistoria Europea del III millennio a.C.,* 98-99. Trento: Ufficio Beni Archeologici.

Pétrequin, P., Chastel, J., Giligny, F., Pétrequin, A.-M. & Saintot, S. 1987-1988, Réinterprétation de la civilisation Saône-Rhône. Une approche des tendances culturelles du Néolithique final. *Gallia Préhistoire, Fouilles et monuments archéologiques en France métropolotaine* 30, 1-89.

Poutignat, P. & Streiff-Fenart, J. 1995. *Théories de l'ethnicité.* Paris: Presses Universitaires de France.

Ruiz-Taboada, A. & Montero-Ruiz, I. 1999. The oldest metallurgy in western Europe. *Antiquity* 73, 897-903.

Sarti, L. 1998. Aspetti insediativi del Campaniforme nell'Italia centrale. In F. Nicolis & E. Mottes (eds), *Simbolo ed enigma. Il bicchiere campaniforme e l'Italia nella preistoria Europea del III millennio a.C.,* 137-53. Trento: Ufficio Beni Archeologici.

Sarti, L. 2004. L'Epicampaniforme en Italie centrale: stratigraphies, datations radiométriques, productions lithiques et céramiques. In J. Czebreszuk (ed.), *Similar but different. Bell Beakers in Europe,* 205-21. Poznań Adam Mickiewicz University.

Sarti, L. & Anastasio, S. 2001. The ox grave from Semitella (Sesto Fiorentino). In F. Nicolis (ed.), *Bell Beakers today. Pottery, people, culture, symbols in prehistoric Europe. Proceedings of the international colloquium Riva del Garda (Trento, Italy) 11-16 May 1998,* 649-51. Trento: Ufficio Beni Archeologici.

Sarti, L. & Martini, F. 1998. Il tumulo di via Bruschi a Sesto Fiorentino. In F. Nicolis & E. Mottes (eds), *Simbolo ed enigma. Il bicchiere campaniforme e l'Italia nella preistoria Europea del III millennio a.C.,* 168-73. Trento: Ufficio Beni Archeologici.

Silvestrini, M. & Piagnocchi, G. 1997. La necropoli Eneolitica di Fontenoce di Recanati. *Rivista di Scienze Preistoriche* 48, 307-66.

Spindler, K. 1997. L'homme gelé. Une momie de 5.000 ans dans un glacier des Alpes de l'Ötztal. L'Homme des glaces dans les Alpes il y a 5000 ans. *Dossiers d'Archéologie* 224, 8-27.

Strahm, C. 2004. Das Glockenbecher-Phänomen aus der Sicht der Komplementär-Keramik. In J. Czebreszuk (ed.), *Similar but different. Bell Beakers in Europe,* 101-26. Poznań Adam Mickiewicz University.

Tecchiati, U. 1998. Velturno - loc. Tanzgasse: un'area megalitica di età campaniforme in Val d'Isarco (Bolzano). In F. Nicolis & E. Mottes (eds), *Simbolo ed enigma. Il bicchiere campaniforme e l'Italia nella preistoria Europea del III millennio a.C.,* 69-72. Trento: Ufficio Beni Archeologici.

Tine, S. & Tine, V. 1998. La Sicile. In J. Guilaine (ed.), *Atlas du Néolithique Européen II. L'Europe occidentale,* 133-63. Liège: Université de Liège (E.R.A.U.L. 46).

Tirabassi, J. 2001. La tomba campaniforme di Ca' di Marco (Brescia). In F. Nicolis (ed.), *Bell Beakers today. Pottery, people, culture, symbols in prehistoric Europe. Proceedings of the international colloquium Riva del Garda (Trento, Italy) 11-16 May 1998,* 637-39. Trento: Ufficio Beni Archeologici.

Tusa, S. 1998a. Prospettiva Mediterranea e integrità culturale del bicchiere campaniforme Siciliano. In F. Nicolis & E. Mottes (eds), *Simbolo ed enigma. Il bicchiere campaniforme e l'Italia nella preistoria Europea del III millennio a.C.,* 205-19. Trento: Ufficio Beni Archeologici.

Tusa, S. 1998b. Il bicchiere campaniforme in alcuni siti della Sicilia occidentale. In F. Nicolis & E. Mottes (eds), *Simbolo ed enigma. Il bicchiere campaniforme e l'Italia nella preistoria Europea del III millennio a.C.,* 220-23. Trento: Ufficio Beni Archeologici.

Tusa, S. 2001. Mediterranean perspective and cultural integrity of Sicilian Bell Beakers. In F. Nicolis (ed.), *Bell Beakers today. Pottery, people, culture, symbols in prehistoric Europe. Proceedings of the international colloquium, Riva del Garda (Trento, Italy), 11-16 May 1998,* 173-86. Trento: Ufficio Beni Archeologici.

Ugas, G. 1998. Facies campaniformi dell'ipogeo di Padru Jossu (Sanluri-Cagliari). In F. Nicolis & E. Mottes (eds), *Simbolo ed enigma. Il bicchiere campaniforme e l'Italia nella preistoria Europea del III millennio a.C.,* 261-80. Trento: Ufficio Beni Archeologici.

Usai, E. 2001. La tomba campaniforme di Santa Vittoria di Nuraxinieddu (Oristano). In F. Nicolis (ed.), *Bell Beakers today. Pottery, people, culture, symbols in prehistoric Europe. Proceedings of the international colloquium Riva del Garda (Trento, Italy) 11-16 May 1998,* 695-96. Trento: Ufficio Beni Archeologici.

van Berg, P.-L. & Cauwe, N. 1995. Figures humaines mégalithiques: histoire, style et sens. *Notizie Archeologiche Bergomensi* 3, 21-66.

Vander Linden, M. 2001. *Archéologie, complexité sociale et histoire des idées: l'espace campaniforme dans l'Europe du troisième millénaire avant notre ère.* Unpublished PhD thesis. Free University of Brussels.

Vander Linden, M. 2004. Polythetic networks, coherent people: a new historical hypothesis for the Bell Beaker phenomenon. In J. Czebreszuk (ed.), *Similar but different. Bell Beakers in Europe,* 35-62. Poznań Adam Mickiewicz University.

Vaquer, J. 1998. Le Mourral, Trèbes (Aude). A fortified late Neolithic site reoccupied by Bell Beakers. In M. Benz & S. van Willingen (eds), *Some new approaches to the Bell beaker phenomenon Lost Paradise...? Proceedings of the 2nd meeting of the 'Association Archéologie et Gobelets' Feldberg (Germany), 18th-20th April 1997,* 15-21. Oxford: BAR.

Vaquer, J., Gandelin, M. & Marsac, R. 2000. L'enceinte Néolithique de Mourral-Millegrand à Trèbes (Aude). In *IVes rencontres méridionales de préhistoire récente. Temps et espace culturels. Actualité de la recherche en préhistoire récente dans le midi. Nîmes.*

Carré d'Art. 28 et 29 octobre 2000. Pré-actes. Nîmes: Société Languedocienne de Préhistoire, 53-55.

Veneroso, P. 1991. Osservationi tecniche sulle ceramiche campaniformi Siciliane. In *La preistoria del Basso Belice e dell Sicilia meridionale nel quadro della preistoria Siciliana e Mediterranea,* 461-81. Palermo: Società per la Storia Patria di Palermo.

Vigliardi, A. 1998. Il campaniforme della Grotta del Fontino (Montepescali, Grosseto). In F. Nicolis & E. Mottes (eds), *Simbolo ed enigma. Il bicchiere campaniforme e l'Italia nella preistoria Europea del III millennio a.C.,* 174-79. Trento: Ufficio Beni Archeologici.

Wenger, E. 1998. *Communities of practice: learning, meaning and identity.* Cambridge: Cambridge University Press.

Weiss, M.C. 1998. La Corse. In J. Guilaine (ed.), *Atlas du Néolithique Européen II. L'Europe occidentale,* 395-412. Liège: Université de Liège (E.R.A.U.L. 46).

Whittle, A. 1996. *Europe in the Neolithic. The creation of new worlds.* Cambridge: Cambridge University Press.

Movement as a *mentalité*: mobile lifeways in the Neolithic and Bronze Age Great Ouse, Nene and Welland Valleys

Jessica Mills

Introduction

Movement forms one of the most important phenomena of human life. It is an essential component of being, action and identity; indeed without it we cease to live (Best 1974; Ingold 2000; Thornton 1971). Notwithstanding, human movement remains little theorised within prehistoric contexts, and when it is considered is usually restricted to seasonal mobilities or the patterns of movements around and within the architectures of Neolithic monuments. This is not surprising as the study of movement is seen as a vast and complicated realm, which forms an irretrievable and invisible part of prehistoric society – something beyond Hawkes' ladder of inference (Hawkes 1954; Close 2000, 50; Osborne 1991, 232). It is the aim of this chapter to introduce how relations formed through the routine actions of human movements within the landscape are a fundamental way of considering the shifting and multiple scales of Neolithic and Bronze Age lifeways.

This chapter will first detail the specific perspective on movement adopted for this research. The salience of movement, its role as a medium through which life is lived, as well as how the world comes into being through movement will be outlined. With such a movement perspective in place, I will then go on to apply this approach to the Neolithic and Bronze Age archaeology of the eastern British river valleys of the Great Ouse, Nene and Welland. Through looking at Neolithic and Bronze Age lifeways from such a perspective, new interpretations can be put forward.

The importance of movement

The first thing to consider when regarding movement is its central role to life itself (see Kador this volume). Certainly, without movement we are no longer living – indeed to live is to move. Therefore, movement can be seen as an essential, physical and metaphorical universal characteristic of human lifeways which forms the most fundamental element of a person (Cratty 1964, 15; Harris 2000, 116; Ingold 1987, 172; Seamon 1979, 33; Smith 1968, 3; Thornton 1971, 1). No person is truly static, there is always some form of movement of the body when living, and the degree to which the body moves varies from person to person. Notably, modern, Westernised conceptions of people focus upon bodies as static and sedentary beings (Farnell 1994, 929). Moreover, through a need to tie and associate people to particular places or spaces in the modern world, people living a mobile existence are often characterised negatively as being different and a potential threat (Cresswell 2001, 16). Having roots and being rooted to a place (both physically and metaphorically) are one of the situating fabrics of modern, Westernised lifeways. Therefore, those who do not comply with this lifestyle are seen as being rootless, and at odds with the norms of modern society (Bender 2001; Creswell 2001, 16; Cuba & Hummon 1993, 547). It is from such a backdrop that archaeological narratives of prehistoric people have been created. As a consequence, the way in which we perceive the importance of movement and mobility within past societies has been biased.

Movement as a medium

Many studies of human movement treat the concept as an abstracted behaviour, mechanistically undertaken for human survival. Movement is seen as an automatic response to a stimulus, received through the neural system of the body (Lamb & Watson 1979, 85; McMahon 1984, 173; Tricker & Tricker 1966, 74). The roles of the mind and body in movement are rigidly separated; the mind processes the stimulus and accords a response which is then transmitted to the body which conducts the correct action (Cratty 1964, 23). These biomechanical accounts reduce movement to a behavioural trait of humankind, while characterising mind and body as dichotomous (Gibson 1979, 225). The role of the individual as a holistic entity is denied, and the individual is seen as passive, reacting solely to the stimuli and responses processed by the body.

Alternative views of human movement have been posited within physical education studies and environmental psychology. Here, the mind and body are one, actively perceiving and negotiating the world through a constant act of engagement (Ingold 2000; Gibson 1979; Lewis 1995; Thornton 1971). There is no separation of the mind and body, as through the action of moving, mind and body become a totality. Hence, studying movement is not to privilege the body as the prime locus for being-in-the-world. The holistic nature of movement enables a person to undertake movements that range from routine regimes where many movements may feel 'automatic' or 'unconscious', to movements that entail the active and intentional negotiation of a situation (usually one we are not familiar with), (Seamon 1980). The mind/body is not a passive reactor to outside stimuli; instead the individual is actively apprehending phenomena and as a result, finding ways of going on in the world. This 'intelligence' manifest within a person cannot be separated into a mind : body dichotomy, and certainly cannot be put down to a corporeal stimulus-response mechanism (Merleau-Ponty 1962, 110-11). It is the combined mind/body knowing that allows for a being-in-the-world to exist.

Such a view of movement leads us to state that it is a socially embedded medium for action (Thornton 1971, 1). It is not an abstract action which lies outside of the meaning of the world, but is a medium through which we conduct our lives (Cresswell 2001, 14; Pandya 1990, 777; Thornton 1971, 31). As movement is a socially-produced phenomenon, its role in the socialisation of people is fundamental (Oglesby 1968). Whether as children growing up and learning, or as adults going about their daily existence, movement enables people's socialisation through participation in the world. This participation is multi-scalar in that a person fluidly exists as an individual, but also (within the same spatial and temporal realms) is participating within group socialities as well as a larger corporate sphere. Therefore, the picking up of information, knowledge, experience and ways of being-in-the-world all become a reality through the movements a person makes, and it is the varying scales at which such movements are undertaken that help produce the multiple ways of being of an individual (Ingold 2000, 203). Notably, emphasising the fluid and multiple layers of identity that a person may have is not to suggest that these identities were unproblematic. Certainly, tensions would have arisen between the various scales of being, and conflicts between, for example, the interests of the individual and those of the larger group would have played a major part in day-to-day existence.

We can, therefore, see how movement feeds into the sense of agency that an individual has. As movement allows for the participation of an individual in society, it is movement that mediates between the agency of a person and the societal structures that they are living within. Recursive patterns of movement help to reinforce knowledge of social rules, norms and behaviours by the habitual exposure to such structures. Ways of being in the world are constantly reaffirmed through the movements an individual makes in their lifetime. Therefore, if patterns of movement change, or become substantially tethered or restricted for instance, then participation in society is affected. The scale, motive and intensity of the movements of an individual not only inhere with the agency of a person, but also, at the same time, reflect the societal bounds a person is living within. So, on the one hand, movement situates an individual within a society, but on the other, it gives that individual the means by which to actively step outside of such structures. Movement therefore can be a reaffirming and situating medium for social discourse, but also a means by which such discourse can be challenged.

Movement, perception and the world

Having highlighted the essentiality of movement to being, it is now necessary to understand how through movement an individual engages with and experiences the world. The work of Tim Ingold (2000), building on studies of perception by James Gibson (1979), has considered how movement is integral to how one perceives the world. Implicitly, perception occurs through movement, and reciprocally, movement is enabled through perception (Bateson 1980, 107; Gibson 1979, 240; Ingold 2000, 203; Rosenbaum 1991, 24). Certainly, within ecological psychology, perceptual activity consists in the intentional movement of the whole being, and this is a constant act (Gibson 1979, 225). Such activity enables individuals to gain information about their surroundings through experiencing and engaging (Ingold 2000, 242).

As movement allows for the world to come-into-being, it is worth noting that the constitution of the world is not seen in the same way by everyone. Ingold (2000, 98, 242) stresses a phenomenological view, where the world

unfolds as individuals move along; phenomena are perceived and engaged with through the movements we make. The world is said to emerge and unfold at the same time the person emerges and perceives (Ingold 2000, 168). Alternatively, the ecological psychology of Gibson (1979) posits the world as being already furnished with affordances which are *a priori*. This pre-formed view of the world comes-into-being through the perception of surfaces and objects (Gibson 1979, 33). Again, movement is the key to both standpoints on perception; it is only how the world is constituted that is different. It is Ingold's (2000) phenomenological view of a world constantly coming-into-being that I believe is the most appropriate for theorising conceptions of being and the world. This is because we can have no conception of the world prior to actively apprehending and engaging with it (Ingold 2000; Thomas 2001, 173). This may be through a physical movement of the body (such as moving through the landscape), or engendered through a sub-conscious, experiential act (such as dreaming and shamanistic activities). Nevertheless, the world does not exist prior to our engagement with it; it emerges as we move along in the world. This emphasises the inherent dynamism and temporality of the world, as places/landscapes are never the same, however many times we visit them (Bender 1998 25; Pandya 1990, 792; Tilley 1994 27). There is always some form of change, which is apprehended through the movements of individuals within the world.

The creation of space through movement

The biggest drawback to the majority of prehistoric narratives that do consider human movement is that they usually see space as an affordance, that is a pre-fabricated backdrop for movement (see Bradley 1993; Thomas 1999; Tilley 1994). The main point of departure of this research, based on a reading of Ingold, is that it is movement that generates a sense of space and place. Often, it is narratives pertaining to the role of monuments within Neolithic and Bronze Age landscapes that emphasise how certain places influence movements. In particular, it is architecture and spatiality that are focused upon, and the configuration of monuments takes precedence over movement. Certainly, little consideration is given to how movement affects the structure of monuments in the first place, and it is normally assumed that monuments are *a priori* fixed entities in the landscape. This is to deny the whole process of the conception, creation, use and decay of monuments, and totally removes the influence of movement from the origins of monumental landscapes. Conversely, I want to put forward the idea that it is movement that generates a sense of space, place and notions of spatiality within the landscape, a sense which ultimately influences the shape monuments take. This standpoint is echoed by the work of Laban (1971) and Pandya (1990):

> …empty space does not exist. On the contrary, space is a superabundance of simultaneous movements and it is through the rhythm of movements that the forms of objects, as well as the shape

97

assumed by living organisms, wax and wane uninterruptedly.

(Laban in Thornton 1971, 28)

...movement alone defines and constructs space; space does not define and construct movement.

(Pandya 1990, 793)

To illustrate this point, let me introduce ethnographic research carried out with the Ongee hunter gatherer people of Little Andaman in the Bay of Bengal, which has revealed a completely different way of looking at the conception and configuration of space (Pandya 1990). The Ongees define space through the practice of movement, which is opposite to the prehistoric narratives mentioned above. Ongee ideology dictates that movement defines and generates space, and invests places with positive or negative values (Pandya 1990, 788). Both space and cosmology are created through movement, and the movements of people, animals and spirits all feed into the creation of space and place. Notably, people, animals and spirits move in different ways and on different paths; however, the intersections where these movements come together enable the hunting of animals, as well as meetings with spirits (Figure 11.1).

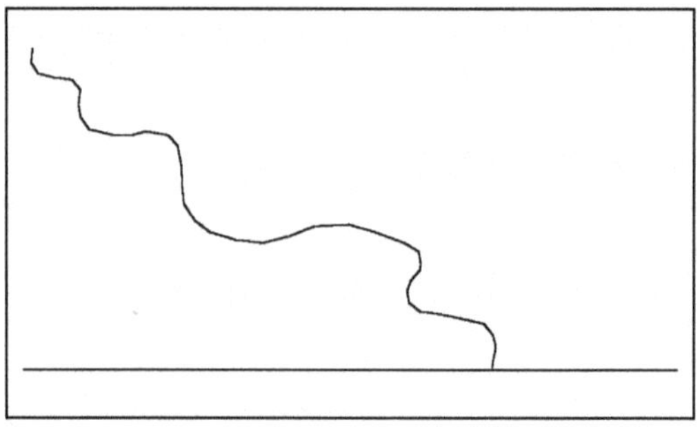

Figure 11.1. The movement paths of Ongee people (straight line) and Ongee spirits (wavy line), (after Pandya 1990, 785, fig. 1a).

The role of spirits is an important fundamental which permeates Ongee ideology at all levels. Generally, unplanned encounters with spirits are dangerous and to be avoided. Hence, knowing and mapping the movements of both people and spirits is a major concern, so as to prevent unplanned meetings. This makes the Ongees very movement-conscious and as a consequence, the world is seen as a perpetually moving stage (Pandya 1990, 779). The landscape is not thought of as a pre-determined backdrop, but as a dynamic place which is continually coming-into-being through human, spirit and animal networks of movement. This ethnographic account illustrates well how the construction of space/place cannot be divorced from movement – movement is fundamental to how space/place is created.

As the world continually unfolds as a person moves, it follows that conceptions of space that see it as a container for movement are inherently erroneous. Therefore, prehistoric monuments should not be viewed as *a priori* features within the landscape, but as features that are constantly coming-into-being through the movements of people around and within them. Emphasising movement shows how monumental places within the landscape are constantly changing – both in a physical (architectural) sense, and a conceptual, ideological one too. Monumental architectures are not waiting as inert backdrops for the movements of individuals - they are actively created as people engage with that part of the world. Architectural features may influence the movements of people, but this is flexible and temporally dependent. Through time, new ways of engaging with places emerge, arising out of patterns of socially constituted practice and current agencies. Posts or stones can be moved, ditches re-dug or filled in, new paths created and so on. In a more subtle way, the erosion/decay of features, regeneration of vegetation, and the gradual migration of old paths to new places all arise out of the ebb and flow of patterns of movement. Movements can be deliberately harnessed to put forward particular expressions of sociality at these places, for instance, the wearing down of areas of vegetation to indicate places that are 'inscribed' into the landscape – highlighting their currency and longevity. Certain monuments or parts of monuments may have been deliberately shunned at times to encourage the re-growth of vegetation and the erosion/decay of architectural features to suggest notions of disuse, evoking views of the distant past. No doubt, combinations of such patterns of movement were deliberately used at times to convey such messages, which would then have been accessed by others as they moved around the landscape. Notably, such phenomena would have also been the unconscious outcome of movement. Experiencing places that were in various stages of 'use' would have indicated to the traveller the biography, history and current social expressions of the group who was associated with the particular monument.

Movement and the multiple scales of identity

As movement is a socially produced medium through which we live our lives, it follows that the movements an individual undertakes feed into conceptions of identity. The locations, motives, intensity and experiences of patterns of movement help to engender differing constructions of identity. Significantly, it is the fluid nature of movement that allows for an individual to realise their multiple scales of identity. A person undertaking routine movements and activities reinforces their core sense of identity and personhood through the type, habitual nature and familiarity of movements (Bourdieu 1977; Ingold 2000, 325). Moreover, the locales of such familiar and routine *praxis* form an important part of identity composition (Buttimer 1981, 167). How an individual fits in with others around them becomes a reality through the paths and intersections of movement. These paths form the inter-relating web of movements of a community and thus enable constructions of small group identity. However, identity is also reinforced and challenged through experiencing situations that are not part of the everyday regime. Movements encountering more unusual and irregular situations may, on the one hand, help reinforce particular identities, but on the other, challenge them through accessing the identities of others and other places.

This is particularly relevant when we consider the notion of a corporate sphere of identity and interaction. With styles of monumentality being similar within the Great Ouse, Nene and Welland Valleys, greater concerns than small group identity can be suggested. Communal monuments (for instance, causewayed enclosures and cursus monuments) follow particular patterns and forms within each valley. This indicates that the expression of a broad scale consensus of valley identity was important during prehistory. This corporate notion would have been accessed and reinforced by the routine journeys of people along the course of each river valley (see Mills forthcoming). However, despite emphasising the fluid nature of the multiple scales of identity an individual may have, tensions between the individual, small group and corporate spheres of identity would have existed. Moreover, the degree to which such identities could be accessed by individuals (which would have been dependent upon the degree of movement an individual could undertake) would have been another source of potential stress. Therefore, movement forms a fundamental mechanism to how we construct identities and become aware of alternative identities, and also how we situate ourselves as beings-in-the-world.

The focused movements of people within particular places help to feed into constructions of place identity, not just through their habitual nature, but through their very physicality (see Mills forthcoming). People not only experience sights, sounds, and smells, but also the very topographies under foot. These 'muscular consciousnesses', as Bachelard (1964, 11) calls them, filter into the mind/body in an overt way (say when negotiating unfamiliar areas), or a non-conspicuous way (when moving around habitual places of movement). Through experiencing these topographies and textures, an individual becomes situated within familiar and unfamiliar places.

Applying a movement perspective: moving around in the Neolithic and Bronze Age

I will now briefly look at the archaeological evidence for the Neolithic and Bronze Age in the Great Ouse, Nene and Welland Valleys from a movement perspective. All three rivers rise in the Cotswolds/Northamptonshire Uplands region and flow in an easterly direction through the East Midlands into the East Anglian Fens (Figure 11.2). Each valley contains rich and diverse palimpsests of past activity, which vary from valley to valley and within different sections of the valleys themselves. The topography of each river valley is typically well defined in the upper and middle stretches, with valley bottoms grading into defined valley sides. However, as each river approaches the flat, low-lying fenlands, it becomes increasingly difficult to pin down where each valley lies.

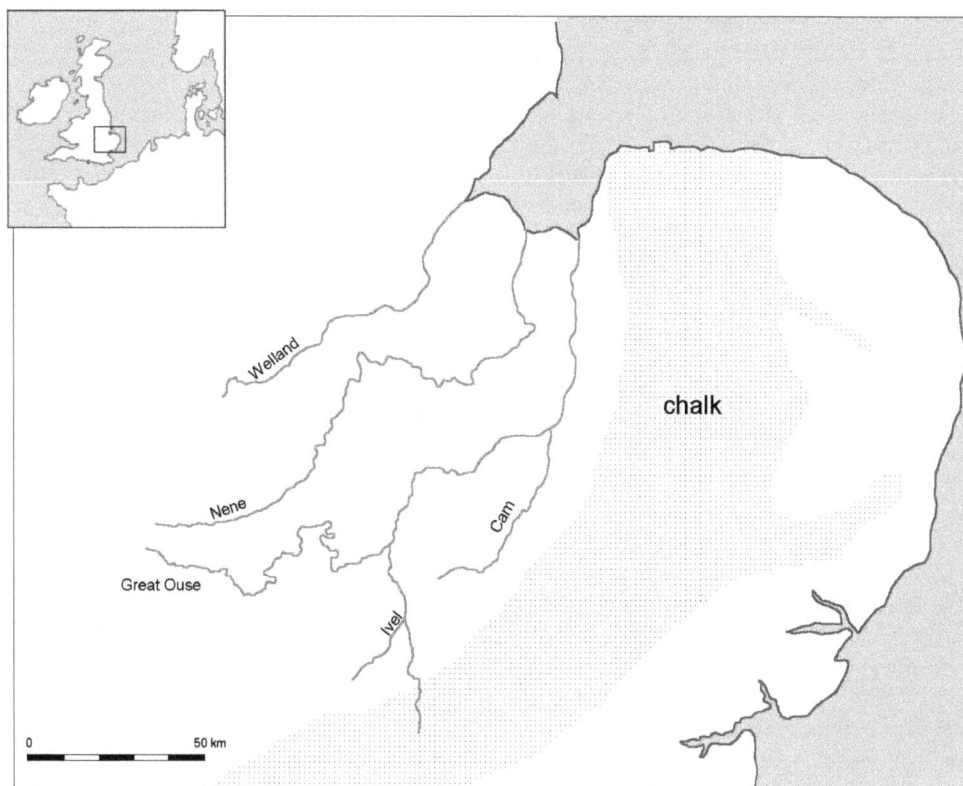

Figure 11.2. Location map showing the Great Ouse, Nene and Welland Valleys, eastern Britain.

99

From the distribution of Mesolithic lithic scatters, it seems that in this period, staying close to the river within each valley seems to have been important. Linear corridors of movement focusing upon the flow of each river were key, with little evidence for forays onto the higher valley sides and interfluves (Dawson 2000; Healy & Harding forthcoming). Gravel islands and ridges were favoured within the floodplain, as exemplified by sites such as Over Site 3, Haddenham and Biddenham in the Great Ouse Valley (Dawson 2000; Evans & Webley 2003; Hodder & Evans forthcoming), West Cotton, Ringstead and Orton Meadows in the Nene Valley (Healy & Harding forthcoming), and Glinton and Rectory Farm, West Deeping in the Welland Valley (French & Pryor forthcoming; Lincolnshire SMR). The floodplain zone would have felt quite enclosed, as woodland had yet to be cleared (French 2003, 89; Scaife 2000, 20), although greater variability and patchiness in vegetation would have been more likely as a result of anthropogenic, faunal and hydrological disturbances (Evans 2003, 77; Field 2004, 155).

Early Neolithic

By the Early Neolithic, evidence for dwelling within all three valleys occurs in the same places that saw Mesolithic occupation. There is a strong floodplain and valley terrace continuity, with linear flows of routine movement focusing on each river being most significant. Notably, it is at this time that the first monuments are constructed within small clearings in the floodplains of each valley. Intersections of paths of floodplain movement appear to be salient, with many of the earliest monuments being deliberately situated in areas of focused Later Mesolithic movements. For instance, the Long Mound (3940-3780 cal BC) at West Cotton in the middle Nene overlies (and incorporates in its turf mound) large quantities of Mesolithic lithics, as well as a number of tree-throw holes (Healy & Harding forthcoming, 31-34). Close by, the density of lithics suggests that this was a significant node within the Mesolithic network of floodplain movements, subject to repeat visits over a long period of time. Again, within the Great Ouse Valley on the Fen-edge, the long barrow at Foulmire Fen, Haddenham was placed at the juncture of repeated Mesolithic movements (Hodder & Evans forthcoming).

Conversely, the unique trapezoidal enclosure further upstream at Godmanchester (4000-3700 cal BC – OxA-3370) does not appear to have been directly placed over previous Mesolithic occupation (McAvoy 2000). Nevertheless, its siting within the floodplain and its orientation on the flow of the river strongly suggest that this monument was referencing past and present flows of movement up and down the Great Ouse – but in a less 'direct' way. This is also repeated at the West Cotton long barrow just south of the monument complex on the river Nene. Here, the long barrow was placed into a recent clearing and covered Early Neolithic lithics and tree-throws. There was evidence for light grazing; however, clearance appears to have occurred just prior to its construction (Healy & Harding forthcoming, 38). From deliberately incorporating the materiality of past activities to the referencing of more general patterns of landscape

movement, the locations of the earliest monuments within the three valleys strongly suggest that they were primarily embedded within significant flows of mobility which had their origins within the Mesolithic. The playing out of new architectures and spatialities was being undertaken in established places where the maximum amount of people would have accessed and experienced these social expressions; they were not placed into backwaters that saw little movement.

The location of causewayed enclosures also poses interesting questions (Figure 11.3). Distributions vary within each valley, with just two known enclosures 50 km apart within the Great Ouse at Cardington and Haddenham (Clark 1991; Evans 1988). In contrast, the Nene saw a pair of enclosures at Briar Hill and Dallington and an oval enclosure at Southwick 40 km downstream. The site of Upton is just 15 km beyond (Bamford 1985; Healy & Harding forthcoming). The difference in enclosure form and location within these two valleys suggests the assertion of a wider-scale identity through the varied form and spatiality of such monuments. Within the lower Welland Valley approaching the Fens, an unprecedented concentration of enclosures occurs. Characterised by their somewhat oval shape, the sites at Etton, Northborough, Barholm and Uffington form a distinct focus of Early Neolithic activity which is missing from the upper and middle stretches, yet mirrors the two oval enclosures on the lower Nene (Oswald et al. 2001, xii; Pryor 1998a). Four other possible Welland sites have been postulated at nearby Glinton and Peakirk, and on land to the west of Etton (French & Pryor forthcoming; Pryor 2002, 20). The large number and unusual spatial proximity of these enclosures to each other has engendered interpretations of this area as a prehistoric cultural boundary (Pryor 2002).

Interestingly, this proliferation of a similar form of causewayed enclosure on the lower Welland and Nene does suggest more focused relations between the two valleys at this point than is witnessed between other areas of all three valleys. Notably, the oval enclosure at Upton is situated close to a pronounced meander of the Nene near Wansford which marks the shortest distance between the Welland and Nene rivers (Figure 11.3). Just to the west of the Upton enclosure, many leaf-shaped arrowheads, flint and polished stone axes have been found in the parish of Thornhaugh (Peterborough SMR). Potentially, this enclosure and surrounding area may have marked a symbolic threshold and corridor of movement between the two valleys which necessitated demarcation. Notably, enclosures have been seen as places where potentially 'polluting', 'risky' or 'liminal' activities may have been carried out (Edmonds 1999, 114; Thomas 1999, 42-43). Perhaps, movement between the two valleys or the coming together of neighbouring groups was a risky or polluting business that was undertaken with recourse to powerful protective rituals and special patterns of movement. Therefore, one can envisage that it may have been necessary to attend the enclosure at Upton, as it mitigated the risk involved in the 7.5km journey over gently rolling interfluves to reach the Welland River at Barnack (and vice versa). Barnack is a significant place, as it later became embellished with a small cursus and hengiforms, and marks the start of the causewayed enclosure zone within

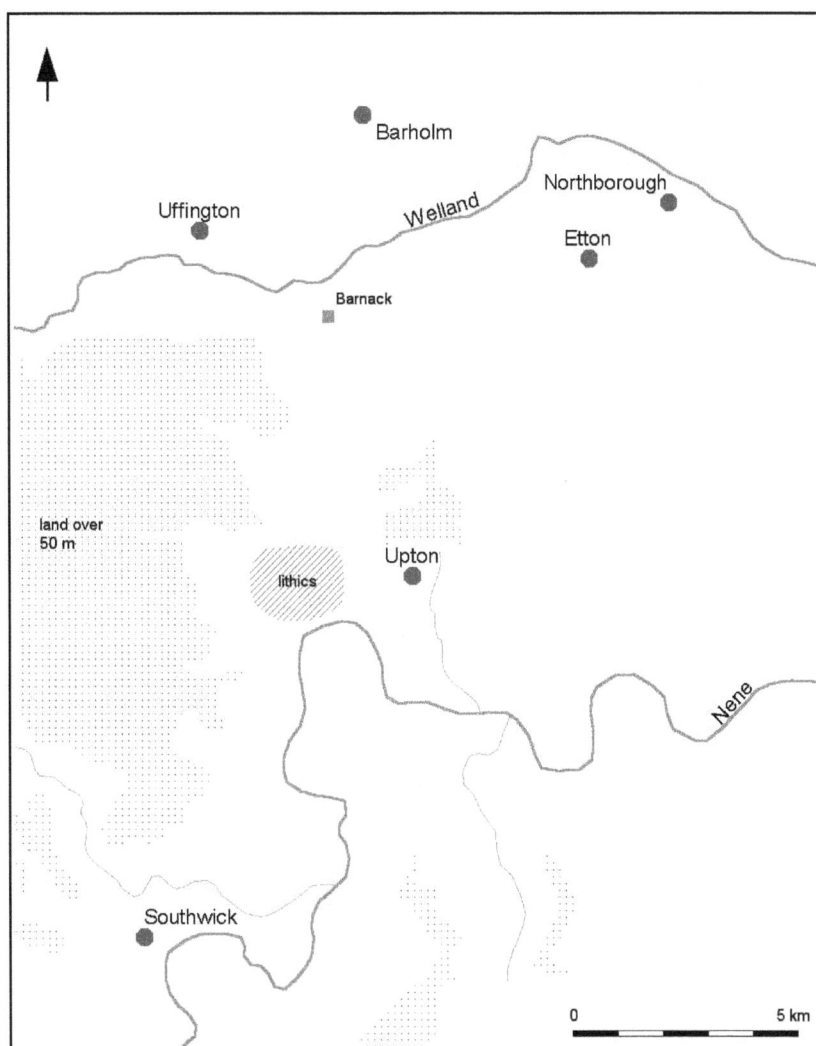

Figure 11.3. The oval causewayed enclosures of the lower Nene and Welland Valleys
(after Oswald *et al.* 2001, 110, fig. 6.3).

the lower Welland (RCHME 1960, 39; Reynolds 1992). The similarity in the oval form of enclosures, plus the small distance between both rivers at this point, suggest that aspects of corporate identity were being asserted through movements at a wider landscape scale (between valleys) than was usually seen elsewhere.

Nevertheless, the causewayed enclosures within the Great Ouse and upper Nene Valleys indicate that inter-valley connections and aggregations were generally of more importance than attending enclosures outside of an individual's 'valley-zone'. This is supported by the variety in enclosure form, as well as the similarity of pottery found at such places. For instance, the pottery assemblages at Briar Hill and Haddenham show different trends pertaining to each enclosure (Bamford 1985; Evans 1988, 130). However, this is not to say that people from further afield did not attend these places. Evidence for non-local artefacts (such as Group VI axes from Cumbria) show that certain people, objects (and probably animals), were travelling much longer distances. Moreover, a more detailed look at the locations of causewayed enclosures suggests that whilst they were located in primary zones of

floodplain movement which pertained to local concerns and was intimately linked with local identities, their siting simultaneously makes them readily accessible to wider networks of movement (Edmonds 1999, 88). For instance, Cardington may have served the upper and middle stretch of the Great Ouse Valley primarily, but via the river Ivel and Hiz may have linked communities in the valley with the chalk ridge of the Chilterns to the south. Haddenham, with its Fen-edge location, may have been concerned with communities in the lower Great Ouse and Fens, however, non-local flint deposited within the façade area of the enclosure (Hodder & Evans forthcoming) shows that again, links with the chalk ridge to the south (via interfluve and the river Cam) were important (Figure 11.3). In the Nene Valley, Briar Hill may have served the southern area of the upper Nene, and Dallington the zone to the north. People within the upper Welland, so far largely devoid of Neolithic monuments, may have focused upon the enclosure at Husband's Bosworth (Butler *et al.* 2002). There are many more examples for close contacts and flows of movement at certain points between the river valleys, but space precludes their mention here.

101

Middle Neolithic

In contrast to the earlier importance of contacts, by the Middle Neolithic period the construction of cursus monuments suggests that assertions of a particular 'valley-specific identity' was becoming more important. Furthermore, localised signatures within the broad tradition of cursus construction were being played out within particular stretches of each valley. For example, within the Great Ouse Valley, from its middle reaches downstream to the Fen-edge, six small cursus sites have been discovered at Cardington, Buckden, Eynesbury, Brampton, Godmanchester and Fen Drayton, (Last 1999, 91; Malim 1999; 2000). Another site at Kempston (quarried away over 50 years ago) is somewhat doubtful (Stephen Coleman pers. comm.). These sites can be placed into Loveday's 'minor' category of cursus, ranging in length from 100+ m at Cardington to 500+ m at Godmanchester (Ellis 2004, 6; Last 1999, 89-90; Loveday 1985; Malim 2000, 72). In complete contrast, this emphasis on cursus monuments is not witnessed to this degree and character in the neighbouring Nene Valley. So far, only two possible sites at Hardingstone and Ailsworth have been discovered (Healy & Harding forthcoming; Peterborough SMR). Further north in the Welland Valley, three cursuses are known from the lower reaches at Barnack, and close to the Fen-edge at Etton and Maxey. The cursuses at Etton/Maxey are unusual for this region due to their combined length, which at approximately 2 km long can be classed in the same 'major' category as Buscot, Benson and Dorchester-on-Thames on the Upper Thames (Barclay & Hey 1999, 72; Last 1999, 92; Loveday 1999, 60).

Such a varied uptake in cursus construction between all three valleys, combined with the much localised differences between cursuses within each valley, strongly suggest that by the Middle Neolithic, communities within each river valley were becoming more focused upon flows of movement that were rooted in more circumscribed places in the landscape. These more focused routine movements would have helped foster increasingly localised senses of group and place identity, partly through feeling the particular topographies and textures in their 'muscular consciousness' (Bachelard 1964, 11). Notably, cursus monuments (just like the Early Neolithic monuments) were placed into the floodplain, the zone of routine movement, thus enhancing their power to engage with moving individuals. Floodplain mobility was still important within each river valley, but by now, such movements were becoming more constrained by the social expression of monuments. The spatial arrangement of each cursus ensured that, whether one had to negotiate its broad-side as it blocked a significant part of the floodplain or whether one walked parallel to its length, following the flow of the river, travelling past these monuments would have impacted upon previous flows of movement. Even after the silting up of cursus ditches, when the cursus no longer posed a physical influence on journeys, the area of the cursus may still have precluded everyday movements through a more enduring symbolic demarcation of the landscape (Harding 1999, 34). Through manipulating the movements of people and animals within the floodplain, the social expression and power of the particular group associated with the monument would have been asserted.

So, whilst moving up and down the floodplain, people encountered monuments which expressed the identities of their builders. The act of moving past such structures enabled those not involved in the construction of such sites to express and reflect upon their own conceptions of identity.

Late Neolithic

By the Late Neolithic, people became more concerned with routine movements around particular sections of each valley. This is evidenced by the location of monuments and the expansion of lithic scatters on the higher terraces and valley sides, and was intimately linked to the increasing clearance of woodland from those areas (Campbell & Robinson forthcoming; French 2003; Robinson 2000; Scaife 2000). Monumentality was expressed at a progressively smaller scale, mainly taking the form of small henges, hengiforms, ring ditches and penannular ring ditches. These monuments were being placed not only into the established monument complexes within each valley, but were spilling out onto previously non-monumentalized places in the floodplain. For example, in the Great Ouse Valley at Goldington, a small henge and ring ditch were placed on the opposite bank of the river to the earlier Cardington monument complex (Mustoe 1988). Other potential examples also occur within this complex (Clark 1991, 10). Further downstream at Over, a small hengiform associated with Grooved Ware pottery was found close to the river (Evans & Webley 2003, 73-5). Within the Nene, potential henges exist at Elton, Woodford, and Raunds (Healy & Harding forthcoming 124). Notably, the attribution of henge status to the large enclosure situated on the valley side at West Cotton is open to speculation. Whilst similar in form to the 'great' henge at Maxey in the lower Welland, both these monuments may be more similar to sites like the large barrow at Duggleby Howe in Yorkshire (Healy & Harding forthcoming, 90). Within the Welland Valley, a number of small henges/hengiforms are located close to the river at Barnack and downstream at Etton (French & Pryor forthcoming; Harding & Lee 1987; Reynolds 1992; RCHME 1960).

The gradual focusing of movement into areas which covered smaller sections of floodplain, but more varied parts of the valley sides and interfluves, is evidenced by the increasing amount of lithics found further away from the river (Healy & Harding forthcoming, 121; Woodward 1978). The degree to which people were able to move up and down each valley as part of routine moves is difficult to ascertain. Whilst fluidity in communications and relations between groups within the valleys would still have been salient, taken together the increasingly small-scale nature of monuments, the growing need to tether individuals to particular places through burial, as well as new places becoming monumentalized all suggest that there was more scope for tensions within the traditional flows of movement that concentrated on the river. Over time, however, the habitual nature of being focused within particular areas would have fed both physically and ideologically into particular affinities and identities that were intimately linked with the locality in which groups were moving. Thus, it may have been increasingly less attractive for groups of people to follow long-ranging linear patterns of routine movement along the course of the river, as people felt more 'situated' within smaller zones of the landscape.

Early Bronze Age

Evidence for Early Bronze Age life within all three valleys is similar, with increasing amounts of lithics occurring on the valley sides and interfluves (Healy & Harding forthcoming, 121; Taylor 1985, 15-23; Woodward 1978). Burial under a round barrow or within a ring ditch becomes prolific, with a floodplain location being favoured within each valley. Clustering of round barrows/ring ditches into groups is significant within the upper and middle sections of the rivers. For example, in the Great Ouse Valley, five barrows mark the confluence of that river with the Ivel (Taylor & Woodward 1985). In the Nene at Fotheringhay/Nassington, a major concentration of ring ditches occurs (RCHME 1975, 67). Where the relief flattens out as each river approaches and enters the Fens, greater numbers of round barrows/ring ditches occur. This is exemplified on the lower Welland around Tallington, Maxey, Etton and Borough Fen (RCHME 1960), the lower Nene around Cat's Water and on the lower Great Ouse at Over/Haddenham (Hall 1987, 175-76; Healy & Harding forthcoming, Fig. 5.15). Furthermore, it is at this time that evidence for the first field system at Fengate has been discovered, located just to the north of the River Nene (Pryor 2001).

The increasing association of particular deceased individuals to specific places, tethering them in the landscape, and the tentative beginnings of field systems, both indicate that a transformation in attitudes towards movement, identity and inter-group relations was occurring. With settlement evidence still very ephemeral within each river valley, lithics and the occasional Beaker pit constituting the typical evidence, it can be assumed that people were still living mobile lives. Therefore, we have a situation where routine movements were being played out within a network permeated by more and more places where movement had ceased. At the same time, groups were becoming more embedded, and moving around in increasingly particular tracts of each river valley. The round barrows/ring ditches may have represented the manifestation of a group's identity and affinity for particular places within each valley. Lineages of kin were being tied to places, creating histories intimately linked to geographical locales. The particular impact of such practices lies in the fact that these individuals were no longer moving. They had reached their final resting point in a particular place in the landscape, and this was commemorated in a very physical way. This contrasts greatly with earlier Neolithic practice, which saw the circulation and movement of individuals even after death. Therefore, by the Early Bronze Age, we can see that the cessation of the particular movements of dead people preceded notions of more permanent settlement for the living. It appears that the dead had to be tethered first, before this could occur for the living. Perhaps this was linked to the potential power that the dead held within Bronze Age society, their long-term presence legitimising/marking out certain places for permanent settlement by the

living. Therefore, we can see that different facets of life were being tethered at different temporal scales, and that despite people being strongly associated to place during the Early Bronze Age, it was not until the Middle Bronze Age that life within each valley became more focused upon longer periods of more settled existence.

Keeping on the move vs. settling down: changes in *mentalité* by the Middle Bronze Age

Over time, associations with specific places were becoming focal within each river valley. Movements were becoming more circumscribed and tethered, with greater numbers of people being overtly 'tethered' to places in the landscape through burial. However, it was not until the Middle Bronze Age that we see more permanent structures with both roundhouses and occasional rectilinear structures and field systems becoming visible, particularly in the Fenland archaeological record. For instance, at Welland Bank on the lower Welland, Middle Bronze Age round and rectangular houses focused behind an Early Bronze Age earthen bank. Various pits containing charcoal and Deverel-Rimbury pottery and six bowl hearths have been excavated. Notably, this settlement ties in with a co-axial, ditched field system that expands to the east of the settlement (Pryor 1998b, 113-23; 1998c, 139-45). Only six km to the south is another similar field system at Borough Fen. Again, the use of long droveways aligned on the Fen-edge was salient at this site (Pryor 2001, 72). Looking west from the Welland Bank settlement, approximately five km away on the lower Welland, another co-axial field system aligned on a series of earlier Bronze Age round barrows has been excavated at West Deeping (Pryor 1998b, 110-13). Further south, on the lower Nene, the infamous fields at Fengate were still in use (Pryor 2001, 409). On the lower Great Ouse, at Over Site 5, two roundhouses, a four post structure, and pits were found associated with a series of rectilinear paddocks (Evans 2002, 46). At neighbouring Barleycroft Farm, Needingworth, a Middle Bronze Age compound contained a long house and roundhouses and was associated with a field system encompassing 35+ hectares (Evans & Knight 2000, 97; 2001). Further upstream from these Fen-edge examples, field systems are also known at Brampton and probably Cardington in the Great Ouse Valley (Evans & Knight 2000; Last 1996; Mustoe 1988), and Raunds in the middle Nene Valley (Healy & Harding forthcoming, 22). Not only were these more permanent architectures highly visual expressions of the sociality of a group, but in a more fundamental sense they curtailed and manipulated many movements within the floodplain of each valley.

By now, it appears that valley communities were not so much governed by a *mentalité* that espoused 'keeping on the move', but one that focused upon the actual 'place' of movement. Therefore, moving around in particular locales which were familiar, rooted and were invested with the histories and biographies of a group was the central concern. The actual action of moving perhaps took more of a backseat. This is not to suggest that people no longer undertook long-ranging movements, as specific roles and events would have warranted various scales of movement within the valleys. For instance, herding livestock, attending inter-group ceremonies, trade, exchange and the manipulation of particular resources may have taken an individual or group outside of their domain of habitual life. However, these movements would have been less defined by the journey itself than by the destination and motive of that journey. Leaving and returning to places that an individual was rooted to would have been at the forefront of such actions, as opposed to the process of 'getting there'. This is in great contrast to previous periods, when places were certainly important but the movements taken to visit such places were the key to a group's *mentalité*.

Conclusion

This chapter has shown why a consideration of movement within a society is fundamentally important. From a much generalised summary of the archaeological evidence from the Great Ouse, Nene and Welland Valleys, we can suggest that movement formed an over-riding facet of Neolithic and Bronze Age ideologies and *mentalités*. The evidence suggests that through time, the motive, intensity, location, manipulation and transformation of movements affected how groups within the valleys viewed themselves and each other. Tensions within more traditional earlier Neolithic movement networks, which focused upon the floodplains, gradually came to the fore as routine spheres became increasingly monumentalized. By the later Neolithic, the progressive tethering of communities to particular places through their dead, and through the very physical expressions of their smaller, but more numerous monuments indicate that *mentalités* were beginning to change. However, this was a very long transformation, which increased in pace during the Early Bronze Age.

Therefore, we can see that through conscious short-term shifts in patterns of movement, almost imperceptible changes in the *mentalité* of valley people were worked through over long periods of time. Over-riding concerns changed from an existence for which 'keeping on the move' was salient to one where being associated with, and tethered to, a particular area was more important. Starting from less encumbered and hindered movements in the Early Neolithic, and after a change towards moving around more circumscribed areas in the Early Bronze Age, controlling movements (and thus claims to areas of the landscape) had become the primary concern by the Middle Bronze Age.

How far back did people remember ancestral trails? Were communities aware of the extent to which they once moved? Or did the gradual circumscription of movements occur so imperceptibly, over a long period of time, that it was not directly challenged? By the Middle Bronze Age, the construction of complexes of fields, as well as some permanent 'domestic' architecture suggests that the tethering of movements in particular parts of the landscape were key. Whilst this would have been borne out of the gradual changes and curtailment of longer range movements that were of importance during the Mesolithic and earlier Neolithic, through time, being related to and physically 'feeling' and sensing the landscape of habitual living led to people wanting to move around in their familiar locales through a conscious choice.

Acknowledgements

I would like to thank Dani Hofmann and Andy Cochrane for comments on previous drafts - needless to say, any errors or omissions are entirely my own. Thanks also to Alasdair Whittle for much discussion and comment over the years regarding movement. Finally, the financial assistance of the AHRC who have funded this PhD research into prehistoric movement is gratefully acknowledged.

References

Bachelard, G. 1964. *The poetics of space.* Boston: Beacon Press.

Bamford, H. 1985. *Briar Hill excavation 1974-1978.* Northampton: Northampton Development Corporation.

Barclay, A. & Hey, G. 1999. Cattle, cursus monuments and the river: the development of ritual and domestic landscapes in the Upper Thames Valley. In A. Barclay & J. Harding (eds), *Pathways and ceremonies: the cursus monuments of Britain and Ireland,* 67-76. Oxford: Oxbow.

Bateson, G. 1980. *Mind and nature: a necessary unity.* London: Fontana/Collins.

Bender, B. 1998. *Stonehenge: making space.* Oxford: Berg.

Bender, B. 2001. Landscapes on-the-move. *Journal of Social Archaeology* 1(1), 75-89.

Best, D. 1974. *Expression in movement and the arts: a philosophical enquiry.* London: Lepus.

Bourdieu, P. 1977. *Outline of a theory of practice.* Cambridge: Cambridge University Press.

Bradley, R. 1993. *Altering the earth.* Edinburgh: Society of Antiquaries of Scotland.

Butler, A., Clay, P. & Thomas, J. 2002. A causewayed enclosure at Husbands Bosworth, Leicestershire. In. G. Varndell & P. Topping (eds), *Enclosures in Neolithic Europe,* 107-9. Oxford: Oxbow.

Buttimer, A. 1981. Home, reach and the sense of place. In A. Buttimer & D. Seamon (eds), *The human experience of space and place,* 166-87. London: Croom Helm.

Campbell, G. & Robinson, M. forthcoming. Environment and land use in the valley bottom. In F. Healy & J. Harding, *Raunds area project: the Neolithic and Bronze Age landscapes of West Cotton, Stanwick and Irthlingborough, Northamptonshire.* English Heritage.

Clark, R. 1991. Bedford Southern Bypass. *South Midlands Archaeology* 21, 8-11.

Close, A.E. 2000. Reconstructing movement in prehistory. *Journal of Archaeological Method and Theory* 7(1), 49-77.

Cratty, B.J. 1964. *Movement behaviour and motor learning.* London: Henry Kimpton.

Creswell, T. 2001. The production of mobilities. *New Formations* 43, 11-25.

Cuba, L. & Hummon, D.M. 1993. Constructing a sense of home: place, affiliation and migration across the life cycle. *Sociological Forum* 8(4), 547-72.

Dawson, M. 2000. The Mesolithic interlude. In M. Dawson (ed.), *Prehistoric, Roman and post-Roman landscapes of the Great Ouse Valley*, 45-50. York: CBA.

Edmonds, M. 1999. *Ancestral geographies of the Neolithic*. London: Routledge.

Ellis, C. 2004. A prehistoric ritual complex at Eynesbury, Cambridgeshire. *East Anglian Archaeology* 17, Salisbury: Wessex Archaeology.

Evans, C. 1988. Excavations at Haddenham, Cambridgeshire: a 'planned' enclosure and its regional affinities. In C. Burgess, P. Topping, C. Mordant & M. Maddison (eds), *Enclosures and defences in the Neolithic of western Europe*, 127-47. Oxford: BAR.

Evans, C. 2002. *Excavations at Over: the Church's Rise sites*. Unpublished report. Cambridge Archaeological Unit.

Evans, C. & Knight, M. 2000. A Fenland delta: later prehistoric land-use in the lower Ouse reaches. In M. Dawson (ed.), *Prehistoric, Roman and Post-Roman landscapes of the Great Ouse Valley*, 89-106. York: CBA.

Evans, C. & Webley, L. 2003. *A delta landscape: the Over lowlands investigations (II) – the 2001 evaluation*. Unpublished report. Cambridge Archaeological Unit.

Evans, J.G. 2003. *Environmental archaeology and the social order*. London: Routledge.

Farnell, B. 1994. Ethno-graphics and the moving body. *Man* 29(4), 929-74.

Field, D. 2004. Sacred geographies in the Neolithic of south-east England. In J. Cotton & D. Field (eds), *Towards a new stone age: aspects of the Neolithic in south-east England*, 154-63. York: CBA.

French, C. 2003. *Geoarchaeology in action: studies in soil micromorphology and landscape evolution*. London: Routledge.

French, C. & Pryor, F. forthcoming. Archaeology and environment of the Etton landscape. *East Anglian Archaeology*.

Gibson, J.J. 1979. *The ecological approach to visual perception*. Boston: Houghton Mifflin.

Hall, D. 1987. Regional fieldwork on the Wash Fenlands of England. In J. Coles & A. Lawson (eds), *European wetlands in prehistory*, 169-80. Oxford: Clarendon Press.

Harding, A.F., & Lee, G.E. 1987. *Henge monuments and related sites of Great Britain*. Oxford: BAR.

Harding, J. 1999. Pathways to new realms: cursus monuments and symbolic territories. In A. Barclay & J. Harding (eds), *Pathways and ceremonies: the cursus monuments of Britain and Ireland*, 30-8. Oxford: Oxbow.

Harris, M. 2000. *Life on the Amazon: the anthropology of a Brazilian peasant village*. Oxford: Oxford University Press.

Hawkes, C.F.C. 1954. Archaeological theory and method: some suggestions from the Old World. *American Anthropologist* 56, 155-68.

Healy, F. & Harding, J. forthcoming. *Raunds area project: the Neolithic and Bronze Age landscapes of West Cotton, Stanwick and Irthlingborough, Northamptonshire*. English Heritage.

Hodder, I. & Evans, C. forthcoming. *A woodland archaeology: the Haddenham Project, volume I*. Cambridge: MacDonald Institute Research Papers.

Ingold, T. 1987. *The appropriation of nature: essays on human ecology and social relations*. Iowa City: University of Iowa Press.

Ingold, T. 2000. *The perception of the environment: essays in livelihood, dwelling and skill*. London: Routledge.

Lamb, W. & Watson, E. 1979. *Body code: the meaning in movement*. London: Routledge & Kegan Paul.

Last, J. 1996. A buried prehistoric landscape at Huntingdon Racecourse, Cambridgeshire. *Mid Anglia Group Bulletin* spring, 30-33.

Last, J. 1999. Out of line: cursuses and monument typology in eastern England. In A. Barclay & J. Harding (eds), *Pathways and ceremonies: the cursus monuments of Britain and Ireland*, 86-97. Oxford: Oxbow.

Lewis, J. 1995. Genre and embodiment: from Brazilian Capoeira to the ethnology of human movement. *Cultural Anthropology* 10(2), 221-43.

Loveday, R. 1985. *Cursuses and related monuments of the British Neolithic*. Unpublished PhD thesis. University of Leicester.

Loveday, R. 1999. Dorchester-on-Thames – ritual complex or ritual landscape? In A. Barclay & J. Harding (eds), *Pathways and ceremonies: the cursus monuments of Britain and Ireland*, 49-63. Oxford: Oxbow.

Malim, T. 1999. Cursuses and related monuments of the Cambridgeshire Ouse. In A. Barclay & J. Harding (eds), *Pathways and ceremonies: the cursus monuments of Britain and Ireland*, 77-85. Oxford: Oxbow.

Malim, T. 2000. The ritual landscape of the Neolithic and Bronze Age along the middle and lower Ouse Valley. In M. Dawson (ed.), *Prehistoric, Roman and Post-Roman landscapes of the Great Ouse Valley*, 57-88. York: CBA.

McAvoy, F. 2000. The development of a Neolithic monument complex at Godmanchester, Cambridgeshire. In M. Dawson (ed.), *Prehistoric, Roman and post-Roman landscapes of the Great Ouse Valley*, 51-56. York: CBA.

McMahon, T.A. 1984. *Muscles, reflexes and locomotion*. Princeton: Princeton University Press.

Merleau-Ponty, M. 1962. *Phenomenology of perception*. London: Routledge.

Mills, J. forthcoming. The role of inter-valley journeys in creating Neolithic identities in the Great Ouse Valley. In V. Cummings & R. Johnston (eds), *Prehistoric journeys,* Oxford: Oxbow.

Mustoe, R.S. 1988. Salvage excavation of a Neolithic and Bronze Age ritual site at Goldington, Bedford: a preliminary report. *Bedfordshire Archaeological Journal* 18, 1-5.

Oglesby, C.A. 1968. Movement and culture. In H.M. Smith (ed.), *Introduction to human movement*, 37-48. Reading, MA: Addison Wesley Publishing Co.

Osborne, R. 1991. The potential mobility of human populations. *Oxford Journal of Archaeology* 10(2), 231-52.

Oswald, A., Dyer, C. & Barber, M. 2001. *The creation of monuments: Neolithic causewayed enclosures in the British Isles.* Swindon: English Heritage.

Pandya, V. 1990. Movement and space: Andamese cartography. *American Ethnologist* 17(4), 775-97.

Pryor, F. 1998a. *Etton: excavations at a Neolithic causewayed enclosure near Maxey, Cambridgeshire, 1982-7.* London: English Heritage.

Pryor, F. 1998b. *Farmers in prehistoric Britain.* Stroud: Tempus.

Pryor, F. 1998c. Welland Bank Quarry, south Lincolnshire. *Current Archaeology* 160, 139-45.

Pryor, F. 2001. *The Flag Fen basin: archaeology and environment of a Fenland landscape.* Swindon: English Heritage.

Pryor, F. 2002. The Welland Valley as a cultural boundary zone: an example of long-term history. In T. Lane & J. Coles (eds), *Through wet and dry: essays in honour of David Hall,* 18-32. Sleaford: Lincolnshire Archaeology and Heritage.

Reynolds, T. 1992. *A buried prehistoric landscape at Barnack.* Unpublished report. Cambridgeshire Archaeological Field Unit.

Robinson, M. 2000. Coleopteran evidence for the elm decline, Neolithic activity in woodland, clearance and the use of the landscape. In A.S. Fairbairn (ed.), *Plants in Neolithic Britain and beyond,* 27-36. Oxford: Oxbow.

Rosenbaum, D.A. 1991. *Human motor control.* San Diego: Academic Press Inc.

Royal Commission on Historical Monuments England, 1960. *A matter of time: an archaeological survey of the river gravels of England.* London: HMSO.

Royal Commission on Historical Monuments England, 1975. *An inventory of the historical monuments in the County of Northampton. North East.* London: HMSO.

Scaife, R. 2000. The prehistoric vegetation and environment of the river Ouse valley. In M. Dawson (ed.), *Prehistoric, Roman and post-Roman landscapes of the Great Ouse Valley,* 17-26. York: CBA.

Seamon, D. 1979. *A geography of the lifeworld: movement, rest and encounter.* London: Croom Helm.

Seamon, D. 1980. Body-subject, time-space routines, and place-ballets. In A. Buttimer & D. Seamon (eds), *The human experience of space and place,* 148-65. London: Croom Helm.

Smith, H.M. 1968. The nature of human movement. In H.M. Smith (ed.), *Introduction to human movement,* 3-7. Reading, MA: Addison Wesley Publishing Co.

Taylor, A. & Woodward, P. 1985. A Bronze Age barrow cemetery, and associated settlement at Roxton, Bedfordshire. *Archaeological Journal* 142, 73-149.

Taylor, M. 1985. The transect survey. In F. Pryor & C. French, *The Fenland Project No. 1: the Lower Welland Valley, vol. 1,* 15-23. Cambridge: East Anglian Archaeology 27.

Thomas, J. 1999. *Understanding the Neolithic.* London: Routledge.

Thomas, J. 2001. Archaeologies of place and landscape. In I. Hodder (ed.), *Archaeological theory today,* 165-86. Cambridge: Polity Press.

Thornton, S. 1971. *A movement perspective of Rudolf Laban.* London: Macdonald & Evans.

Tilley, C. 1994. *A phenomenology of landscape: places, paths and monuments.* Oxford: Berg.

Tricker, R.A.R. & Tricker, B.J.K. 1966. *The science of movement.* London: Mills & Boon.

Woodward, P. 1978. Flint distribution, ring ditches and Bronze Age settlement patterns in the Great Ouse Valley. *Archaeological Journal* 135, 32-56.

Reopening old trails – Rethinking mobility: a study of mesolithic northeast Ireland

Thomas Kador

Abstract

This paper takes the position that, as a routine activity, mobility in the present as well as the prehistoric past cannot be explained in a singular manner as simply either an economic, social or ideological phenomenon. It therefore strives towards an approach which challenges the dominant black and white narratives of human movement in early prehistory. The distinct treatment mobility has consistently received in interpretations of the earliest – pre-neolithic[1] – parts of prehistory, focusing on 'basic issues', compared to a much stronger emphasis on the social aspects in recent accounts of later periods, has resulted in a marked rift in how the subject has been approached, especially between mesolithic and neolithic researchers. This in turn has compounded the difficulties comparing these periods with regard to continuity and change. In this paper it shall be demonstrated that narratives focusing on social and ideological aspects, in addition to the common economic ones, are possible throughout early prehistory. At the core of the study lies an assumption that movement is a means of expression and is therefore strongly linked to people's social relationships, identities and ideologies. Therefore, by studying people's movements we should be able to make interesting statements about aspects of their lives beyond the purely economic domain. The study presented here is based on ongoing research with particular regard to a study area in northeast Ireland. As outlined above, the concept of mobility is employed as a way of understanding the myriad factors interacting in people's everyday lives. In so doing, it is hoped the paper may help to make inroads into territories that have so far remained largely closed to early prehistoric and in particular mesolithic research.

Introduction

'From their [hunter-gatherer] point of view both moral and physical movement, the religious journey and the economic quest for food, are part of the same process: namely *living*' (Ingold 1986, 153; emphasis in original).

Human movement is very much an everyday practice, it is the lifeblood for a healthy body and mind and being mobile is an important part of our human identity. Yet in archaeology mobility has received rather generalised treatment and would often appear to be taken for granted as simply a consequence or reflection of more pressing concerns, be they economic, social or ideological ones.

This has resulted in mobility often being discussed only implicitly with little attention dedicated to people's movements themselves as a subject worth studying. This implicit treatment of mobility has a long history in early prehistoric scholarship and the resulting very broad views of people's movements are deeply entrenched in the subject (e.g. Spikins 1999, 64-65). Such a longstanding tradition of a generic and simplified understanding of prehistoric movement can make it quite difficult to conceive of an entirely new way to approach the subject, free of the baggage of former approaches.

Hunters of the northern forests

A common custom among many hunters of the northern forests – from Siberia to the American Northwest – when exploring new ways to traverse the land is to reopen disused tracks (e.g. Tanner 1979; Nelson 1973; 1983). This could be compared to the concept of mobility in this paper, which is by no means new to early prehistoric research. Similar to the hunters' reopening of redundant tracks, the aim here could be defined as an attempt to find new ways forward by making inroads into a territory once frequented but since abandoned and all but forgotten. In other words, my aim is to take this old and well-used concept and attempt to discover new potential and directions within it. There is a need to reassess the question of mobility across prehistory and in particular from both sides of the 'mesolithic/neolithic divide' and it is encouraging to see that others (e.g. Mills this volume) are also granting this fascinating and important subject more explicit attention. In the following pages I will discuss some ideas relating to the study of movement and mobility before reviewing the most dominant models traditionally used to interpret prehistoric and in particular hunter-gather mobility. I will then propose some alternative strategies and present an example of how these could be put into practice, in the form of a case study based on my research in northeast Ireland, focusing primarily on the later parts of the mesolithic.

Why mobility?

"It is important that we learn to recognise the various forms of mobility archaeologically, because the ways people move exert strong influences on their culture and society" (Kelly 1992, 43).

Before starting to worry about how to recognise mobility archaeologically, it is vital to briefly consider the importance it holds in people's lives. Without wanting to generalise too much, it would appear fair to say that people value movement highly right across the world, even though the individual expressions may vary significantly. For example, for the Lumbee of Robeson County, North Carolina "movement itself has a positive meaning, for it suggests life, vitality, connection to others" (Blu 1996, 214). It "is a metaphor for health, well-being, and

---

[1] In the following, capitalisation of periods, like the mesolithic, is consciously avoided to stress that these are modern constructs and not in any way real entities in the past. As de-capitalised adjectives, they are simply used to denote a chronological period, rather than an objectifiable and distinct entity.

connectedness" as well as a symbol for political power and autonomy and hence important for defining personal and community identity (Blu 1996, 215-16). Similarly, in many African societies the metaphor of pathways applies to social relationships as well as to individual anatomy and physiology (Jackson 1989, 146). The Kuranko, small scale cultivators of Sierra Leone and Guinea, use the word *kile* ('path'/'road') as a metaphor for social relationship. They explain the reason for giving a gift with the phrase "so that the path does not die". If relations between affines or neighbours are strained, however, it is often said that "the path is not good between them" (Jackson 1989, 145).

These examples illustrate that mobility is invariably rich in meaning, symbolism and cultural value – regardless of what the specifics may be. In other words, the idea of moving, and by implication the physical act as well, is important to people, though probably for numerous different reasons. It would, therefore, seem safe to assume that mobility was equally viewed as significant by early prehistoric communities, whose lives would have involved routine movement. Ethnography tells us that such communities tend to emphasise notions of places and paths as central to their existence (Ingold 1986, 147-8 & 153). For example, the Mistassini Cree of northwest Canada refer to their hunting grounds as 'my path', 'my road' or 'my river', "indicating the temporary social appropriation of terrain with a path of movement" (Tilley 1994, 54). This idea of life as a path or journey is a very common one and can extend even beyond death. The Koyukon of northwest interior Alaska see their afterlife as a journey on which the wandering spirit follows one of two trails; either a poor 'trail of suffering' if the person has lived badly, or an easy trail without hardship, if the person lived well, yet ultimately both will reach the same afterlife place (Nelson 1983, 245).

Thus, in addition to its functional dimension, mobility would appear to be a social phenomenon and a means of expression which cannot be reduced to a singular explanation, be it ideological, economical, behavioural or otherwise. It is also an everyday or routine practice and could be compared to other activities discussed by Whittle (2003, 22-49) as part of the 'daily round'. "They [routines] may be both generated by and in their turn help to generate culturally specific principles and worldviews" (Whittle 2003, 22). Like most of these, mobility does not serve only one – usually practical – purpose but at the same time is used to communicate, linked to the creation and maintenance of social relationships, and is thus essential in forming and negotiating identities. By moving around the world people participate in different levels of social discourse, they get to know themselves, the world around them and their position within society. Furthermore, through understanding these relationships and learning to manipulate them, people can change their own position within society by changing the way they move and consequently the people they meet and activities they participate in.

Dominant models of prehistoric mobility

Despite this apparent link between mobility and social identity the most frequently employed models discussing

mobility in archaeology, and especially in the study of hunter-gatherers, are primarily concerned with economic considerations. Among these models two stand out as having been particularly influential in archaeological discourse for the past few decades. Although these models, which were devised with quite different research agendas in mind and were not necessarily intended as catch-all solutions to questions of hunter-gatherer mobility, soon took on a 'life on their own', far beyond their creators' intentions (e.g. Kelly 1992, 45; Warren 2001, 90). They have come to be known as the 'Upland/Lowland' and the 'Forager/Collector' model, respectively.

While the latter has been derived from observations in the form of ethnographic studies of hunter-gatherer groups in the present to help interpret archaeological evidence, the former was produced mainly with the aim of explaining evidence for mesolithic activity as encountered, especially in certain parts of Britain. Its proponents observed the occurrence of larger artefact scatters in lower lying areas and in particular coastal locations, on lake shores, or along river valleys. These finds were dominated by so-called 'balanced assemblages', consisting usually of some 30-60 percent microliths and 25-50 percent flake and blade scrapers (Mellars 1976, 389-90). In contrast to these lowland sites, finds from the uplands appeared to be much smaller in scale and extent and were strongly dominated by microlith industries. Given that microliths were traditionally seen as almost exclusively used as projectile points (for an alternative view see Finlay 2000, 71-74) the upland sites were interpreted as hunting camps, whereas the larger lowland scatters were seen as base camps and aggregation sites. The resulting model thus saw mesolithic hunters congregating in larger coastal and lowland settlements during the winter months and dispersing into the uplands in the summer (Clark 1972; Mellars 1976, 379-80). Economically, this was justified based on hypothetical movement patterns of red deer and an assumption that this mammal provided the prime source of nutrition. It has since been found that the importance of red deer has been over-exaggerated (e.g. Finlay 2000, 69), the proposed movement patterns have been called into question (e.g. Spikins 1999, 68-70; Myers 1987 143-44), and serious problems with regards to chronology have been identified (e.g. Myers 1987 139-40; Warren 2001, 91). The traditional model for Ireland, with a marked absence of red deer during the earliest parts of prehistory (Woodman *et al.* 1997), is in many ways quite similar to the upland/lowland model. Like its British counterpart it has been primarily based on the hypothetical seasonal availability of the presumed main food sources, salmon, eel, wild pig and, to some extent, hazelnuts. As a result, and in contrast to the British model, for Ireland it was proposed that the coastal areas were occupied in the spring, people moved to rivers and lakeshores during the summer and early autumn and on to the uplands during late autumn and winter (Woodman 1978, 176-91, Fig. 61). Again, although initially many problems and difficulties were identified by the model's proponent (Woodman 1978, 188-90; 1985,161) the model itself took on a life of its own and has since been described as a 'self-evident truth' (Woodman *et al.* 1999, 142). Despite some shift away from the idea of dependence on such a narrow range of major food sources, as Spikins (1999, 54) points out, the basic paradigm of mobility, involving long term seasonal base camps and more dispersed short term camps, has remained undisputed.

Equally, the parameters of the Forager/Collector model are still being widely used in discussing hunter-gatherer mobility (e.g. contributions in Fisher & Eriksen 2002). The distinction between foragers and collectors has firstly been drawn by Binford (1980) and caught on with the archaeological community almost immediately. The main principle is that "foragers typically do not store foods but gather foods daily. They range out gathering food on an 'encounter' basis and return to their residential bases each afternoon or evening" (Binford 1980, 5). In "contrast to the foragers where a group 'maps onto' resources through residential moves and adjustment in group size", collectors are logistically organized and "supply themselves with specific resources through specially organized task groups" (Binford 1980, 10). Hence the main argument in relation to mobility is that foragers are characterised by residential moves, as they move consumers to the resource while collectors move mainly logistically in the form of small specialist task groups bringing the resources back to the bulk of the consumers (Binford 1980, 18). An alternative to Binford's Forager/Collector model, if less influential, has been provided by Bettinger and Baumhoff (1982) who proposed a continuum from travellers to processors. Travellers are characterised by a high degree of mobility – presumably both residential and logistical – and by taking only high return rate food resources such as large game. Processors are less mobile and intensively use a diversity of resources, especially plant foods. Furthermore, a difference in subsistence is seen to generate a difference in demography. For instance, high rates of female infanticide are thought to lower growth of group size among travellers. According to the authors, the model specifies precise relationships between population and resources, and settlement and subsistence (Bettinger & Baumhoff 1982, 488). Yet neither Binford's nor Bettinger and Baumhoff's model actually help us understand how people move as part of their everyday life, let alone the question of addressing what their mobile lifestyle means to them.

Problematic dichotomies
In an attempt to "introduce some order and coherence" to the chaotic manner in which movement among human societies, and especially hunter-gatherers and pastoralists is treated, Ingold (1986, 165) questions the usefulness of the term 'nomadic', often applied to such societies. He sides with Salzman (1971, 193), who suggests that we could learn most about nomadism by comparing its manifestations among the various categories of people who lead a mobile lifestyle. For our purpose then, if it is our goal to study mobility, or more specifically early prehistoric mobility, it would be most advisable to compare and contrast the different ways of moving evident in the archaeological record, rather than constantly attempting to produce or work within evolutionary economic dichotomies (*cf.* Wylie 1985, 68). Yet, all the models discussed above are built on such dichotomies; be they 'sedentary-mobile', 'embedded-logistical procurement' or 'dispersal-aggregation'. These traditional dichotomies are rather problematic and it needs to be questioned to what extent they can actually help our

understanding of movement. Firstly, sedentism and mobility are not either/or phenomena, nor are they opposite ends of a continuum (Eder 1984, 837-38; Varien 1999, 9) and most communities engage in both types of 'lifestyle' on different levels and to a different extent. In Kelly's (1992, 60) words, "No society is sedentary, not even our own industrial one – people simply move in different ways." Furthermore, it needs to be pointed out that increasing sedentism does not necessarily mean that residential mobility decreases in importance (Varien 1999, 11) and in fact "sedentary people may be characterised by a more pronounced 'shiftiness', or impermanence, in their ties to specific locales, than are nomads" (Ingold 1986, 180). Equally, given the large degree of variation among the world's hunting-gathering societies, the forager-collector dichotomy and with it that between logistical and residential mobility do not appear to hold up, in relation to mobility and every other facet of their lives (e.g. Binford 2001; Kelly 1995). Binford (1980, 19) himself argued that "logistical and residential variability are not to be viewed as opposing principles but as organizational alternatives which may be employed in varying mixes in different settings." This however, would make it all but impossible to apply his model practically to any concrete archaeological problem that does not conform to the ideal conditions assumed for the model.

Another problematic dichotomy, and often an obstacle in the way of understanding prehistoric mobility, is that drawn between mesolithic and neolithic and the general equation of either period with a distinct lifestyle; hunting and gathering and farming respectively (e.g. Eder 1984, 837; Tolan-Smith 2003, 113). Furthermore, the subject of mobility has been treated quite differently by researchers mainly interested in 'neolithic farming communities' and those whose prime interest are 'mesolithic hunter-gatherers'. In terms of the neolithic, being mobile is often portrayed as an active 'lifestyle choice' (e.g. Thomas 1999, 1996; Whittle 1996, 1997) while for the mesolithic it is seen as necessity and part of a survival strategy. The concept of a mobile neolithic lifestyle was intended to break down the standard view of sedentary farmers (Thomas 1993, 362-64), but was quickly established as a 'new orthodoxy' (Cooney 2000, 56) and has consequently been criticised for applying a blanket rule to the period without allowing for regional variations (Cooney 2000, 51).

Away from the problems posed by the artificial dichotomies, the dominant models used to study mobility create further difficulties. Firstly, the often large-scale spatial and temporal resolution within which most of the models operate seems to be inadequate to approach people's movements, which take place on many different levels and at several interlinking spatial as well as temporal scales. Secondly, virtually all of the models reviewed here are almost exclusively interested in subsistence economy and thus portray movement and mobility as purely a function of the latter. It seems that the notion of "mobile man pursuing food, shelter, and satisfaction in different places in his environment" (Binford 1980, 39) still dominates mesolithic research. This of course is why certain prehistorians felt justified in describing prehistoric hunters and gatherers as having "ecological relations with hazelnuts" (Bradley 1984, 11) rather than social relationships. Overall the treatment of people's movements has remained entirely in the generic and large-scale domain, primarily focusing on broad differences across – often questionable – chronological and cultural divides. This does not help our understanding of what people's actual day-to-day movements were like, what they were about or how they were experienced.

Recent alternative approaches and interpretive accounts of mobility

In contrast to the above models, mobility has seen some more explicit consideration in the light of interpretive accounts and in particular those described as phenomenological perspectives of landscape (e.g. Tilley 1993; 1994; Thomas 1996). These approaches stand out, as they made it their goal to also investigate the experience and meaning of individual journeys. The link with the prehistoric past, in the form of archaeological evidence, is generally provided by the presence of prehistoric (mostly neolithic) landscape features and monuments, such as tombs, causewayed enclosures or cursus monuments. The problem in relation to earlier, pre-neolithic times is that this rich and highly visible architectural dimension is absent from the landscape. Therefore attempts to engage with 'mesolithic landscapes' in a similar manner can appear somewhat far-fetched, as the connection to actual evidence for mesolithic activity may be rather spurious. In order to produce more interesting accounts in relation to early prehistoric movement, concepts such as ancestral travel, mythical journeys and metaphors have been introduced, often superimposed directly from ethnographic accounts. "The methodological problem is that these concepts grant abundant poetic license but fail to demand rigorous engagement with the *specificity* of particular archaeological data sets" (Jordan 2003, 130; emphasis in

original). If our aim is to say something more specific as well as interesting about early prehistory in northern Europe, we need to re-engage with the actual evidence (Jordan 2003, 130). This re-engagement requires recognising the particular nature of the material and formulating our questions accordingly. These questions should then be tested in the form of detailed case studies employing methodologies that are consistent whilst also allowing for the varied and often circumstantial nature of the evidence.

Engaging with the material evidence for mobility in Irish early prehistory

As apparent from the discussion above, mobility would clearly seem to be much more than merely an economic necessity and it would be reasonable to suggest that this is particularly true for people who see routine movement as a central part of their existence. The way people move also reflects their intentions, perceptions and ideas. In other words it would appear that mobility is intrinsically linked to most other aspects of people's lives, their relationships with one another and with the world around them. This link between mobility and social relations could help an archaeological investigation. If we accept that people express aspects of their social lives, ideologies and identity through the way they move, then in turn reconstructing movement patterns archaeologically should enable us to make some interesting statements about their lives. Following on from this, the two questions at the centre of this study are firstly, how to reconstruct people's mobility patterns in the past, based on archaeological evidence, and secondly how these relate to other aspects of their lives? (Figure 12.1).

Key Relationships

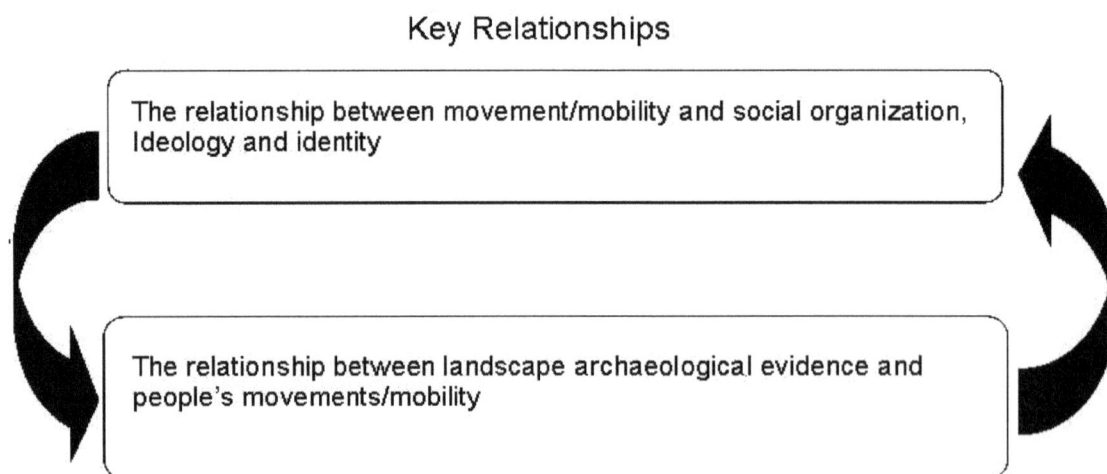

The relationship between movement/mobility and social organization, Ideology and identity

The relationship between landscape archaeological evidence and people's movements/mobility

Figure 12.1. Relationships between mobility and archaeological evidence.

The main source of early prehistoric evidence, especially in an Irish context, is represented by lithics. Since the latter occur frequently and continuously throughout prehistory, they also allow us to transcend the traditional chronological divides and consider continuity and change across time. However, stone tools are by no means the

only type of evidence to be considered. They should rather be seen as a point of entry into a surprisingly diverse range of data. Various methods can be utilised to access these different sources of information, many of which may grant useful pointers as regards mobility. For example, lithic analysis can provide important insights into material selection, tool use and manufacture, all of which in turn can offer vital clues in relation to people's movements and mobility patterns (e.g Odell 1994; 1996; Carr 1994). This could include macroscopic approaches, such as identifying stages of reduction, retouch and rejuvenation (e.g. Andrefsky 1998; Finlayson *et al.* 2001), or more specialised use-wear, microwear or residue analysis (e.g. Kooyman 2000). In addition, lithic sourcing could be employed – at a rather basic macroscopic and experimental level (e.g. Kooyman 2000, 39; Odell 1996, 15-20) as well as utilising technically advanced and chemical methods (e.g. Kooyman 2000, 40-44) – to identify the origins of raw materials used and thus the distances they have been moved. While it may not be possible to relate the movement of materials directly to people's movements, practically lithic sourcing has proved to be very informative in relation to discussing the possibility of different modes of movement, communication and exchange of materials within and between early prehistoric communities (e.g. Griffith & Woodman 1987; Odell 1996, 16-20; Cunliffe 2001, 127-29).

Yet even without directly analysing the stone tools, their presence at certain locations in the landscape provides in itself a wealth of information. Taking into account issues relating to taphonomy and artefact curation, investigation can commence from these locations, by placing them in their landscape setting and examining them at different scales. It is mainly this latter form of analysis that has informed the data gathering for this paper. The methodology utilised here, as detailed in my MA thesis (Kador 2003), employs a number of interlinking scales of analysis. It starts out from the relatively small or local scale of individual object finds and their locations, moves on to a regional scale of how these locations relate to their wider landscape setting and eventually leads to a broad scale to place the findings from the study region into the wider setting of Ireland and beyond. Different methods and means of investigation are employed at each of these scales. This entails recording and cataloguing observations of the landscape setting of each location, at the local scale. The ensuing regional scale is primarily based on Cost Surface Analysis, utilising Geographic Information Systems (GIS). Using these techniques, ideal – or least cost – paths (e.g. van Leusen 2002, 6.8-6.9) through the landscape can be projected and placed in relation to the individual find locations. Finally, the broad scale combines a synthesis of the two smaller scales with data from other regionally based surveys and investigations, in order to identify broader patterns and re-evaluate other research on early prehistoric Ireland, with special regard to movement and mobility. It also needs to be pointed out that the scales employed here are purely heuristic, enabling access to the evidence and a discussion of mobility at different levels. Hence I do not wish to claim that these dimensions are in any way representative of the different scales and levels at which people moved in prehistory. Nonetheless, I hope that employing interlinking resolutions in analysing the evidence and discussing mobility will serve as a helpful reminder that human movement always takes place at many different levels; from everyday 'short hops' to occasional long distance travels and mass migrations.

To illustrate the methodology I will now present a case study based on my research in the Glens of Antrim, Co. Antrim, northeast Ireland (Figure 12.2). This area was chosen for a number of reasons. Firstly, it provides a varied but well-defined landscape, which could be broadly divided into a coastal strip, low-lying inland areas of the Glens, and hilly uplands. All of these areas show quite distinct environmental characteristics, and contemporary land use patterns. Palynological evidence (Francis 1987; Weir 1993; Smith & Goddard 1991; Jessen 1949) would suggest that – to some extent – this was also the case in the past. The availability of such environmental data was considered important for the study and thus provided a second reason for this area to be selected. Secondly, the area has produced a reasonable number of early prehistoric find locations, including a considerable amount of mesolithic evidence to allow a meaningful investigation of this material from a landscape perspective. Incidentally, all the mesolithic find locations identified within the area have produced later mesolithic material; dating c. 5500 – 4000BC. Evidence for earlier mesolithic activity was discovered at four locations, yet in all of these it occurred alongside later mesolithic material. Consequently, I will limit the discussion to the later mesolithic, as this allows to operate within a more restricted chronological framework. In relation to earlier mesolithic evidence, it was felt that the low density of finds from that period would make it rather difficult to make any meaningful statements as regards people's movements.

Scales of practical investigation

Local scale

As briefly outlined above, the local scale set out from each individual find location of mesolithic material within the study area, to investigate its position in the immediate surroundings. Before presenting a summary of the findings of the analysis at this scale, a word of caution is required. The resolution of the data set available for early prehistoric finds leaves a lot to be desired. As in many areas that have a long-standing history of antiquarian collecting prehistoric assemblages from northeast Ireland are riddled with biases (e.g. Woodman 1978, 2-5; 2003, 7-11), which to discuss in detail would demand a research paper in itself. The issue of most interest for this study is the question of spatial distribution of finds and thus how accurately they have been recorded. The fact that a large amount of the objects from the study area have been recovered during the second half of the nineteenth and the first half of the twentieth centuries means that, unfortunately for our purposes, the overall standard of recording of find locations is rather poor. Locational information of most items held in collections and museums is generally restricted to townlands. To make things worse, different spellings of townland names and the reoccurrence of similar names in several counties, mean that in some cases several different find locations for the same object are possible. I have attempted to keep this possibility to a minimum and only selected those finds for further analysis for which the find location

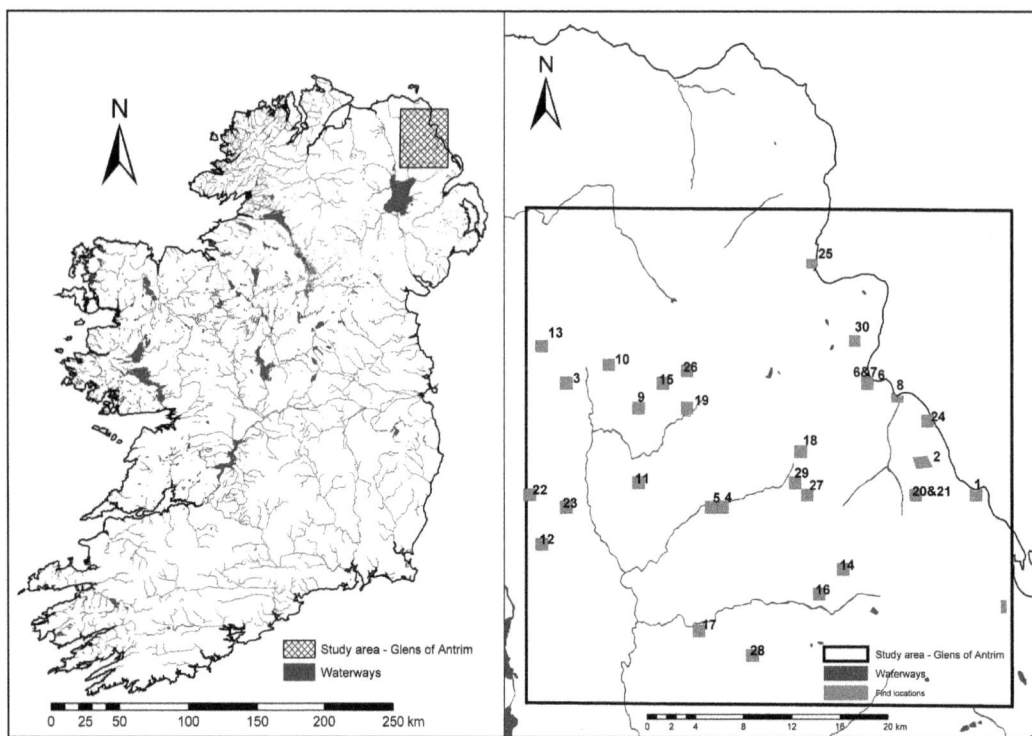

Figure 12.2. Study area in northeast Ireland and find locations.

seems most certain. However, it is impossible to give an absolute guarantee and exclude any possibility for an error occurring in this regard. The limit in terms of the least acceptable resolution required for a meaningful investigation was set at roughly one square kilometre and locations documented less accurately were excluded. The rationale behind this was that any distance inside a one kilometre square could be easily covered within half an hour's walk, even in rough or difficult terrain (e.g. Rose *et al.* 1994, 60-62). While this situation is certainly not ideal, with the exception of material from recent fieldwork and excavations, this is often the best possible accuracy that can be expected. Consequently, working at this admittedly coarse resolution provides the only conceivable strategy to utilise the material in a landscape context at all. Archival research and a search of published literature allowed me to identify thirty-eight locations of mesolithic material within the study area. However, for reasons discussed above eight of those had to be excluded, leaving thirty for further analysis. Even within this group the accuracy of recording varies greatly and thus not all could be subjected to the same level of detailed investigation. Furthermore these locations represent the whole spectrum from large, excavated sites, which produced several thousand artefacts, to single object finds (Table 12.1).

The difference in size and extent of the finds has obvious implications on the scales of movements and activities which contributed to their creation; however, I will not be able to address these issues in the course of this paper.[2] For this paper, the mere presence of artefactual material at these locations was taken to indicate a human presence.

The inclusion of locations of single object finds may prove to be a contentious point, as it could easily be argued that there are many possible ways a single object could have been moved subsequent to its original deposition. However, only through including these small scale and low-key finds – which as a matter of course account for the majority of the available evidence – can we truly hope to devise a 'bottom up' approach to early prehistory, as opposed to the traditional 'top down' perspective (see Spikins 1999, 52). Furthermore, without evidence to the contrary it would not seem likely that the bulk of the objects concerned have been moved a significant distance from their original context. The conceivably more frequent displacement of objects through ploughing and other agricultural activities should not result in the objects moving great distances (e.g. Brady 2002; Boismier 1997, 35-46; contributions in Schofield 1991) and was therefore considered to have had little impact on the findings of this study. Practically, research at the local scale involved landscape investigation carried out through surveying every find location in relation to local topography, direction and aspect of slope and general position in the landscape. Moreover, numerous ethnographic accounts of small-scale societies illustrate the importance of features such as mountains, lakes, peninsulas, caves, islands, waterfalls and springs (e.g. Bradley 2000, 6; Morphy 1995; Basso 1984; 1996), which often "invoke common responses in human beings – feelings of awe, power, majestic beauty, respect, enrichment among them" (Taçon 1999, 36). Accordingly the investigation also set out to establish whether any relation between the location of early prehistoric finds and landscape features – either through proximity or visibility – could be identified and if it is therefore possible to claim that any of these features also played an important role for people in early prehistoric in Ireland.

---

[2] For a more thorough treatment of issues relation to the scale and nature of the finds see Kador 2003.

No	Location	Description of find	Collection details	Source
1	Ballygally	100 blades, incl. 8 butt trimmed forms	Coll. Grainger	EHSNI
2	Ballygilbert	30 late mesolithic flakes and cores	Coll. Gray	Ulster Museum Records
3	Bellaghy	1 mesolithic flint scraper	Wellcome Trust	Ulster Museum Records
4	Birchwood	1 butt trimmed flake	Coll. Milligan	Woodman 1978
5	Broughshane	1 'bann flake'	Coll. Knowles	Woodman 1978 & Ulster Museum
6	Carnlough, Bay Farm 1	Site of extensive flintworking, several flakes and blades	Coll. Stuart/ exc. Woodman	Woodman & Johnson 1996
7	Carnlough, Bay Farm 4	unrolled late mesolithic material near top of raised beach	exc. Woodman	Woodman & Johnson 1996
8	Cloney, Glenarm	raised beach, late mesolithic flint working site	exc. Movius	Movius 1937
9	Clough	2 'bann flakes'	Coll. Knowles	Woodman 1978
10	Clough Mills	1 mesolithic flint axe	Coll. Dr Evelyn	Ulster Museum Records
11	Dernaveagh	1 'bann flake'	Coll. Knowles	Woodman 1978
12	Drumraw	1 'bann flake'	Coll. Knowles	Woodman 1978
13	Dunloy	1 small face trimmed axe	Coll. Knowles	Woodman 1978
14	Glenhead	Several 'bann flakes' & 2 needle points	Coll. Knowles	Woodman 1978
15	Glenleslie	c.20 early& late mesolithic implements	Coll. Knowles	Woodman 1978 & Ulster Museum
16	Glenwhirry	1 crude micro awl, 1 barbed and tanged (bann) flake	Coll. Knowles	Woodman 1978 & Ulster Museum
17	Kells Fort	small hoard of laminar 'bann flakes'	Coll. Knowles	Woodman 1978 & Ulster Museum
18	Killicarn/Ticloy	1 'bann flake', 7 late mesolithic flakes & blades	various collections	Ulster Museum Records
19	Knockinally Junction	1 'bann flake', 1 late mesolithic tanged flint point	Coll. Knowles	Woodman 1978 & Ulster Museum
20	Linford/Glenarm	tanged blades (number unknown) dated c.7000BP	MacDermot	Woodman & Johnson 1996
21	Linford/Glenarm 2	1 large mesolithic flint flake	Record specimen (UM)	Ulster Museum Records
22	Lisnahunchin	1 'bann flake' & 1 pointed pick (at L. Tamin)	Coll. Knowles	Woodman 1978
23	Loan Hill	1 leaf shaped needle point, 1 late mesolithic flint flake	Coll. Knowles	Woodman 1978 & Ulster Museum
24	Minnis (N/S)	Selection of flint flakes (late mesolithic)	various collections	Ulster Museum Records
25	Red Bay	Several flint blades & flakes	various collections	Ulster Museum Records
26	Skerry	1 'bann flake'	Coll. Knowles	Woodman 1978
27	Stoneyquater	2 'bann flakes' (one marked 'nr. foot of Slemis')	Coll. Knowles	Woodman 1978 & Ulster Museum
28	Tardree	1 mesolithic flint axe roughout	Wellcome Trust	Ulster Museum Records
29	Three Towns	1 'bann flake'	Coll. Knowles	Woodman 1978
30	Windy Ridge	1 butt trimmed flake	exc. Glencloy Project	Woodman et. al. 1992

Table 12.1. Find locations and details.

One of the most striking findings of the survey was perhaps that the largest part of the find locations within the study area was located at a distance of more than 10km from the sea, conversely to the general assumption about Irish mesolithic sites being predominantly found in coastal areas. Only ten of the thirty locations are closer than 10km, and only seven are within 1km (Table 12.2), though it needs to be acknowledged that the sea levels and the coastline of County Antrim have undergone significant changes during the early Holocene (e.g. Prior 1966; Prior *et al.* 1981). Equally, a comparison of elevations and terrain types suggested that the majority of the locations are not situated in low-lying areas, as commonly assumed, but are found at elevations between 100–200m in an area

which could be characterised as in a medial position between the uplands and lowlands. This upland-lowland boundary often provides the "paths of least resistance" for traversing the land, as it is frequently associated with a change or break in vegetation (Hind 1998; 2000, 222). These findings are interesting, as they actually seem to work against the research bias in the area which, due to both land development and collecting history, should favour the coastal and lowland locations. The importance of the medial position is further strengthened by more detailed analysis of the inland locations, which revealed that nineteen of the twenty one were indeed in areas with significant breaks of slope and vegetation often overlooking a large river valley. The remaining three

No	Location	General location	Elevation	Proximity to sea	Resolution
1	Ballygally	Coastal, Urban (village)	5 – 50m OD	less than 100m	10m
2	Ballygilbert	Coastal - Upland	20 - 350m OD	less than 100m	1km
3	Bellaghy	Hilly Uplands	100 - 150m OD	more than 20km	1km
4	Birchwood	Slope overlooking river valley	50 - 110m OD	more than 20km	1km
5	Broughshane	Urban, Valley bottom	50 - 80m OD	more than 20km	1km
6	Carnlough, Bay Farm 1	Coastal / Lowland	10 - 20m OD	less than 100m	10m
7	Carnlough, Bay Farm 4	Coastal / Lowland	5 – 10m OD	less than 100m	10m
8	Cloney, Glenarm	Coastal/estuarine and village	0 – 10m OD	less than 100m	10m
9	Clough	Hilly Uplands	150 - 165m OD	15 - 20km	500m
10	Clough Mills	Upland / lowland Border	90 - 100m OD	more than 20km	1km
11	Dernaveagh	Rolling lowlands, marsh	100 - 110 m OD	more than 20km	1km
12	Drumraw	Hilly Uplands	140 - 160m OD	more than 20km	1km
13	Dunloy	Village, Uplands	100 - 150 m OD	more than 20km	1km
14	Glen Head	Mountainlous uplands	270 - 370m OD	15 - 20km	1km
15	Glenleslie	Hilly Uplands	200 - 220m OD	15 - 20km	1km
16	Glenwherry	Upland border overlooking valley	170 - 250m OD	15 - 20km	1km
17	Kells Fort/Connor	Hilly forelands, outside village	70-100 m OD	more than 20km	20m
18	Killicarn/Ticloy	Hilly Uplands	150-170m OD	15 - 20km	1km
19	Knockinally Junction	Lowland / Valley bottom	130 - 150m OD	15 - 20km	200m
20	Linford/Glenarm 1	Mountainous uplands	260 - 270m OD	3 - 5km	500m
21	Linford/Glenarm 2	Mountainous uplands	240 - 270m OD	3 - 5km	500m
22	Lisnahunchin	Edge of the upland zone	140-160m OD	more than 20km	1km
23	Loan Hill	Hilly Uplands	150-180m OD	more than 20km	500m
24	Minnis (N/S)	Coastal - Upland	20 – 200m OD	100 - 500m	1km
25	Red Bay	Coastal Promontory	5 – 20m OD	less than 100m	20m
26	Skerry	Hilly Uplands	230 - 270m OD	10 - 15km	1km
27	Stoneyquater	Hilly Uplands (border)	160 - 200m OD	15 - 20km	1km
28	Tardree	Hilly Uplands	180 - 240m OD	more than 20km	1km
29	Three Towns	Hilly Uplands	130 - 150m OD	more than 20km	500m
30	Windy Ridge	Upland	280 - 300 m OD	1 - 3km	10m

Table 12.2. Spatial attributes of find locations.

inland locations are all in rather low-lying positions and close to the banks of a river, which begs the question of the importance of movement in relation to rivers (Spikins 1996, 88) and the importance of fording points (Table 12.2).

While it may be impossible to reconstruct mesolithic travel routes as such, the findings at the local scale would certainly seem to highlight the possibility that mesolithic activity centred around parts of the landscape favourable for the location of travel routes and paths of movement, such as the upland-lowland boundary and water courses. Though expressed previously (e.g. Tilley 1994, 86; 1995, 11; Cummings 2000, 93) this notion has hitherto found little substantiation through practical research.

Furthermore, given the distribution of finds between the

coast and hinterland, it would appear that the networks such routes were part of covered most parts of the land, linking locations across the entire study area. In the following section I will explore the relationship between artefact distribution and potential travel routes somewhat further.

Branching out – a regional perspective
The main objective of the regional scale was to project ideal paths of movement (Llobera 2000) across the study area and to analyse them in relation to the find locations. This was done with the help of GIS cost surface analysis (e.g. Wheatley & Gillings 2002; 151ff).[3] The theoretical background and methodology of this scale, as well as the

---

[3] For a recent critique of the use of Cost Surface Analysis in archaeology see van Leusen (2002, 6.8 – 6.9).

discussion of the findings, have been treated in greater detail elsewhere (Kador 2003). The core idea of the model relies on an assumption that there exists a predictable correlation between the energy expended to walk in a given terrain and the gradient of the slope (see Llobera 2000, 75-76; Wheatley & Gillings 2002, 154-56). Based on this relationship, it is then possible to infer the most cost efficient path across any defined area within this terrain. For the pilot model as presented here, ideal paths were created from every find location in the northern half of the study area to Carnlough and Glenarm beach, which represent the two most likely origins of the flint utilised (Griffith & Woodman 1987; Woodman & Anderson 1990). When considering the results of this model, it is vital to bear in mind that the paths are entirely based on the terrain and do not account for vegetation, soil types or hydrology. Ideally, all these factors should be taken into consideration, however, it would be very hard to predict how these factors would have affected people's movements and apparently little research has been done in this regard (see van Leusen 2002, 6.4–6.6). Therefore, it was decided, for this study, to rely on the impact of slope alone, as this appears to be reasonably predictable and could be supported by a substantial body of research (eg. Minetti 1995; Helbing *et al.* 1997; Batty 1997; Llobera 2000). Furthermore, the use of cost surface analysis in general and especially with cost surfaces based entirely on terrain, derived from digital terrain models (DTMs)[4], restricts the projected movements to the functional and economic domain. In other words the models themselves cannot tell us anything about people's social relations, ideologies or experiences. However, assuming that there existed some relationship between the physical shape of the land and the way people moved through it (Rose *et al.* 1994, 60-62; Llobera 2000, 75; van Leusen 2002, 6.6-6.7), the approach was nonetheless considered useful with regard to providing an insight into people's movement patterns in prehistory. The idea was to employ the model with its obvious limitations in mind, strictly to represent potential paths in relation to known findspots and without making any further statement about the motivation or the meaning of the journeys that may have taken place along these paths. Hence it serves merely as a point of departure open to subsequent critique and further interpretation, with a particular view to discussing the social and ideological aspects of the movement patterns mapped.

One of the most interesting findings of the regional scale

---

[4] The Digital Terrain Model (DTM) employed was supplied by the OSNI (© Crown copyright 2003) written in units of 2km squares, with a unit of elevation of 100mm. Data values were given in ASCII format using 80 character records representing ground elevations at the intersections of 50m square grid on the Irish National Grid. Cost surfaces were created in ESRI ArcGIS 8.1 from the DTM using Dijkstra's shortest-path algorithm (Cormen *et al.* 1990, 527-32). With this algorithm the cost of moving between nodes (cells) can be calculated, which can then be expanded to calculate the minimum cost path of going from one node to any other one in the graph. Thus potential or ideal pathways across the landscape can be projected.

was that the paths from the find locations in the hinterland which were divided into the two groups of; Clough [9], Glenleslie [15], Skerry [26], Knockanully [19] and of Bellaghy [3], Cloughmills [10] and Dunloy [13] – appear to converge at a certain point and from then on follow the same route to the coastal locations of Carnlough and Glenarm (Figures 12.3 & 12.4). In relation to Carnlough the routes for these two groups are different. Those pertaining to the first group comprising the find locations north of the Braid River [9, 15, 19 & 26], converge and make their way past the mountain path and early prehistoric site at Windy Ridge [30] (see Woodman *et al.* 1992). The paths from the locations to the west [3, 10 & 13] take a route further south and make their way to Carnlough through Glencloy glen (Figure 12.3). In relation to Glenarm the paths from both groups appear to be taking the same route after converging southeast of Knockanully [19] (Figure 12.4). Similarly, the picture could of course be reversed, showing a distinct dispersal of paths away from the coast and into the hinterland.

In employing this scale of analysis I aimed to further examine the possibility of a relationship between the distribution of mesolithic material across the landscape and the location of potential travel routes and communication networks (see above). Given the simplicity of the model it is perhaps rather surprising that it indeed appears to lend further support to this possibility.

Widening the path – broad scale
Having discussed the individual find locations within the study area and their position in the landscape as well as the possibility that these locations may represent points along paths of movement across the land, I will now move to consider the wider implications of the findings and how they relate to early prehistoric evidence gathered elsewhere in Ireland. During the discussion of the local and regional scales, I have suggested the existence of a correlation between mesolithic find locations and people's movement patterns, although I do not wish to imply that this correlation is always direct or straightforward. Research into early prehistory in other parts of Ireland has revealed an apparent concentration of artefact scatters along river valleys, and in particular on the boundary between the low-lying alluvial floodplain and the higher glacial till (Ramsden *et al.* 1995, 330; Woodman & Anderson 1990; Zvelebil *et al.* 1996,). Above, I have drawn attention to the possibility that such border zones between two areas of "major differences in sediment, slope and drainage" (Ramsden *et al.* 1995, 330) would have been ideally suited to facilitate movement. Furthermore, river courses themselves would have held great potential for movement in prehistory, whether this concerns travel on the water or overland travel along floodplains and riverbanks (Spikins 1996, 88).

Another common current in relation to Irish early prehistoric evidence is the movement of objects and materials over considerable distances. In relation to neolithic material, this situation has been widely acknowledged and discussed (e.g. Cooney 2000, 58-60), yet the considerable movement of later mesolithic material has received far less attention.

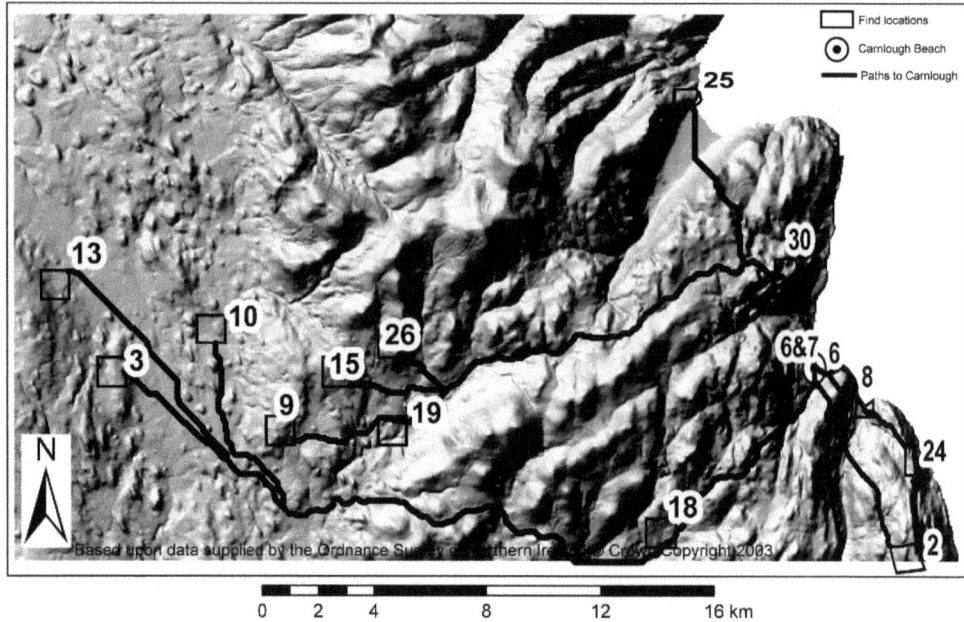

Figure 12.3. Ideal paths between find locations and Carnlough Beach

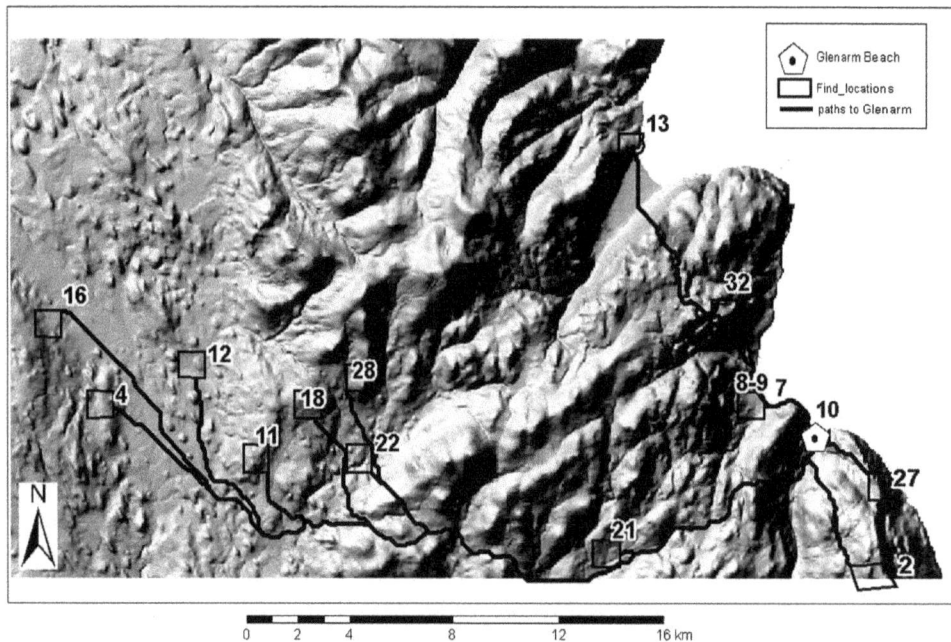

Figure 12.4. Ideal paths between path locations and Glenarm Beach.

The case of northeast Ireland, where literally tonnes of flint were moved largely during later mesolithic times, from the east Antrim coast across the Antrim plateau and into the Bann Valley (Woodman 1981; 1986; 1987; Griffith & Woodman 1987; Woodman & Anderson 1990), may well be exceptional in terms of the vast amounts of material shifted. However, the general practice of introducing objects of later mesolithic date made from non-local raw materials has also been identified in many other parts of the country. This has been documented in the southeast (Ramsden et al. 1995, 331), at Ferriter's Cove, County Kerry (Woodman 1987, 144; Woodman et al. 1999, 50), at Bay Farm (Woodman & Johnson 1996,

163), the north Leinster coast (e.g. Mitchell 1949, 17) and the north Midlands (Woodman et al. 1999, 142). Most of these areas produced a small proportion of introduced materials in addition to a larger amount of locally available stone. This would suggest that contacts and communication across Ireland, and often between quite distant areas, were rather widespread and it also highlights the possibility of several agents being involved in the procurement, production, transportation and use of objects (Hind 1998; Finlay 2003). The fact that the introduced materials are not necessarily superior to locally available stone (e.g. Woodman & Johnson 1996, 142; Rynne 1983, 328) should serve as a reminder that these artefacts were probably not the main reason behind people's movements, but are merely the most durable form of evidence for these journeys. I would favour the idea that there existed elaborate and often complex social networks between communities in different parts of Ireland and that the movement of objects and raw materials represents only one facet of them.

It is also clear that communication was not restricted to travel over land. This is supported by the recently discovered part of a mesolithic log boat from Lough Neagh – dated to 5490-5246 cal. BC (Fry 2000, 116) – but also by ample evidence for mesolithic activity on Irish offshore islands (e.g. McCartan 2000; Mitchell 1956; 1972; Liversage 1968). An interesting conundrum is therefore the apparent absence of material evidence for pre-neolithic contacts between Ireland and western Britain (e.g. Woodman 1978, 205ff; Wickham-Jones & Woodman 1998; Saville 2003, 346-47), especially in the light of such evidence from the Isle of Man (McCartan 1991; 2003). It would seem inconceivable that people did not attempt the rather short sea crossing between northeast Ireland and southwest Scotland, and thus that there were no contacts between these two regions at all. Yet if there was contact, the fact that archaeologists have not been able to find evidence for it clearly highlights the need to take a fresh look at our use of typologies as an indicator for the presence or absence of such contacts.

Moving to a close

This paper set out from the position that routine activities are always social. They are means of expression and can serve to create, maintain and renegotiate social relationships, while at the same time also having mundane or functional purposes. Mobility is clearly one of the most common and most routine of all human practices and, as I have argued, has strong links to people's engagement with the world and others around them. It thus presents an important part of people's social, economic, ideological and spiritual life spheres. However, in prehistoric research movement has largely been dealt with implicitly, been viewed as a means to an end or simply been taken for granted. I hope to have demonstrated that a specific and explicit treatment of mobility in relation to early prehistoric evidence can help us discover new ways of interpreting this evidence and cross-cut the deeply entrenched dichotomies, such as social-economic or sedentary-mobile, currently dominating our understanding. To do this we need to approach mobility at several interlinking levels with the aim of accessing the different scales at which human movement actually takes place as well as to accommodate and optimise the different sources of evidence available. I would suggest that this is best accomplished in the form of regionally based case studies, as these appear to have most potential for an intimate and direct engagement with the evidence available, given the strong degree of regional variation throughout prehistory. By striving to recognise people's movements archeologically we should be in a good position to gain insights into the social processes underlying the practice, offering us new means to interpret prehistoric lives.

Acknowledgements

I wish to thank the Irish Research Council for the Humanities and Social Sciences for funding provided under the 'Government of Ireland Scholarship Scheme' and the Humanities Institute of Ireland for providing me with office facilities. Furthermore I am very grateful to Sinéad McCartan for her support and permission to access the collections of the Ulster Museum, Professor Peter Woodman for kindly offering his advice and expertise on Irish early prehistoric collections and finally Graeme Warren for his assistance and guidance throughout my work as well as his comments on a draft version of this paper. Finally I wish to thank Daniela, Andrew and Jessica for organising the TAG session at which the first version of this paper was presented and for inviting my contribution to this volume.

References

Andrefsky, W. 1998. *Lithics: macroscopic approaches to analysis.* Cambridge: Cambridge University Press.

Basso, K. H. 1984. Stalking with stories: names, places, and moral narratives among the Western Apache. In E. M. Bruner (ed.), *Text, play, and story: the construction and reconstruction of self and society,* 19-55. Washington D.C.: Proceedings of the American Ethnological Society.

Basso, K. H. 1996. Wisdom sits in places: notes on a Western Apache landscape. In S. Feld & K. H. Basso (eds), *Senses of place,* 53-90. Santa Fe: School of American Research.

Batty, M. 1997. Predicting where we walk. *Nature* 388, 19-20.

Bettinger, R. L. & Baumhoff, M. A. 1982. The Numic spread: great basin cultures in competition. *American Antiquity* 47(3), 485-503.

Binford, L. R. 1980. Willow smoke and dogs' tails: hunter-gatherer settlement systems and archaeological site formation. *American Antiquity* 45, 4-20.

Binford, L.R. 2001. *Constructing frames of reference: an analytical method for archaeological theory building using ethnographic and environmental data sets.* Berkeley: University of California Press.

Blu, K. I. 1996. "Where do you stay at?" Home place and community among the Lumbee. In S. Feld & K. H. Basso (eds), *Senses of place,* 197-227. Santa Fe: School of American Research.

Boismier, W. A. 1997. *Modelling the effects of tillage processes on artefact distributions in the ploughzone: a simulation study of tillage-induced pattern formation.* Oxford: BAR.

Bradley, R. 1984. *The social foundation of prehistoric Britain.* London: Longman.

Bradley, R. 2000. *An archaeology of natural places.* London: Routledge.

Brady, C. 2002. Earlier prehistoric settlement in the Boyne Valley. *Archaeology Ireland* 16, 8-12.

Carr, P.J. 1994. Technological organization and prehistoric hunter-gatherer mobility: examination of the Hayes site. In P.J. Carr (ed.), *The organization of North American prehistoric chipped stone tool technologies*, 35-44. Ann Arbor: International Monographs in Prehistory.

Clark, J.G.D. 1972. *Star Carr: a case study in bioarchaeology*. Reading: Addison-Wesley.

Cooney, G. 2000. Recognising regionality in the Irish Neolithic. In A. Desmond, G. Johnson, M. McCarthy, J. Sheehan & E. Shee-Twohig (eds), *New agendas in Irish Prehistory*, 47-65. Dublin: Wordwell.

Cormen, T.H., Leiserson, C.E. & Rivest, R.L. 1990. *Introduction to algorithms*. Cambridge: MIT Press.

Cummings, V. 2000. Myth, memory and metaphor: the significance of space, place and landscape in Pembrokeshire. In R. Young (ed.) *Mesolithic lifeways: current research from Britain and Ireland*, 87-96. Leicester: Leicester University Press.

Cunliffe, B. 2001. *Facing the ocean: the Atlantic and its peoples, 8000 BC-AD 1500*. Oxford: Oxford University Press.

Eder, J.F. 1984. The impact of subsistence change on mobility and settlement pattern in a tropical forest foraging economy: some implications for archaeology. *American Anthropologist* 86, 837-53.

Finlay, N. 2000. Deer Prudence. *Archaeological Review from Cambridge* 17(1), 67-79.

Finlay, N. 2003. Microliths and multiple authorship. In L. Larsson, H. Kindgren, K. Knutsson, D. Loeffler, & A. Åkerlund (eds), *Mesolithic on the move: papers presented on the sixth international conference on the Mesolithic in Europe, Stockholm 2000*, 169–176. Oxford: Oxbow Books.

Finlayson, B., Finlay, N. & Mithen, S. 2001. The cataloguing and analysis of lithic assemblages. In S. Mithen (ed.), *Hunter-gatherer landscape archaeology: the Southern Hebrides Mesolithic Project 1988 – 98, Vol. 1*, 61–72. Cambridge: McDonald Institute for Archaeological Research.

Fisher, L.E. & Eriksen, B.V. (eds), 2002. *Lithic raw material economies in late glacial and early postglacial Europe*. Oxford: BAR.

Francis, E. 1987. The palynology of the Glencloy Area. Unpublished PhD thesis, Belfast: Queens University.

Fry, M.F. 2000. *Coiti: logboats from Ireland*. Belfast: Greystone Press.

Griffith, D. & Woodman, P.C. 1987. Cretaceous chert sourcing in N.E. Ireland: preliminary results. In G. Sieveking & M.H. Newcomer (eds), *The human uses of flint and chert: proceedings of the fourth International Flint Symposium*, 249-52. Cambridge: Cambridge University Press.

Helbing, D. Keltsch, J. & Molnár, P. 1997. Modelling the evolution of human trail systems. *Nature* 388, 47-50.

Hind, D. 1998. Chert use in the Mesolithic of Northern England. *Assemblage* 4, http://www.shef.ac.uk/assem/4/, accessed 28/10/2004.

Hind, D. 2000. *Landscape and technology in the Peak District of Derbyshire: the fifth and forth millennia BC*. Unpublished PhD Thesis, University of Sheffield.

Ingold, T. 1986. *The appropriation of nature: essays on human ecology and social relations*. Manchester: Manchester University Press.

Jackson, M. 1989. *Paths toward a clearing: radical empiricism and ethnographic inquiry*. Bloomington: Indiana University Press.

Jessen, K. 1949. Studies in the late-Quaternary deposits and floral history of Ireland. *Proceedings of the Royal Irish Academy* 52B, 85-290.

Jordan, P.D. 2003. Investigating Post-Glacial hunter gatherer landscape enculturation: ethnographic analogy and interpretative methodologies. In L. Larsson, H. Kindgren, K. Knutsson, D. Loeffler, & A. Åkerlund (eds), *Mesolithic on the move: papers presented on the sixth international conference on the Mesolithic in Europe, Stockholm 2000*, 128-38. Oxford: Oxbow Books.

Kador, T. 2003. *Moving off the beaten track: mobility as a way of understanding the mesolithic in northeast Ireland*. MA Thesis in Landscape Archaeology, University College Dublin.

Kelly, R.L. 1992. Mobility/sedentism: concepts, archaeological measures and effects. *Annual review of Anthropology* 21, 43-66.

Kelly, R. L. 1995. *The forager spectrum: diversity in hunter-gatherer lifeways*. London: Simthsonian.

Kooyman, B.P. 2000. *Understanding stone tools and archaeological sites*. Calgary: University of Calgary Press.

Liversage, G.D. 1968. Excavation at Dalkey Island, Co. Dublin, 1956-1959. *Proceedings of the Royal Irish Academy* 66, 53-233.

Llobera, M. 2000. Understanding movement: a pilot model towards the sociology of movement. In G. Lock. (ed.), *Beyond the map*, 65-84. Amsterdam: IOS Press.

McCartan, S.B. 1991. A later Mesolithic site at Rhendhoo, Jurby, Isle of Man. *Proceedings of the Isle of Man Natural History and Antiquarian Society* 10, 87-117.

McCartan, S.B. 2000. The utilisation of island environments in the Irish Mesolithic: agendas for Rathlin Island. In A. Desmond, G. Johnson, M. McCarthy, J. Sheehan & E. Shee Twohig (eds), *New agendas in Irish prehistory*, 15-30. Dublin: Wordwell.

McCartan, S.B. 2003. Mesolithic hunter-gatherers in the Isle of Man: adaptions to an island environment? In L. Larsson, H. Kindgren, K. Knutsson, D. Loeffler, & A. Åkerlund (eds), *Mesolithic on the move: papers presented on the sixth international conference on the Mesolithic in Europe, Stockholm 2000*, 331-39. Oxford: Oxbow Books.

Mellars, P.A. 1976. Settlement patterns and industrial variability in the British Mesolithic. In G. Sieveking, I.H. Longworth & K.E. Wilson (eds), *Problems in economic and social archaeology*, 375-99. London: Duckworth.

Minetti, A.E. 1995. Optimum gradient and mountain paths. *Journal of Applied Physiology* 79, 1698-1703.

118

Mitchell, G.F. 1949. Further early kitchen middens in County Louth. *Journal of the County Louth Archaeological Society* 12, 14-20.

Mitchell, G.F. 1956. An early kitchen-midden at Sutton, Co. Dublin. *Journal of the Royal Society of Antiquarians of Ireland* 86, 1-26.

Mitchell, G.F. 1972. Further excavation of the early kitchen-midden at Sutton, Co. Dublin. *Journal of the Royal Society of Antiquarians of Ireland* 102, 151- 59.

Morphy, H. 1995. Landscape and reproduction of the ancestral past. In E. Hirsch & M. O'Hanlon (eds), *The anthropology of landscape: perspectives on place and space,* 184–209 Oxford: Clarendon Press.

Myers, A. 1987. All shot to pieces? Inter-assemblage variability, lithic analysis and Mesolithic assemblage 'types': some preliminary observations. In A.G. Brown, and M.R. Edmonds (eds), *Lithic analysis and later British prehistory*, 137–153. Oxford: BAR.

Nelson, R.K. 1973. *Hunters of the northern forest: designs of survival among the Alaskan Kutchin.* Chicago: University of Chicago Press.

Nelson, R.K. 1983. *Make prayers to the raven: a Koyukon view of the Northern Forest.* Chicago: University of Chicago Press.

Odell, G.H. 1994. Assessing hunter-gatherer mobility in the Illinois Valley: exploring ambiguous results. In P.J. Carr (ed.), *The organization of North American prehistoric chipped stone tool technologies,* 70-86. Ann Arbor: International Monographs in Prehistory.

Odell, G.H. 1996. Stone tools and mobility in the Illinois Valley: from hunter-gatherer camps to agricultural villages. Ann Arbor: International Monographs in Prehistory.

Prior, D.B. 1966. Late Glacial and Post-Glacial shorelines in north-east Antrim. *Irish Geography* 5, 173-87.

Prior, D.B., Holland, S.M. & Cruickshank, M.M. 1981. A preliminary report on late Devensian and early Flandrian deposits on the coast at Carnlogh, County Antrim. *Irish Geography* 14, 75-83.

Ramsden, P., Zvelebil, M., Macklin, M.G. & Passmore, G. 1995. Stone age settlement in southeastern Ireland. *Current Anthropology* 36, 330-32.

Rose, J., Ralston, H.J. & Gamble, J.G. 1994. Energetics of walking. In J. Rose & J.G. Gamble (eds), *Human walking (second edition),* 45-72. Baltimore: Williams and Wilkins.

Rynne, E. 1983. An Antrim 'Bann flake' from County Kildare. *Journal of the Kildare Archaeological Society 16/4,* 328-31.

Salzman, P.C. 1971. Movement and resource extraction among pastoral nomads: the case of the Shah Nawazi Baluch. *Anthropological Quarterly* 44, 115-31.

Saville, A. 2003. Indications of regionalisation in Mesolithic Scotland. In L. Larsson, H. Kindgren, K. Knutsson, D. Loeffler, & A. Åkerlund (eds), *Mesolithic on the move: papers presented on the sixth international conference on the Mesolithic in Europe, Stockholm 2000,* 340-50. Oxford:

Oxbow Books.

Schofield, A.J. (ed.) 1991. *Interpreting artefact scatters: contributions to ploughzone archaeology.* Oxford: Oxbow Books.

Smith, A.G. & Goddard, I.C. 1991. A 12,500 year record of vegetational history at Sluggan Bog, Co. Antrim, N. Ireland. *New Phytologist* 118, 167-87.

Spikins, P. 1996. Rivers, boundaries and change: a hypothesis of challenging settlement patterns in the Mesolithic of Northern England. In T. Pollard and A. Morisson (eds), *The early prehistory of Scotland,* 89-107. Edinburgh: University of Edinburgh Press.

Spikins, P. 1999. *Mesolithic Northern England: environment, population and settlement.* Oxford: BAR.

Taçon, P.S.C. 1999. Identifying ancient sacred landscapes in Australia: from physical to social. In W. Ashmore & A.B. Knapp (eds), *Archaeologies of landscape: contemporary perspectives,* 33-57. Oxford: Blackwell.

Tanner, A. 1979. *Bringing home animals: religious ideology and mode of production of the Mistassini Cree hunters.* London: C. Hurst.

Thomas, J. 1993. Discourse, totalisation and 'the Neolithic'. In C. Tilley (ed.), *Interpretative archaeology,* 357-94. Oxford: Berg.

Thomas, J. 1996. *Time, culture and identity: an interpretive archaeology.* London: Routledge.

Thomas, J. 1999. *Understanding the Neolithic.* London: Routledge.

Tilley, C. 1993. Art, architecture, landscape [Neolithic Sweden]. In B. Bender (ed.), *Landscape politics and perspectives,* 49-84. Oxford: Berg.

Tilley, C. 1994. *A Phenomenology of landscape: places, paths and monuments.* Oxford: Berg.

Tilley, C. 1995. Rocks as resources: landscape and power. *Cornish Archaeology* 34, 5-57.

Tolan-Smith, C. 2003. Social interaction and settlement patterns in hunter-gatherer societies – application of the 'amity-enmity' model. In L. Bevan & J. Moore (eds), *Peopling the Mesolithic in a Northern Environment,* 113-18. Oxford: BAR.

van Leusen, P.M. 2002. *Patterns top process: methodological investigations into the formation and interpretation of spatial patterns in archaeological landscapes.* Groningen: VanRijksunversiteit.

Varien, M.D. 1999. Sedentism and mobility in a social landscape: Mesa Verde and beyond. Tucson: University of Arizona Press.

Warren, G.M. 2001. *Towards a social archaeology of the Mesolithic in eastern Scotland: landscape, contexts and experience.* Unpublished PhD Thesis, University of Edinburgh.

Weir, D.A. 1993. Pollen analysis of a small basin deposit, Tievebulliagh, Co. Antrim. *Ulster Journal of Archaeology* 56, 18-24.

Wheatley, D. & Gillings, M. 2002. *Spatial technology and archaeology: the archaeological applications of GIS.* London: Taylor & Francis.

Whittle, A. 1996. *Europe in the Neolithic: the creation of new worlds.* Cambridge: Cambridge University Press.

119

Whittle, A. 1997. Moving on and moving around: Neolithic settlement mobility. In P. Topping (ed.), *Neolithic landscapes,* 16-22. Oxford: Oxbow.

Whittle, A. 2003. *The archaeology of people: dimensions of Neolithic life.* London: Routledge.

Wickham-Jones, C. and Woodman, P.C. 1998. Studies on the earliest settlement of Scotland and Ireland. *Quaternary International* 49/50, 13-20.

Woodman, P.C. 1978. *The Mesolithic in Ireland: hunter-gatherers in an insular environment.* Oxford: BAR.

Woodman, P.C. 1981. The post-glacial colonization of Ireland: the human factors. In D. O'Corrain (ed.), *Irish antiquity: essays and studies presented to Professor M. J. O'Kelly,* 93-100. Cork: Tower Books.

Woodman, P. C. 1985. *Excavations at Mount Sandel 1973-1977.* Vol. 2. Belfast: Northern Ireland Archaeological Monographs.

Woodman, P.C. 1986. Problems in the colonisation of Ireland. *Ulster Journal of Archaeology* 49, 7-17.

Woodman, P.C. 1987. The impact of resource availability on lithic industrial traditions in prehistoric Ireland. In P. Rowley-Conwy, M. Zvelebil & H.P. Blankholm (eds), *The Mesolithic in north-west Europe: recent trends,* 138-49. Sheffield: Department of Archaeology and Prehistory.

Woodman, P. C. 2003. Pushing back the boundaries for early human settlement in Ireland. *John Jackson Memorial Lectures. Occasional papers in Irish science and technology.* Dublin: The Royal Dublin Society.

Woodman, P.C. & Anderson, E. 1990. The Irish later Mesolithic: a partial picture. In P.M. Vermeersch & P. van Peer (eds), *Contributions to the Mesolithic in Europe,* 377-87. Leuven: Leuven University Press.

Woodman, P.C., Anderson, E & Finlay, N. 1999. *Excavations at Ferriter's Cove 1983 - 1995: last foragers first farmers in the Dingle Peninsula.* Dublin: Wordwell.

Woodman, P.C., Doggart, R. & Mallory, J.P. 1992. Excavations at Windy Ridge, Co. Antrim, 1981-82. *Ulster Journal of Archaeology* 54– 5, 13-35.

Woodman, P.C. & Johnson, G. 1996. Excavations at Bay Farm 1, Carnlough, Co. Antrim, and the study of the 'Larnian' technology. *Proceedings of the Royal Irish Academy* 96C, 137-235.

Woodman, P.C., McCarthy, M. & Monaghan, N. 1997. The Irish Quaternary Fauna Project. *Quaternary Science Reviews* 16, 129-59.

Wylie, M.A. 1985. The reaction against analogy. *Advances in Archaeological Methods and Theory* 8, 63-112.

Zvelebil, M., Macklin, M.G., Passmore, D.G. and Ramsden, P. 1996. Alluvial archaeology in the Barrow Valley, Southeast Ireland: the 'River Ford' Culture re-visited. *Journal of Irish Archaeology* 7, 13-40.